FAST TIMES AT

AT

RIDGEMONT HIGH
A True Story

by CAMERON CROWE

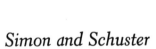

Simon and Schuster   New York

1 2 3 4 5 6 7 8 9 10
1 2 3 4 5 6 7 8 9 10 *pbk.*

Library of Congress Cataloging in Publication Data

Crowe, Cameron, date.
Fast times at Ridgemont High.

I. Title.
PS3553.R589S8   813'.54   81-8945
AACR2

ISBN 0-671-25290-9
0-671-25291-7 *pbk.*
A portion of this book originally appeared in Playboy *magazine.*

For My Parents

"ALL KIDS CAN'T GROW UP TO BE MOVIE STARS OR ROCK PERFORMERS. DON'T MAKE NOT WORKING EASY FOR THEM. IF AT FIRST THEY HAVE TO SETTLE ON JOBS THAT AREN'T INTELLECTUALLY FULFILLING, SO WHAT? HAS EVERY JOB YOU'VE EVER HAD BEEN 'INTELLECTUALLY FULFILLING'?"

—THE SURVIVAL KIT FOR PARENTS OF TEENAGERS, by David Melton

For seven years I wrote articles for a youth culture magazine, and perhaps not a day went by when this term wasn't used—"the kids." Editors assigned certain articles for "the kids." Music and film executives were constantly discussing whether a product appealed to "the kids." Rock stars spoke of commercial concessions made for "the kids." Kids were discussed as if they were some enormous whale, to be harpooned and brought to shore.

It began to fascinate me, the idea of The Kids. They were everywhere, standing on street corners in their Lynyrd Skynyrd t-shirts, in cars, in the 7-Eleven. Somehow this grand constituency controlled almost every adult's fate, yet no adult really knew what it was nowadays—to be a kid.

In the summer of '79, I had just turned twenty-two. I discussed the idea for this book with my New York publisher. Go back to high school, he said, and find out what's really going on in there with *the kids*. I thought about it over a weekend, and took the project.

I had attended Ridgemont Senior High School in Redondo Beach, California, for a summer session seven years earlier, and those eight weeks had been sublime and forbidden days, even if it did mean going to school in the summer. I normally attended a rather strict Catholic school, and there were many of us who believed that all our problems would be solved, all our dreams within reach if we just went to Ridgemont public high school.

In the fall of '79 I walked into the office of Principal William Gray and told him the plan. I wanted to attend classes at Ridgemont High and remain an inconspicuous presence for the full length of the school year. The object, I told him, was to write a book about real, contemporary life in high school.

Principal Gray was a careful man with probing eyes. He

was wary of the entire plan, and he wanted to know what I had written before. I explained that I had authored a number of magazine profiles of people in the public eye.

"Like who?" he asked.

I named a few. A president's son. A few rock stars. A few actors. My last article had been on the songwriter-actor Kris Kristofferson.

Principal Gray eased back in his chair. "You know *Kris Kristofferson?*"

"Sure. I spent a few weeks on tour with him."

"Hell," said the principal. "What's he like?"

"A great guy." I told him a few Kris stories.

"Well now," said Principal Gray, "I think I can trust you. Maybe this *can* be worked out."

It was. Principal Gray called in an English teacher, Mrs. Gina George, and gave me a homeroom for the year. Four other teachers were also informed. I started school the next week as a seventeen-year-old senior.

Walking the halls of Ridgemont was at first an unnerving experience. I wore standard Southern California attire—tennis shoes, t-shirt, and backpack, but as I pushed past the other students I began to wonder. Was I *walking* too much like an adult? Was there some kind of neon light blinking on me— Imposter?

I was never found suspicious. In fact, for the first month, I was completely ignored at Ridgemont. I eavesdropped on conversations around me, made copious notes, winked at the teachers who knew, and made my way. I began to feel like a third-rate spy.

One day after school I wandered into journalism class and saw a girl I'd noticed before but had not met. She was hunt-and-pecking on the typewriter, looking caught in the midst of writer's block.

"Sorry to bother you," I said.

"You're not bothering me," she responded. She switched off her typewriter.

Her name was Linda Barrett, and she began asking rapid-fire questions, as if she was making a mental computer card out on me. Do you have a girlfriend? Where do you work? Who's your favorite teacher?

We talked until the janitors kicked us out, and then we sat in her car in the parking lot. She began pointing out campus notables through her windshield. She knew them all, and they knew her. Linda Barrett worked in the local mall, at a popular ice cream parlor.

I soon realized what a valuable friend I had made. Through Linda Barrett I met her best friend Stacy, Stacy's brother, Brad, and many others I would come to write about. It was the beginning of my social acceptance at Ridgemont High. As the year progressed, they became my group, and they were the characters I spent most of my days with. They were my friends.

As it happens with any writer, the temptation was to continue the research forever. My entire lifestyle changed that year. I went to malls, to slumber parties, to beaches, to countless fast-food stands. I can't remember all the times I left situations to "go to the bathroom" and furiously scribble notes on conversations and facts I'd just heard. Back at Ridgemont, no doubt, some still remember me as the guy with the bad bladder.

I found it was all too easy to recapture one's adolescence. The hard part was growing up again. I would return to my home in Los Angeles to visit former cohorts and old friends more and more infrequently. Their look was distant and puzzled.

"Still alive?" they'd ask. "Still writing?"

(Magazine journalists, like P.O.W.'s and Turkish drug prisoners, are presumed dead if not heard from over two major holidays.)

Even my own mother looked at me sadly as I passed through the living room one day.

"You used to be such a mature person," she said. "I remember when things like cars and the prom didn't mean anything to you." She shook her head. "You've changed. What happened to you?"

By the end of the school year I had become so accepted

that even Principal Gray had forgotten about my project. I attended the prom and passed by his table near the entrance, where he sat with Mrs. Gray, greeting students and introducing them to his wife. When he saw me, a fleeting look of panic crossed his face. Nine months later it was as if he couldn't quite recall my name or where he knew me from.

"It was a great year," I told him. "Thanks."

I returned to a prom table with a group of Ridgemont students and began to think. I had developed close friends and had come to follow their thoughts and movements so carefully, that I wondered exactly how important my own undercover scheme really was. I did not want to become yet another adult writing about adolescence and *the kids* from an adult perspective. This story, I felt, belonged to the kids themselves.

Over the next summer I visited many of the students I'd lived with that school year. I told them the story of my project. Their reaction was almost always the same.

"A book?" they said. "About *Ridgemont?*"

I later interviewed the main characters extensively, corroborating stories and notes from the previous year. I have tried to capture the flow of day-to-day high school life, as well as the life that begins as soon as the last bell rings. It was my intention to write of the entire business—from academic competition to the sexual blunders—of teenage adulthood. In all cases the people I have written about have been given names other than their own. I have taken the liberty of changing superficial identifying characteristics, but all the incidents are true.

It was an experience that will forever change the way I perceive the word *kids.* The only time these students acted like kids was when they were around adults. What follows is a year in the life of Ridgemont High.

—*Cameron Crowe*
February 1981

The Night Before

Stacy Hamilton lay under the covers, still fully dressed, and stared at the ceiling. Some- where in the course of the long and uneventful summer she  had come to an important decision. There was no way she was going to start senior high school still a virgin.

She listened to the noisy floorboards above her bed, fol- lowing her parents throughout their entire ritual of preparing for sleep. Every night at 11:30 precisely, off went the upstairs television. Then all the lights. Then came the rattling of the bathroom pipes. Finally, Frank and Evelyn Hamilton came to rest on their upstairs mattress with two resounding thuds. They were grateful, heavy sleepers. Stacy's brother, Brad, liked to say that nothing short of a ballistic-missile test in the living room could raise their parents after those last two thuds.

On this night, Stacy rolled out of bed and tied on a pair of tennis shoes. She took a red wool sweater for the cold night air. Soundlessly, she slid open her bedroom window and hopped out.

This was to have been Stacy Hamilton's Summer of Wild Abandon. Just turned fifteen, she was the youngest hostess at Swenson's Ice Cream Parlor—the prestigious Town Center Mall location. Stacy's friend Linda Barrett, who was two years older and a senior at Ridgemont High, had found her the job. She'd come to Stacy last April and put it to her plain and sim- ple—come to work at Swenson's and *your life will change.*

Well, it was now September. She'd been imprisoned all summer long in a hot, floor-length Peppermint Pattie hostess dress. Maybe her life *had* changed, Stacy figured, but it sure wasn't from seating the same immature boys she'd known since grade school, and it definitely wasn't from listening to all the parents jacked up on coffee and telling their kids to "just *stop* playing with the ice cream." No, if anything, Stacy's life had changed by listening to all the twelfth-grade waitresses in the back kitchen at Swenson's.

The Swenson's waitresses, most of whom went to Ridgemont, were not allowed to chat among themselves in the main dining room. Talking was permitted only in the kitchen area. It was a Swenson's tradition that whenever anything interesting happened, whenever an eligible male sauntered into the place, the waitresses would discreetly disappear into the back kitchen. Once in the back kitchen, the Peppermint Pattie act went right out the window. The Swenson's girls got down to business.

"Did you see that guy in B-9?"

"That's Bill from Toys 'R Us. He still lives at home."

"Really?"

"Christie went out with him and said he's a mama's boy."

"*Pass.* Is that Tuna Melt up yet?"

From the back kitchen talk at Swenson's, Stacy Hamilton had learned that the world of girls could be divided up into two distinct groups—those who spent the weekend with their parents, and those who spent it with *Allen* or *Bob*. The latter group was a special sorority. They spoke of their older boyfriends in a certain way. Their accounts of dates ended at a certain point, with a smile and a click of the tongue. The message was clear enough—there was fun, and then there was *sex*.

Stacy Hamilton was not yet a part of this group. She sensed that all the other waitresses knew, but accepted her anyway. Stacy was just a hostess and no threat to anyone's tips. She listened quietly. She was Linda Barrett's friend. The girls at Swenson's all liked Stacy. Sometimes they would even pat her on the head.

"You are really going to be beautiful," they told her, "*someday . . .*"

Stacy was a sweet-looking girl with long blond hair and only the last traces of adolescent baby fat. An interesting thing had happened over the summer. She had caught the flu and had lost weight and slimmed down to what her mother constantly reminded her was a "voluptuous figure." Stacy was not quite used to it yet. She had noticed increased attention from boys, but, as Linda Barrett pointed out, boys didn't count. The idea was to interest *men*.

Stacy had been working the cash register on the August night that The Vet first walked into Swenson's. He looked to be in his early twenties. He sat down alone at table C-9, clasped his bandless fingers in front of him, and ordered a French-dip sandwich. Stacy watched as the main-floor waitresses all vanished into the back kitchen. He was kind of cute, she decided, in a blow-dry sort of way.

He kept staring at her. It wasn't Stacy's imagination. Even the other girls noticed. The man finished his sandwich, by-passed any ice cream order, and walked directly over to Stacy with his check.

"So," he said with a ready smile, "are you working hard? Or hardly working?"

Stacy smiled back—they were supposed to enjoy all customer jokes unless obscene—and punched up the amount.

"Working hard," she said with studied indifference. She took his ten-dollar bill. "Out of ten."

"Listen," the man said, "my name is Ron Johnson."

She counted back his change. "I'm Stacy."

"You really look like someone I'd like to know. I never really do this, but . . ." He pulled a business card from his wallet and wrote his home number on the back. "Why don't you give me a call sometime. I'd love to take you out for dinner. What do you say?"

Caught by surprise, Stacy reverted to the tone and phrasing she usually reserved for customers asking for substitutions on to-go orders. "I'll see what I can do."

"I look forward to hearing from you."

"Okay. Thank you, and have a nice evening."

As soon as he walked out of Swenson's, three waitresses beelined for Stacy.

"What's his name? What's his name?"

"What a total fox!"

"Does he work in the mall?"

They crowded around the business card he'd left behind. He worked at a veterinary clinic in nearby Redondo Beach. His name was Ronald M. Johnson, but from that moment on he would always be known around Swenson's as The Vet.

On the advice of Linda Barrett, Stacy waited an appropriate three days to call The Vet. She reached him at home, where he lived with two college-buddies-turned-stereo-salesmen. They had a pleasant conversation about Swenson's, ice cream parlors in general, and veterinary school. Ron Johnson was very smooth about working in his key question.

"So," he said, "you look like you could still be in high school."

"I know," said Stacy, who was due to start high school in three-and-a-half weeks. "Everyone says that."

"How old *are* you?"

"Nineteen. How old are you?"

"Twenty-five," said The Vet. "Think we can still be friends?"

They had been on two dinner-and-movie dates before Stacy called her friend Linda Barrett for a special consultation. They met at Bob's Big Boy Restaurant. The issue—Stacy's Vanishing Summer of Wild Abandon.

"I'm depressed," said Stacy.

"About The Vet?"

"I guess," said Stacy. "I like him. He's a nice guy. He's good-looking. We go out, we have a fun time, but . . . *nothing happens.*"

"I don't believe this guy," said Linda. "You know what he reminds me of?" The words fell from her lips like spoiled clams: "A *high school* boy. Haven't you figured men out yet, Stacy? Most guys are just . . . pussies. For years I chased after every guy I thought was cute. I thought if I was nice to them, they'd get the idea and call me up. Well, guess what? They didn't call. I got impatient. So *I* started making the first move, and you know what else? Most guys are just too insecure and too chicken to do it themselves."

Stacy nodded. You didn't argue with Linda Barrett. Their two-year age difference made a world of difference. Linda was taller and quite striking, with dark, perm-styled hair and an always skillful make-up job. Linda knew men, and she knew how to carry herself. She had what she called "a sexual overview."

"I don't care *who* he is," Linda continued. "Two dates is *enough*. Are you sure he's not a fag?"

Talk suspended while a Bob's Big Boy waitress arrived, took the girls' order for coffee and Big Boy combinations, and then stood by the table totaling other checks. Linda and Stacy glared at her until she left.

"I don't think he's a fag," said Stacy. "He said he broke up with his girlfriend a few months ago."

"Well then, what are you waiting for? You're *good-looking*. You've just got to learn to get what you want. I know it sounds hard making the first move, but think of it like this. Three years from now you'll be eighteen and it won't matter either way."

The words made sense to Stacy. Two nights later she called The Vet and asked him to meet her that night for a drive. It didn't matter where they went, she said, she just had to get out of the house. The Vet agreed.

She met him out in front of her family's condominium complex, in the shadows next to the mailbox, where she was out of sight from the neighbors.

"Thanks for picking me up," she said, shivering despite her sweater. "I can't wait until I move out."

"No problem," said The Vet. "Where do you feel like going?"

"I don't know. Do you know where the Point is?"

"The Point?" The Vet looked at Stacy curiously, and for a moment she was sure she had given away her age. The Point was a notorious make-out spot for Ridgemont teenagers with parents at home. "The Point sounds good to me!"

They drove up Ridgemont Drive, past all the neon-lit fast-food restaurants, up the hill toward the campus of Ridgemont Senior High School. The parking lot was empty. The Vet found a space near the back corner. From there they walked across the baseball field to the cliff behind the Ridgemont High backstop. The Point.

The Point was the best spot to overlook the whole town. The Point was dark and secluded, with only one drawback. The Ridgemont High Point was always covered with milk cartons. Hundreds of milk cartons. Milk cartons with the straws still stuck inside. Milk cartons without. Squashed milk cartons. Milk cartons still half full. More milk cartons than you had ever seen in any one place at any one time, ever. There was the usual smattering of premixed Mai-Tai cans and shattered Bacardi bottles, sure, but the emphasis was always on milk cartons.

The Point was deserted. Only Stacy and The Vet stood there, arms touching, on their third summer date, looking out at the blinking lights of the condo developments below, listening to the distant sounds of the Pacific Ocean lapping up onto the shore of Redondo Beach.

"Let's sit down," said The Vet. But there were only rocks out on the Point. The Vet was the type, as Stacy would later tell Linda Barrett, who could probably have a lot more fun if he didn't wear slacks all the time.

"We can sit over there," said Stacy. "There's probably a seat in the baseball dugout."

They cleared their way through a summer's worth of trash, more milk cartons, and found a nice, concrete seat inside the visiting team dugout. Stacy and The Vet sat side by side. Above them shone a single light bulb. There was no view of the city from the dugout.

"You look nice tonight," said The Vet.

"You do, too."

Silence. Stacy rearranged her hands in her lap.

"It's pretty warm out tonight."

"It is. It's real warm. I wonder how long it will last."

The Vet leaned over and kissed Stacy on the cheek. *Was that the first move?* She sat quietly for a moment, her hands folded in her lap. *It had to be the first move.* She waited another monent. *When I'm eighteen it won't matter either way.*

She lunged for The Vet and kissed him squarely on the mouth. At first surprised, he held her there and kissed her even more deeply. She began to run her fingers through his blow-dry haircut.

It was The Vet who spoke first. "Are you really nineteen?"

"Yes," said Stacy. "I am *really* nineteen."

She kissed him again.

"I'd better take you home," he said.

"What about those other guys you live with?"

"I mean back to *your* home."

But they made no moves in any direction. A few minutes later, The Vet had apparently resolved his inner conflict. He began tugging lightly at Stacy's red corduroy pants. She looked down at his hand on the snap.

This was it, Stacy thought. The Real Thing. A thousand schoolyard conversations and tips from Linda Barrett jumbled in her head. Would it hurt? Would it be messy? Would she get pregnant? Would they fall in love?

"Do you really want to do this?" Stacy heard herself ask. "I mean, it's your final decision."

"I think we both want to."

Slowly, awkwardly, Stacy reached down to help him. She unsnapped her pants, and suddenly The Vet needed no more reassurance. He tilted her backward onto the concrete dugout bench. They continued kissing, feverishly, his hand slipping up into her blouse. He massaged her breasts. Then he pulled off her shoes. Then her pants. Then his own pants. Ron "The Vet" Johnson was different from the other boys she'd made out with. He had Technique.

"Is this your first time?" he whispered.

"Yesssssssss . . ."

As she held onto The Vet's shoulders and felt a man enter her for the first time, Stacy looked up at the top of the Ridgemont dugout. She would always remember reading the graffiti above her:

Heroin in the neck

Lincoln was here—Sieg Heil

Led Zeppelin

Dan y Roberto (Disco Fags)

Stacy Hamilton, fifteen, slipped back into her room at three that morning. Already her room felt different to her. Those frilly pillowcases, those Scholastic Book Services paperbacks she'd ordered in junior high, that bubblegum chain on the dresser . . . they all seemed out of place to her now.

She was giddy, wide awake. She sat on the edge of her bed and examined herself in the mirror—no difference. Somehow it was just like Linda Barrett had explained it to her. Her first feeling would be one of relief, the second, that she would want to go out and sleep with all the cute guys in the world because it was *so much fun*. Stacy smiled and turned on her clock radio. Then she picked up the telephone extension and punched out a number.

Linda Barrett answered her phone in a sleep-laden murmur. "Did you get him?"

"*Yes.*"

Linda laughed and cleared her throat. "Congratulations."

"See you tomorrow."

"See you tomorrow."

Stacy clicked off and dialed yet another number. This one was the request line for the local FM rock station.

"Good morning. KXLY." The disc jockey had her on a speaker box.

"Hi!" said Stacy. "Could you play 'Stairway to Heaven,' by Led Zeppelin?"

"Don't you have that record by now?" It was nothing personal. Led Zeppelin's "Stairway to Heaven" was just the most requested rock track of the last ten years. Any disc jockey knew it came with the territory. You answered the request line, chances were one in three it was some kid asking you to play "Stairway to Heaven."

"*Yes.* But the stereo is in the living room. And I like it better when you play it anyway."

The disc jockey must have liked the tone in her voice. "I'll try and get it on for you," he said.

It was Stacy's idea of the perfect touch—the supreme lullaby for her rite of passage. "Stairway to Heaven," with all its mythic optimism and thundering guitar soloing, had been her favorite song since fourth grade.

Stacy had already fallen asleep by the time KXLY played her song. She was dreaming of Swenson's Ice Cream Parlor, and the rock star David Bowie. In her dream, David Bowie had walked into the Town Center Mall location Swenson's and applied for a job. He was pregnant by the actor-comedian Chevy Chase, he said, and Linda Barrett had suggested he come in and see about busing tables. David Bowie was pleading for the position—"to support my baby"—when real life interrupted.

Stacy's clock radio clicked back on. She lay in her bed, face pressed into the pillow. It was 6:45 A.M.

"Get up, Stacy honey," came her mother's voice through the door. "These are the best years of your life!"

Green

The Ridgemont Senior High School official colors were red and yellow. But anyone who had ever attended the school did not think of red and yellow when it came to Ridgemont. They thought of green.

The whole place was green. Green walls in the gymnasium. Green classrooms. Green bungalows. Even the blackboards were green. New graffiti? Roll on some green. Crack in the wall? Slap on some green. It was a Ridgemont High joke that if all other disciplinary measures failed, they called in the janitors and painted you green, too.

There was a problem on this first day of regular classes at Ridgemont Senior High School, a problem beyond even the reach of green. In the early morning hours after Stacy and The Vet had left the Point, someone else had paid the school a visit. Someone had taken the steel letters.

The first sight any student saw upon turning off Ridgemont Drive into the school parking lot was Ridgemont High's green brick vanguard. Built as a memorial to the Ridgemont students slain in the Vietnam War, the vanguard was meant to spell out the school's name with "honor and omnipotence."

But on this first morning the steel letters said only: IDG MON SEN OR HI HO.

There was more. The rest of Ridgemont High was wrapped in toilet paper. Toilet paper, that most versatile of high school vandalism weapons. Toilet paper wafted from the trees out front and tangled in the branches where it was virtually impossible to remove without a janitor on a ladder having to unhook each piece. Toilet paper had been applied to the 200 Building windows with an egg-and-wax mixture that adhered to it with true permanence. There was even toilet paper strewn through the yards of those unfortunate homeowners across the street from Ridgemont High, on Luna Avenue. Someone had really done a job. And the toilet paper was green.

A spray-paint message had been left along the side of the front office building: LINCOLN SURF NAZIS.

Lincoln High School, located several miles inland, was Ridgemont's crosstown rival.

"I know who did it," said Brad Hamilton, seventeen. "It was those *little* fuckers. They're wild. They come up out of Paul Revere Junior High, and they're out to ruin *our* senior year."

Standing by the A-B-C-D-E registration counter in the gymnasium, waiting to pick up his red add card on the first day, Brad Hamilton had the unmistakable aura of Important Man on Campus. He stood surrounded by four buddies, all of them dressed in the same ventilated golf caps with brand logos like CAT and NATIONAL CHAINSAW on the front. They all nodded vigorously at everything Brad said. They all worked together at the same Carl's Jr. hamburger franchise on Ridgemont Drive, where Brad was head fryer.

"They ought to just waste those guys," said Brad, "one by one, as soon as they leave junior high."

Every June, Paul Revere Junior High held a graduation procession for the outgoing ninth graders. Several hundred of the fourteen-year-olds crossed Ridgemont Drive en masse, a symbolic passage toward higher education. Ridgemont High

School upperclassmen usually launched water balloons at them from strategic locations. For them, the Paul Revere procession was like a dirty river about to empty into their backyard.

The kids from Paul Revere would find that things change quickly in high school. Suddenly it was considered in bad taste to continue adolescent behavior into tenth grade. High school brought on new responsibilities and a whole new set of priorities. It was different from what it had been ten, or even five years earlier. One of the most common phrases heard in high school was now: "I went through my *drug* phase in junior high."

Once in high school a kid could drive, and a car necessitated a certain cash flow. An allowance from your parents was not only demeaning, it wasn't enough. It didn't take long for a kid to see the big picture—you were nothing unless you had a job. But well-paying teen jobs were scarce, especially since the abolishment of training wages.

Ah, but there was always one bastion of teen employment left. That one business where a guy like Brad Hamilton was king.

"I'm in fast food," Brad would say with professional dignity.

Brad's job as chief fryer at Carl's Jr. was no trifling matter, but what was particularly impressive was Brad's *location*. He worked at the Carl's Jr. at the very top of Ridgemont Drive.

Like most of his friends, Brad worked six days a week. School was not a major concern. Actually it was fourth on his list, after Carl's and Girls and Being Happy. School was no problem, especially this year. Brad could have graduated as a junior last year—he had enough units—but why do that? It had been a major task to reach a social peak in junior high and then work up again through high school. After two years at Ridgemont, Brad was on top. He knew practically everyone, and he was well liked. For Brad, the best part of school was being with his friends and seeing them every day.

This, as Brad had been saying since last year and all summer long at Carl's, would be his Cruise Year. He had selected only four classes—Mechanical Arts, Running Techniques, Advanced Health and Safety, and Public Speaking. He wanted to enjoy the year, take it easy, and not rush things.

"Hi, Bradley!" It was his sister, Stacy, a sophomore.

"What are *you* so happy about?"

"Sor-ry," said Stacy.

"Who do you have fifth period?" Brad asked.

"U.S. History. Mr. Hand."

"Hey-*yo*," said Brad.

"Hey-*yooooooo*," said his friends in the ventilated golf caps.

"You'd better get to class," Brad instructed. "The show begins after the third bell."

After Stacy left, one of Brad's friends turned to him. "Your sister is really turning into a fox."

"You should see her in the morning," said Brad.

Mr. Hand

Stacy Hamilton took her seat in U.S. History on the first day of school. The third and final attendance bell rang.

He came barreling down the aisle, then made a double-speed step to the green metal front door of the U.S. history bungalow. He kicked the door shut and *locked* it with the dead bolt. The windows rattled in their frames. This man knew how to take the front of a classroom.

"Aloha," he said. "The name is Mr. Hand."

There was a lasting silence. He wrote his name on the blackboard. Every letter was a small explosion of chalk.

"I have but one question for you on our first morning together," the man said. "Can you attend my class?"

He scanned the classroom full of curious sophomores, all

of them with roughly the same look on their faces—there goes another summer.

"Pakalo?" It was Hawaiian for Do you understand?

Mr. Hand let his students take a good long look at him. In high school, where such crucial matters as confidence and social status can shift daily, there is one thing a student can depend on. Most people in high school look like their names. Mr. Hand was a perfect example. He had a porous, oblong face, just like a thumbprint. His stiff black hair rose up off his forehead like that of a late-night television evangelist. Even at eight in the morning, his yellow Van Heusen shirt was soaked at the armpits.

And he was not Hawaiian.

The strange saga of Mr. Hand had been passed down to Stacy Hamilton by Brad. Arnold Hand, Ridgemont's U.S. history instructor, was one of *those* teachers. His was a special brand of eccentricity, the kind preserved only through California state seniority laws. Arnold Hand had been at Ridgemont High for years, waging his highly theatrical battle against what he saw as the greatest threat to the youth of this land—truancy.

According to Stacy's brother, you had to respect a teacher like Mr. Hand. Hand was one of the last *teacher* teachers, as Brad had put it. Most of the other members of the Ridgemont faculty subscribed to the latest vogue in grading, the "contract" method. Under the contract system a student agreed to a certain amount of work at the beginning of the year, and then actually signed a legal form binding him to the task. The contract teacher argued that he or she was giving the student a lesson in Real Life, but in fact it was easier on the teacher. Grades were given according to the amount of contract work done, and such matters as attendance didn't matter to the contract teacher.

Mr. Hand wanted no part of the contract system. The only thing worse than a lazy student, he said, was a lazy teacher. Even the hardcore truant cases had to agree. The last thing they wanted to see was somebody up there looking for loopholes just like them. For them, Mr. Hand was one of the few surviving teachers at Ridgemont who still gave a shit about things like weekly quizzes or attendance slips—who gave a shit, period. That's what Brad had told Stacy.

Mr. Hand's other favorite activity was hailing the virtues of the three bell system. At Ridgemont, the short first bell meant a student had three minutes to prepare for the end of the class. The long second bell dismissed the class. Then there were exactly seven minutes—and Mr. Hand claimed that he *personally* fought the Education Center for those seven minutes—before the third and *last* attendance bell. If you did not have the ability to obey the three bell system, Hand would say, then it was Aloha Time for you. You simply would not function in life.

"And functioning in life," Hand said grandly on that first morning, "is the hidden postulate of education."

At age fifty-eight, Mr. Hand had no intention of leaving Ridgemont. Why, in the last ten years he had just begun to hit his stride. He had found one man, *that one man* who embodied all the proper authority and power to exist "in the jungle." It didn't bother Mr. Hand that his role model happened to be none other than Steve McGarrett, the humorless chief detective of "Hawaii Five-O."

First-year U.S. history students, sensing something slightly odd about the man, would inch up to Hand a few days into the semester. "Mr. Hand," they would ask timidly, "how come you act like that guy on 'Hawaii Five-O'?"

"I don't know what you're talking about."

It was, of course, much too obvious for his considerable pride to admit. But Mr. Hand pursued his students as tirelessly as McGarrett pursued his weekly criminals, with cast-iron emotions and a paucity of words. Substitute truancy for drug traffic, missed tests for robbery, U.S. History for Hawaii, and you had a class with Mr. Hand. Little by little, Mr. Hand's protean personality had been taken over by McGarrett. He became possessed by "Five-O." He even got out of his Oldsmobile sedan in the mornings at full stand, whipping his head both ways, like McGarrett.

"History," Hand had barked on that first morning, "U.S. or otherwise, has proven one thing to us. Man does not do any-

26

thing that is not for his own good. It is for your own good that you attend my class. And if you can't make it . . . I can make *you.*"

An impatient knock began at the front door of the bungalow, but Mr. Hand ignored it.

"There will be tests in this class," he said immediately. "We have a twenty-question quiz every Friday. It will cover all the material we've dealt with during the week. There will be no make-up exams. You can see it's important that you have your *Land of Truth and Liberty* textbook by Wednesday at the *latest.*"

The knock continued.

"Your grade in this class is the average of all your quizzes, plus the midterm and final, which counts for one-third."

The door knocker now sounded a lazy calypso beat. No one dared mention it.

"Also. There will be no *eating* in this class. I want you to get used to doing *your* business on *your* time. That's one demand I make. You do your business on your time, and I do my business on my time. I don't like staying after class with you on detention. That's *my* time. Just like you wouldn't want me to come to your house some evening and discuss U.S. history with you on *your* time. Pakalo?"

Hand finally turned, as if he had just noticed the sound at the door, and began to approach the green metal barrier between him and his mystery truant. Hand opened the door only an inch.

"Yes?"

"Yeah," said the student, a surfer. "I'm registered for this class."

"*Really?*" Hand appeared enthralled.

"Yeah," said the student, holding his all-important red add card up to the crack in the door. "This is U.S. History, right? I saw the globe in the window."

Jeff Spicoli, a Ridgemont legend since third grade, lounged against the door frame. His long dirty-blond hair was parted exactly in the middle. He spoke thickly, like molasses pouring from a jar. Most every school morning Spicoli awoke before dawn, smoked three bowls of marijuana from a small steel bong, put on his wet suit, and surfed before school. He was never at school on Fridays, and on Mondays only when he could handle it. He leaned a little into the room, red eyes glistening. His long hair was still wet, dampening the back of his white peasant shirt.

"May I come in?"

"Oh, *please*," replied Hand. "I get so *lonely* when that third attendance bell rings and I don't see all my *kids* here."

The surfer laughed—he was the only one—and handed over his red add card. "Sorry I'm late. This new schedule is totally confusing."

Hand read the card aloud with utter fascination in his voice. "Mr. *Spicoli?*"

"Yes, sir. That's the name they gave me."

Mr. Hand slowly tore the red add card into little pieces, effectively destroying the very existence of Jeffrey Spicoli, fifteen, in the Redondo school system. Mr. Hand sprinkled the little pieces over his wastebasket.

Spicoli stood there, frozen in the process of removing his backpack. "You just ripped up my card," he said with disbelief. "What's your *problem?*"

Mr. Hand moved to within several inches of Spicoli's face. "No problem," he said breezily. "I think you know where the front office is."

It took a moment for the words to work their way out of Jeff Spicoli's mouth.

"You *dick.*"

Mr. Hand cocked his head. He appeared poised on the edge of incredible violence. There was a sudden silence while the class wondered exactly what he might do to the surfer. Deck him? Throw him out of Ridgemont? Shoot him at sunrise?

But Mr. Hand simply turned away from Jeff Spicoli as if the kid had just ceased to exist. Small potatoes. Hand simply continued with his first-day lecture.

"I've taken the trouble," he said, "to print up a complete schedule of class quizzes and the chapters they cover. Please pass them to all the desks behind you."

Spicoli remained at the front of the class, his face flushed, still trying to sort out what had happened. Hand coolly counted out stacks of his purple mimeographed assignment sheets. After a time, Spicoli fished a few bits of his red add card out of the wastebasket and huffed out of the room.

Hand had made his entrance, just as Brad said he would. But the strange saga of Mr. Hand wasn't the only item Brad Hamilton handed down to his sister. He had also passed her a fairly complete set of Mr. Hand's weekly quizzes. Hand did not change them from year to year, a well-known fact that rendered him harmlessly entertaining.

"So," said Hand just before the last bell, "let's recap. First test on Friday. Be there. Aloha."

Linda Barrett

Stacy Hamilton's second-period class was Beginning Journalism/School Newspaper, the only class she would share this year with her friend Linda  Barrett. Ridgemont High prided itself in a strong and sophisticated school newspaper. The *Ridgemont Reader* covered world and school news alike, all in six pages. It was infrequent that an underclassman like Stacy was allowed to join the staff, but Linda Barrett had arranged that, too.

The teacher was a young woman in her early thirties, a slightly frazzled-looking brunette who wore her hair in a short ponytail. Her name was Mrs. Sheehan, but most of her returning students called her Rita. On the first day of class, Mrs. Sheehan was seated at one of the beige plastic desks arranged in a semicircle around her classroom. At the front of the room, sitting on Mrs. Sheehan's desk and kicking her legs rhythmically against the front panel, was Angie Parisi, the student editor of the *Ridgemont Reader*. She wore a tight Black Sabbath t-shirt.

"Okay," said Angie, "does everybody have their assignments for the first issue?"

A beefy kid in a red-and-yellow letterman's jacket spoke louder than the others. "When do I have to have my column in?"

Angie cast a wicked sidelong glance at the rest of the class. "How about Friday *afternoon?* Like everybody else, *William.*"

"But football is this Friday, and I want to include some observations about the first football game. You know?"

Groans.

"Be grateful you have the column at all, William."

The remark seemed to roll right off William. You got the feeling he was used to it.

"Okay," continued Angie, "where is Alan Davidson?"

"Here." He was short, and wore an oversized blue down vest, winter and summer.

"Alan, how is that piece coming on angel dust smokers out on Luna Street?"

"They don't talk much. I ask them questions and they just kind of *look* at me . . ."

The class was disrupted by the arrival of Linda Barrett. Late, as always, she bustled through the door of journalism class carrying an armload of books. She headed straight for the empty seat beside Stacy Hamilton, and plopped her cargo on the desk. Everything stopped in journalism class—Linda was wearing tight jeans and a filmy blue blouse with three buttons undone.

"Well," she said in a sparkling voice, "do you want to hear my excuse now or later, Rita?"

Mrs. Sheehan watched her with tired eyes, even on this first day. This was her third year with Linda Barrett.

"Please try and be on time, Linda."

"But my locker broke, Mrs. Sheehan!"

"Just try and be on time, Linda."

"I'm sorry, Rita."

The class resumed.

Linda leaned over and punched Stacy's arm. They had not seen each other yet this morning, and they hadn't talked since the phone call at 3 A.M. "God, you look so good," she whispered. "Where did it happen?"

Stacy smiled.

"*Where?*"

"The baseball field."

"The *baseball field?*"

"Well, not really the baseball field. The dugout."

"The *dugout?*"

"Well, where else do you go?"

Linda punched Stacy's arm again. "I don't believe you. Is this serious?"

"Come on," Stacy cracked. "It's just sex."

They both laughed, and Linda feigned great shock at her younger friend's use of one of Linda's favorite lines.

Somehow all roads at Ridgemont High led to Linda Barrett. Everyone knew her. She left an indelible mark on most students who came in contact with her. She was chronically exuberant, usually in a relentlessly good mood. She knew how to *dress*, and she knew how to *walk*.

Even as far back as grade school, other girls came to Linda Barrett for counseling. Her mother was a nurse at University Hospital, and somehow Linda knew all the facts of life before any other kid her age in Ridgemont.

Linda's view of sex was, basically, that everyone had blown it way out of proportion. "A lot of girls *use* sex," she had told Stacy Hamilton long ago. "They use sex to get a guy closer. To really nail him down or something. To say 'I had sex with you, you owe me something.' Well, that's terrible. They're not having sex to have sex. They're having sex to *use* it as something. I'd hate myself if I did that."

No question about it. Linda Barrett was an authority. While the other girls were just abandoning their tricycles, Linda was underlining and memorizing all the sex scenes from *Shōgun*. Some had *Seventeen* magazine in their lockers; she had *The Hite Report*.

Linda and Stacy had been sitting at a bus stop the winter before, when Stacy turned to Linda. "Linda," she asked, "will you help me get birth control pills?"

Linda, then sixteen, turned all pro. "We'll go down to the clinic and get them tomorrow."

"You just *go* down there?"

"Yeah. They give them to you free. But you've got to need them first."

"Linda," Stacy had said with determination, "I'm getting ready to need them."

The next day they ditched third period and took a bus to the downtown free clinic. They were too late for the noon session, so they walked around downtown for an hour. The two girls looked so young, not even the sailors bothered them.

"When you get in there," Linda had advised, "you tell them that you have sex twice a week."

Stacy nodded.

"If you tell them the truth, they won't give you the right pills. They'll try to talk you into a diaphragm or something, and that might really hurt. You've got to hold out for the pills."

It took forever. The free clinic, Stacy thought at the time, was like anything else—they made you wait a long time for what you really wanted. First, three nurses led the group of girls into a high-ceilinged "rap room," public service jargon for a room with bean bags instead of chairs, and proceeded with a half-hour presentation of Responsibilities of Sex. They used the same diagrams Stacy had seen in eighth- and ninth-grade sex-education classes. Then, finally, each girl waited for a private examination and prescription from one of the free clinic doctors.

When Stacy Hamilton finally reached her examination room, a nurse sat her on a steel table and asked her to wait a moment for a Dr. Betkin. Fifteen minutes later Dr. Betkin breezed into the room.

"Good afternoon."

"Good afternoon."

He gave Stacy the once-over. "You look a little young. Why are you here?"

Stacy responded with all the spontaneity of a war prisoner under interrogation. "I have sex twice a week."

"*Twice* a week? How old are you?"

"Fifteen."

The doctor nodded once. He took out a pad. "Uh-*huh*.

Well, I'm going to start you on Norinyl I Plus 50s. I'm giving you three months' worth. Now what I want you to do is please, and this is very important, wait thirty days before you have sex again. Okay? That's not impossible, is it?"

"No. Thank you, doctor."

Dr. Betkin paused before he left the room. "Are you a virgin?"

Stacy almost admitted it. "Sort of."

Dr. Betkin nodded and left the room.

On the way out of the free clinic, Linda and Stacy passed a donation box.

"Do you have any change?"

"No," said Linda, "we'll get it next time."

Linda and Stacy hadn't been friends in junior high. Stacy was in sixth grade and worked in the attendance office. Linda was a haughty eighth grader who hadn't had time for the likes of Stacy.

Linda Barrett always had a score of boyfriends. She acted as if she didn't know why, which only compounded the jealousy of girls like Stacy. Linda was the first girl at Paul Revere Junior High to get tits. Large, full-grown breasts. Even at twelve, she would pull a sweater over her head like she was Ursula Andress.

Linda began dressing out of *Vogue*, wearing stylish raincoats on sunny days. She developed a distaste for males in the same age group. Linda went out with *high school boys* then, and she logged long nights out in the parking lot of Town Center Mall. One of her boyfriends turned her on to smoking pot, and Linda pursued it with her typical uninhibited zeal. She began buying and selling whole kilos out of her room. Then she added speed and coke to the trade. The only drugs Linda Barrett, then thirteen, never sold were heroin and LSD.

But it was not as if her activities as a junior high drug kingpin suddenly changed Linda. She was the same freckle-faced Linda. There was just no way she was ever going to save up for her dream car—a red Chevy Ranchero—with household chore money. No way could she buy make-up, food, clothes, and records . . . forget about records. Everything was too expensive. So she sold dope. And she went out with high school boys who paid for everything.

One Saturday night Linda and a gang of Ridgemont High boys planned a visit to the Regal Theatre to see a midnight showing of *Jimi Plays Berkeley*, the famous Hendrix concert movie. Linda sneaked out of her house and met the boys in the alley behind the Ridgemont Bowl.

Standing in the alley, Linda and the three boys smoked some hash and drank a little tequila from the bottle. A kid named Gary drove to the Regal. They all bought tickets and went inside.

Five minutes into Jimi Hendrix's first guitar solo of the film, two of Linda's friends let loose with bloodcurdling war cries. "AAAAHHH-WOOOOOOOOO!!!!! RIGHTEOUS!!!!!"

As their howls continued, paper cups and boxes began to fly at them from all sections of the theatre. Someone threw a bottle. A scuffle broke out around Linda and her friends. They were all kicked out of the Regal.

At ten minutes after twelve there was not much to do around Ridgemont. The kids sat in Gary's car in the parking lot, and Linda plucked from her purse some finely ground speed. She laid out four lines on a pocket mirror, and each of them snorted it through a Carl's Jr. straw. Then they finished off the rest of the tequila. It was quite a car party.

Someone got the idea to return to the Town Center Mall parking lot, and Gary fired up the car. Halfway back to the mall, Linda Barrett tapped on Gary's shoulder. Her voice was soft, shaking. "I think I'm going to get sick."

"Open the window! Stick your head out and you'll feel . . ."

Linda had the window down halfway when it hit. It was the most ungracious thing she had ever done. She vomited down the inside of the door of Gary's car.

"GODDAMN IT!" shouted Gary. "This is gonna stink for days!"

One of the other boys came to Linda's defense. "Just shut up, *asshole*, and pull into a gas station. We'll clean it up."

34

"What am I running here," said Gary. "A *Barf* Mobile?"

"Just pull into this Arco."

Through it all, Linda stayed in the back with her head on the side armrest.

Gary and his Ridgemont High buddies were just driving into Town Center Mall when they noticed Linda wasn't speaking any more. She wasn't making any sound at all.

They tried to slap her awake, and when that didn't work the boys started to panic. They tried discreetly walking her around the mall parking lot. They tried cold water on her face. They pressed the nerve in her shoulder. Nothing. Then Linda's high school friends arrived at their solution. They propped Linda up against a closed jeans store and called Town Center Mall Security, just before tearing ass *out* of there.

The mall security force referred the call to the Ridgemont Police Department, and when the police arrived, the first thing they did was search Linda Barrett's purse. The Ridgemont police then called Mr. and Mrs. Barrett at two in the morning and informed them that their daughter was not safely asleep down the hall, but instead on her way to University Hospital to have her stomach pumped, with a charge of amphetamines, crystallized speed, and marijuana possession.

Linda Barrett awoke to a scene out of TV drama. Mrs. Barrett was standing over her daughter's bed, screaming at the ceiling as if it were the heavens.

"*Where* did I go wrong? Oh, GOD IN HEAVEN, where did I go wrong with this child?"

Linda looked up feebly. Her first words were, "I don't know why they pumped my stomach. I already threw up everything."

Her mother fell silent for a moment. Then she started screaming at the ceiling again. "DEAR JESUS IN HEAVEN . . ."

Linda Barrett told the complete story to her parents. It had happened for the best, she told them. Now she knew how immature boys were, and how immature she had been. Linda took all the blame herself and promised to change.

Amazingly enough, she did.

Linda set about courting the straightest girl she knew,

Stacy Hamilton. Stacy, who lived in the same condominium complex, worked in the attendance office of Paul Revere. Linda began dropping by, making conversation. She called Stacy constantly. She wrote Stacy notes. She sat next to her at lunch. And slowly, very slowly, Stacy Hamilton, a somewhat plump and prudish young honor student, came to view Linda Barrett as a friend.

When Linda Barrett moved over to Ridgemont High, many of the same boys she had gone out with before the bust were still attending the school. The same boys who abandoned her in the mall pretended it never happened. They took one look at Linda Barrett, then fifteen and gorgeous, in full bloom, and they began crowding around her. They asked her out. They proposed. They complimented her until, as she told Stacy, they turned blue. Linda Barrett still would not go out with another high school boy. It made her more desirable than ever.

As part of her Juvenile Hall rehabilitation program, Linda Barrett had joined a Christian youth organization called Campus Life. Campus Life met once a week during third period—no Algebra—and on irregular weekends for prayer outings at various sites around the county.

Linda had been on a weekend retreat in the country, praying with a group of other girls under a tree, when she first met Doug Stallworth.

"Hey," said Doug Stallworth, "anybody seen a little gold chain around here?"

Their eyes met. Linda Barrett gazed at a young man who was older than the high school boys, but not too old. He had a face that was a little too thin, a nose that was a bit too big, but he did have that one great asset of maturity. He had a beard.

They began going out, Linda and her "older man." Doug Stallworth was then twenty years old. He had just graduated Lincoln High School. Not only was he older, but he was also from the forbidden *rival high school.* To Doug, Linda Barrett was the complete fox girlfriend he had never had before. They fell in love, and had stayed that way throughout her entire sophomore and junior years at Ridgemont. Almost every day after her last class, Doug would be waiting for her out on Luna

Street, on a break from his job at Barker Brothers Furniture. It was one of the sights Ridgemont students were used to.

Pictures of Doug Stallworth filled Linda Barrett's green Velcro wallet. She showed them to everybody. Doug, clowning. Doug, sexy. Doug, indignant. Doug. His name appeared on all of Linda's Pee-Chee folders and notebooks and free pages of her textbooks. Douglas Raymond Stallworth. Mrs. Raymond Douglas Stallworth. Stallworth Raymond Douglas. Dougie. The names of their kids.

And that was how Linda Barrett had come to be the retired sex expert of Ridgemont Senior High School, giving her young neighborhood friend, Stacy Hamilton, the many benefits of her years of field experience.

One day last May, Linda had called Stacy to break the news. She and Doug were engaged to be married. Doug had just asked her on a drive-in date to see *A Force of One*, and she had accepted, and they were going to be married on an undisclosed date. The local papers printed a blurb with a picture.

From that moment on, their relationship began a downhill slide. Other boys started slipping back into her peripheral vision. The engagement was still on, of course, but Christ, she didn't know *when*.

Lunch Court

Finding the right spot at Ridgemont High's outdoor lunch area was tougher than getting the best table at the finest restaurant. It was a puny swimming-pool-sized courtyard dominated by a stocky oak tree in the center, and it was always packed with students. Even by the first day, they had sectioned off into different cliques and staked out their lunch-court territory for the year.

All this for a twenty-six-minute lunch period.

The closer one looked at lunch court, the more interesting

it became. The object had always been to eat near the big oak tree at the center, and in the beginning at Ridgemont it was the surfers and stoners who ruled this domain. Seven years later, they had moved to the parking lot and the cafeteria (which was twice the size of lunch court, but tainted with a reputation as an underclassmen's hangout).

Now each group clustered around lunch court was actually a different contingent of Ridgemont fast-food employees. Lunch-court positions corresponded directly with the prestige and quality of the employer. Why, a man was only as good as his franchise.

Working inward from the outskirts of Ridgemont High's lunch court were the lowly all-night 7-Eleven workers, then the Kentucky Fried Chicken and Burger King crowd, the Denny's and Swenson's types, all leading to the top-of-Ridgemont-Drive-location Carl's Jr. employees. And at the center of lunch court, eating cold chicken under the hallowed big oak tree, was Brad Hamilton.

Brad was popular around Ridgemont. In the world of fast food, once you had achieved a position of power, the next sign of influence was to bring in your friends. Brad had paid his dues. He had loaded his Carl's Jr. with buddies. And why not? He even helped train them.

"No friend of mine," Brad once said, "will ever have to work at a 7-Eleven or in a supermarket."

And for that Brad's friends admired and respected him.

Carl's Jr. was at the top of the Ridgemont fast-food hierarchy for several important reasons. It had a fine location at the top of Ridgemont Drive. Anybody headed anywhere in Ridgemont passed that Carl's Jr. It was clean, with a fountain in the middle of the dining area and never too many kids on their bicycles. Brad, like the other employees, even came there on his off-hours, and that was the ultimate test. By evening, Carl's would be crawling with Ridgemont kids.

But why Carl's? Why not some other fast-food operation? Why not Burger King? Why not McDonald's? Or Jack-in-the-Box?

The answer was simple enough, as Brad himself would tell you. Their food wasn't as good. And places like Burger

King were always giving away glasses and catering to small kids who came whipping into the restaurant on their bicycles. McDonald's was McDonald's. Too familiar, too prefab, too many games. McDonald's was good only if you had no other choice, or if you just wanted fries.

Jack-in-the-Box was suspect because all the food was pre-cooked and heated by sunlamps. It was also common knowledge that the whole Jack-in-the-Box franchise was owned by Ralston-Purina, the well-known dog-food manufacturer. Kentucky Fried Chicken was too boring, and Wendy's was too close to Lincoln High School.

The top-of-Ridgemont-Drive Carl's Jr., on the other hand, had achieved that special balance between location and food quality. At Carl's, the burgers were char-broiled. This crucial fact not only meant that the meal was better, but it returned a little bit of the fast-food power to the kid behind the counter. A guy like Brad Hamilton felt like a real chef.

"Hey Brad," people were always saying to him, "your fries are even better than McDonald's."

"You know it," Brad would say, as if they were, in fact, *his* fries.

Brad had settled into a nice, comfortable pattern, in life and in work. In life, he had a petite and popular girlfriend named Lisa. Lisa was one of the intercom girls at Carl's.

Brad's three best friends, his golf-cap buddies, also worked at Carl's. They were David Lemon, Gary Myers, and Richard Masuta. When they weren't hanging out at school together, they were either at Carl's or driving around Ridgemont together in The Cruising Vessel.

In work Brad had his own method, and at it he was the best. Working the fryer at Carl's was a system governed by beeps. One high beep—the fries were done. One low—change the oil. But Brad didn't even have to go by the beeps. He *knew* when the fries were perfect. He *knew* when to change the oil, and he knew his fryer.

Normally quiet in class, once Brad got behind the fryer at Carl's he was in command. He'd carry on a running dialogue with his coworkers. Or he would listen to the drive-up customers in their cars trying to decide what to order, not realizing the intercom was on and everybody in the kitchen could hear them.

("Look, do you want goddamn cheese or not, Estelle? Hey, quit that! I'm not your punching bag!")

Intercom customers killed Brad. Sometimes, when Lisa was working the intercom, she'd get some little Romeo trying to pick her up. She had a nice, cute voice.

"Do you want anything else with that?" Lisa would say.

"Only if you come with the food, babe."

Then the Romeo would drive up to the window and Brad would be standing there with a professional Carl's smile.

"Hi. How are you tonight?" he'd say. "That'll be $4.35."

"You know, you *do* sound like a girl on the intercom."

"Oh, really?"

"Yeah. Who was I talking to?"

And Brad would count back the change. "You were talking to me, *babe*."

Then he would hand them hamburgers with patties he'd rubbed on his shoe.

Being the main fryer at Carl's meant that everybody had to be nice to you. The other workers depended on Brad for their orders. The only real problem came when company sales were down and the franchise added a "specialty" item, like a cheese-steak or The Hungry Guy (sliced turkey breast on a freshly baked roll with mayonnaise and butter). Forget it. That stuff took forever to make. And some recreation-center clown with a whistle around his neck would always come in and order *fifteen* of them.

But Brad was the calmest guy in the building.

"I need eight double-cheese, Brad!"

"No problem."

"I gotta go. Can you bag them?"

"Go ahead and take off."

When Brad was a sophomore, he wanted to be a lawyer. His parents were delighted. His school counselor set him up in an apprenticeship program with a local law firm. He was there three weeks and became disillusioned. He'd gone to a criminal law defense attorney and asked him a question: "If you got a guy freed on a little technicality, even though you knew he had committed a murder, wouldn't that be on your conscience for the rest of your life?"

"Why don't you try corporate law," was his answer.

Brad spent the next week with a woman lawyer from Redondo Beach Gas and Electric. It was so boring that he'd taken up drinking coffee. He had decided not to think about what to do now that his "lawyer phase" had ended. Right now Brad was the best fryer at the best location around, and that was what was important at Ridgemont High School—especially for his senior year, and things like lunch court.

The topic of conversation at the center of lunch court today was the Hand-Spicoli incident. Three periods later, it had been blown into enormous proportions.

"He almost pulled a gun on Mr. Hand," said Brad Hamilton. "Spicoli had a piece on him. He came right over to Mechanical Drawing and told us."

"Hey Brad," said one of his Carl's friends, "did he say 'dick off' or 'suck dick'?"

"He just got *right* in Mr. Hand's face," said Brad, "and he goes . . ." Brad contorted his face as he recreated the moment. " 'Yoooou fuckin' *DICK!*' And Mr. Hand didn't do anything. Spicoli said if he'd tried anything, he would have pulled the gun. He was going to blow Mr. Hand away. But he came over to Mechanical Drawing instead."

"Whoa."

"He ain't coming back here," said Brad.

But Spicoli would be back the next day in all his glory. The lure of lunch court was too great even for him.

And while everyone was telling and retelling the "you-dick" story, few even noticed an even bigger Ridgemont event that had occurred quietly over the summer. The administration had hired a new dean of discipline. They had replaced Vince.

There had never been much serious trouble at Ridgemont High. Every now and then there was a fight or a locker search, but mostly it was a calm, middle-class high school. Much of that peace, students figured, had to do with the presence of a 260-pound dean of discipline. His name was Vince Lupino, and one look at him stomping around campus made any student feel a little closer to the law.

But this year Vince was gone. Word had it that he had made friends with too many students, had pinched the wrong butt. Vince had had a weakness for eating lunch with the "older girls," the ones who wore the most expensive clothes, ran for student offices like director of social activities, and always looked as if they'd just winged in from Acapulco with the son of Ricardo Montalban.

In Vince's place this year was a different kind of disciplinarian altogether. His name was Lieutenant Lawrence "Larry" Flowers, and he let you know it by wearing a gold name plate directly over his left breast. He was a lean-and-quick-looking black man, and he wore dark blue police suits. He was also distinguished by a pencil-thin moustache, carefully clipped to a wisp. His overall appearance was that of Nat King Cole with a license to kill. The administration had brought in Flowers from some hellhole junior high in Pittsburgh. As he walked, his eyes darted in all directions, as if he half-expected some PCP-crazed teenager to leap at him with a machete.

Lieutenant Flowers passed through lunch court virtually unnoticed on the first day of school. That would soon change.

On the outskirts of lunch court sat Linda Barrett and Stacy Hamilton. Not too close to the inner sanctum, not too far away. Linda, cheese sandwich in hand, casually pointed out some of the Ridgemont personalities to Stacy.

"See over there," she said. She nodded to a frizzy brown-haired boy accepting cash from a small crowd of students around him. "That's Randy Eddo. He's the Ridgemont ticket scalper. He probably makes more money than both of our dads put together."

"Really? A ticket scalper?"

"He says he's not a scalper. He says he provides a service for concert goers. And that the service costs extra money."

"I see."

Linda went on to explain. Although Led Zeppelin was still king of the Ridgemont parking lot after ten years, each new season brought another band discovery. A new group then influenced the set lists of the Ridgemont school dance bands, and usually one main-focus rock star dictated the dress code. This year that star was the lead singer of Cheap Trick, Robin Zander, a young man with longish blond hair cut in bangs just above his eyes. This year on Ridgemont lunch court there were three Robin Zander lookalikes.

"None of them talk to each other," noted Linda Barrett.

A couple, arms around each other's waists and oblivious to everyone, walked past her and Stacy.

"Now *that*," said Linda, "is Gregg Adams and Cindy Carr."

The school couple.

Gregg Adams was equal part sensitive drama student and school funny guy. He looked like a contestant on "The Dating Game." Gregg's jokes never got too dirty, his conversation never too deep. He just strode down the hallways, said hi to people he didn't know, and methodically wrapped up all the leads in the school drama presentations. Everyone, including Gregg Adams, was sure he would be famous one day.

Cindy Carr was a clear-complexioned, untroubled Midwestern beauty. She was a cheerleader, coming from a part of the country where cheerleaders still meant something. She did not leave her room in the mornings until she believed she compared favorably with the framed photo of Olivia Newton-John on her wall. She was a part-time hostess in a Chinese restaurant where a singer named Johnny Chung King sang nightly.

Both Adams and Carr were masters of the teeth-baring smile. This, more than anything else, was the true sign of a high school social climber known as the "sosh." The teeth-baring sosh (long o) began as a glimmer in the eye. Then the sosh chin quivered, and then the entire sosh face detonated into a synthetic grin. Usually accompanied by a sharp "hi," it was an art form that Adams and Carr had taken to its extreme.

The Gregg Adams–Cindy Carr story was thick with tales of overwhelming devotion. When one was sick, the other spent every in-between period on the pay phone, talking to the one at home. Every day they paraded across lunch court, cuddling and holding each other. They were the king and queen of the Public Display of Affection, or P.D.A. Every lunch period they would take their prescribed seats on lunch court and gaze longingly at each other for whatever was left of the twenty-six minutes.

"If there's one thing that never changes," commented Linda, "it's a cheerleader."

"Think they're actually doing it?"

"No way they can't be doing it."

"I just can't picture it," said Stacy with a shrug. "They're too much like my parents."

"They've got to be doing it," said Linda, "or else Gregg would be blue in the face by now."

"I see a little green, but no blue."

Linda Barrett bit into her cheese sandwich. "Everything starts to look green around here after a while," she said.

Biology Class

Stacy Hamilton's next class was Biology II. Most classes at Ridgemont were notorious for one reason or another—perhaps the teacher was someone like Mr. Hand, or the room was lopsided, or the students were allowed to grade themselves—but none had quite the macabre lure of Biology II with Mr. Vargas.

Walking into the room, Stacy was at first struck by the all-white interior of the biology lab. Each student was to sit at his own lab/workshop, complete with Bunsen burner, around the perimeter of the room. Stacy took her seat. Then she noticed something odd. There was a large formaldehyde jar sitting on the windowsill in front of her, and it contained a strange bug-eyed animal that was staring directly at her. She looked at the label: Pig Embryo, 6 months.

Stacy moved to another seat and found yet another form-aldehyde jar poised directly in front of her. This one wasn't as menacing—just a baby squid. She looked around the room. There was a jar on every windowsill, facing every student.

Stacy began to key into all the student conversations around her. Everyone seemed to know one thing going into this class. Somewhere, sometime toward the end of the year, the class was going to be taken on a mandatory field trip to the bottom floor of nearby University Hospital. It was there that Biology II culminated in the display and study of human ca-davers. Cadavers were said to be the private passion of Mr. Vargas, the biology teacher.

Even before the third bell rang on the first day, there was only one topic of conversation around the room.

"I'll tell you right now," a girl two seats up was saying, "I'm not going to go. I'm going to get sick or something. I'm not going into a room with a bunch of dead bodies."

"You'll go," said the boy next to her.

"Have you heard what they do, Mike?"

"What?"

"I'm serious. Have you heard?"

"What?"

"The bodies are dissected, Mike, and Mr. Vargas pulls out parts of the dead body and *holds them up.* Okay?"

"You mean he reaches in and pulls this stuff out?"

"Yes."

"Like a heart?"

"Like a heart."

Mike beamed. *"Bitchin'."*

Mr. Vargas arrived in the classroom, a diminutive man with an inscribed coffee mug in hand. He looked nothing like his ghoulish reputation.

"Good day," said Mr. Vargas in sprightly tones. "I just switched to Sanka. I'm running a little slow today." He pulled on a smock. "So have a little heart."

Mike turned and faced the students behind him, eyes wide with mock terror, as Mr. Vargas began passing out his own purple mimeographed assignment sheets.

So this was high school, Stacy thought. Weird, exotic

teachers and a lot of purple mimeographed sheets. It was enough to make her long for Swenson's Ice Cream Parlor.

A School Night

When Stacy Hamilton arrived home from school, her brother, Brad, was in the driveway washing his LTD sedan. He called the car his Cruising Vessel. Some went for a sporty domestic like a Camaro, others went straight for a Datsun or Toyota. Brad liked to drive to work at Carl's in a nice big clean American machine, even if the car ate up most of his fast-food money. It was a small price to pay for style, as far as he was concerned.

"So how do you like high school?" asked Brad.

"Some pretty strange teachers," said Stacy.

"You'll get used to it."

Stacy stood there for a moment, watching Brad lovingly polishing the windows of his car.

"Brad," said Stacy, "how come I never see you with Lisa anymore?"

"*Jesus,*" said Brad. He threw a chamois rag onto his windshield. "Everybody wants to know about Lisa. Everybody is such *big friends* with Lisa . . ."

"Sorry I asked."

"You got some flowers," said Brad. "They're right inside the door."

Stacy went inside. There, sitting on the living room coffee table, their fragrance cascading throughout the Hamilton home, was a summer floral arrangement. Stacy read the attached note, marked "personal": Memories of You, Ron Johnson.

Stacy's heart quickened. This was a perilous situation, one that set off all her inner alarms. This involved her mother, the notorious Evelyn. For Mrs. H., the word *strict* was weak. First she had refused Stacy a bra, then, two years later, she wouldn't let Stacy out of the house *without* one. She banned any mention of alcohol or drugs in the house. Allowing rock music in the Hamilton home was enough of a battle. Once Evelyn threw away a copy of AC/DC's *If You Want Blood* album because there was blood gushing from the lead guitarist's mouth and chest on the cover. She wouldn't even consider discussing the subject of dating until Stacy had reached the age of sixteen.

Evelyn also had a nose like a foxhound. Once, when Stacy had come home from her first concert (a major fight), her mother even sniffed her clothes.

"I smell marijuana smoke! I smell it all over you!"

"No you don't, mother. You're crazy."

"Don't call me *crazy*, young lady! And don't you ever come home smelling like a *marijuana factory* again. Do you hear me?"

"Yes, mother. But there was no marijuana smoke around me. You're wrong this time."

But, of course, Evelyn was right. Marijuana had been all around her, all night long. Stacy did not relish the act of lying to her mother, that much she knew. In fact, she had made a private pact with her conscience that called for a moratorium after her sixteenth birthday on white lies and sneaking out. Until then, however, it was a matter of survival.

Stacy gathered up the floral arrangement and headed back outside to her brother. She fanned the door a few times.

"Brad! Have Mom or Dad seen this?"

Brad was concentrating on his chrome job. "Not home yet."

"Brad," said Stacy, "what would you say if I asked you to just put these flowers in the trunk of the LTD and get rid of them at work?"

"I'd say," responded Brad, "who the hell is Ron Johnson?"

Stacy had expected her brother to give her a lot more trouble about their both attending the same high school. But

Brad had been supportive, almost helpful. Brad, his little sister had decided, was in the "I'm an adult" phase.

Growing up, they had argued a lot. Almost every fight had been over The Phone. When Brad wanted to use The Phone, he wanted to use The Phone. He would make Stacy give up the line by the cruelest of methods—by listening in on her conversation. Stacy would yell, threaten to go to Mom and Dad. Then Brad would sing into the extension, hum, laugh, anything to destroy the conversation entirely. When Stacy ran to complain to their parents, Brad would simply use the phone, just like he wanted to, while everyone else fought.

Evelyn and Frank Hamilton were easy on Brad, the oldest child. It had been their philosophy that the male should be fully prepared to go out into the world and provide for a family. How this had translated into the family chores, Stacy was not sure. Brad "the provider" didn't have to do the dishes. Or his own sewing. Or clean the floors. No, all her parents had asked Brad to do was "the man's chore," Taking out the trash.

"You're a wimp," Stacy would tell her brother. "How come when you were fifteen, Mom and Dad never even cared what you did on a school night?"

" 'Cause I'm not going to get raped," Brad would respond.

"You can say that again."

Once Brad had started working at Carl's Jr. Stacy noticed an immediate change in her brother. He started with bad weekend hours, a busboy making $2.90-an-hour wages. But even Stacy could see he loved the whole idea of going to work, clocking in, getting paid, and rolling home still wearing his Carl's name tag with a few bucks in his pocket.

Not long after that Stacy spotted Brad with a bus station paperback called *Power with Class*. She noticed he had made graphs of his hours and wages and taped them to his closet door. Someone taught Brad how to work the fryer at Carl's, and there was no looking back. It was the classic example, as she wrote Linda in a note last year, "of a guy finding his niche."

They hadn't squabbled much about The Phone lately.

Stacy had taken to asking Brad first, before she even picked up the receiver.

"Do you need to make a call, Brad?"

"No," said Brad. "I use the phone at work."

There was a muffled knock at Stacy's bedroom door late that night.

"Who is it?"

"Brad."

"Come on in." He looked tired from a night at Carl's. "What's going on?"

"I got rid of those flowers for you."

"Oh, thanks a lot," said Stacy. "That was pretty embarrassing."

"What did you do? Die?"

Stacy looked at the rug. "It's just some guy from Swenson's. You don't know him."

"Does he go to our school?"

"No. You don't know him."

"I don't care if you tell me or not," sighed Brad. "I've got something else on my mind."

"Is everything okay at work?"

"Oh yeah," said Brad. "Oh yeah. Work is fine."

"What's wrong?"

"Lisa," said Brad. "That's what's wrong."

"Are you going to break up with Lisa again?"

Brad got up and started to pace. Lisa had been his girlfriend for the past year and a half. They'd met in typing class. She was pretty. She was friendly. Too friendly, Brad was always saying. He had no idea how popular she was until scores of Lisa's girlfriends starting coming up to him every day, passing notes, telling him, "Lisa likes you." They went out once; they started going together. They'd been together ever since. Brad had gotten her the intercom job at Carl's, and now her hours were almost as good as his. She was even an excellent student. All in all, as Brad once told Stacy, Lisa was the kind of girl who "makes friends with your parents."

"I've been with her almost two years," said Brad. "I've

been doing a lot of thinking. It's a new school year. My *last* high school year. I think I want my freedom."

"Why? Because she won't *sleep* with you?"

Brad glared at his younger sister. After all, it was he who had the sticker on his car that said Sex Instructor.

"Where did you hear that?"

"I'm just guessing."

Brad shrugged. "It's true."

"What do you mean?"

Stacy felt Brad study her face. Everything about him said *this is serious*. He continued in a tone of voice that was meant to cut across the years of brother-sister squabbles.

"I don't know what to do," he said. "We've gotten close, but she always says that she 'can't go any farther.' She has this *thing* about sex. She doesn't think it will feel good or something. We make out for a while, and then she always goes, 'I don't want to have to use sex as a *tool*.' She says that all the time. You know, and I say, 'Tool for *what?* We've been going together almost two years!' Then she says she doesn't want to talk about it anymore, because that ruins everything, and she's out of the *mood*, anyway. It kills me! I go to school and everyone goes, 'HEY HEY HEY, how's Lisa? She's such a fox!'" Brad shook his head. "And I'm thinking, 'Tool for WHAT?'"

"Maybe you just need to give her some time. She's so nice, Brad. That girl really *loves* you."

"Everyone loves Lisa. Everyone loves Lisa. But everyone doesn't have to be her boyfriend."

Brad and Stacy talked for several hours that night. It was one of their first meetings on equal turf. They knew that it wasn't usually wise to entrust a family member with information that could later be used against them, but on this night Stacy and Brad broke the rules. Stacy had waited for the perfect time, and then she popped the big question.

"Hey Brad," she said, "are you still a virgin?"

"Why?"

"I don't know. I was just curious."

Brad grinned. "Maybe yes, maybe no."

"You're not a virgin!"

"I didn't say that."

"But your face did!"

They laughed.

"Are you still a virgin?" Brad asked his sister.

"Maybe yes, maybe no."

"Don't give me that shit! I *know* you're still a virgin!"

Stacy kept smiling, and changed the subject back to Lisa. "What are you going to do, Brad?"

"I've made up my mind," said Brad. "I've got to break up with her. I've got to do it once and for all. There's a world of girls out there. When you're young you have to play the field." Sometimes Brad stayed up and watched late-night "Love American Style" reruns. Stacy had noticed the dialogue cropping up in his speech. "I'm a single, successful guy, and I've got to be *fair to myself.*"

"Just do it in person," said Stacy. "That's the right thing to do. Lisa is so nice." She caught herself. "This is weird. I'm supposed to have an older brother telling *me* stuff. Here I am giving *you* all the good advice."

"Give me a break," said Brad. "It's not like I'm asking you the meaning of life."

There was a parental rap at Stacy's door.

"*Whatever* the meaning of life is, it can wait." It was Mr. Hamilton, turning out the houselights. "Do you kids realize it's past eleven on a school night?"

"Okay, Dad."

Brad smiled at his sister and padded down the hall to his room. Stacy thought about their talk as she turned off the lights and listened to her clock radio in the dark. In the maturity sweepstakes of life, she felt as if she had begun to overtake her brother.

The Attitude

It was one of the cruel inevitabilities of high school, right up there with grades and corn dogs. After thirteen, girls tended to mature at a rate of two- to three-times faster than boys. This led to a common predicament around Ridgemont High. Two kids were in the same grade. The girl was discovering sex and men. The boy, having just given up his paper route, was awakening to the wonders of gothic-style romance. High school could be murder on a guy like Mark "The Rat" Ratner, sixteen.

He was not blessed with the personal success or the looks of a Brad Hamilton. To junior Mark Ratner, high school girls were mystical, unattainable apparitions. So close and yet so far away.

"I am in *love*," said Mark Ratner. He clutched his heart, spun in a circle, and landed on his buddy Mike Damone's bed. It was after school, three weeks into the school year. "In looooove."

"Oh yeah?"

"Oh yeah," said Ratner. "This girl is my exact type. It's her. It's definitely her."

"It's definitely your *mama*," said Damone distractedly. He was in the middle of his after-school ritual. Every day, Mike Damone came home, set his books down, mixed himself a tall Tia Maria and cream, and blasted Lou Reed's live *Rock and Roll Animal* album on the family stereo.

"Damone, you gotta listen to me." Ratner turned serious very quickly. In high school everyone had a coach. For Ratner this was Mike Damone, and Damone wasn't even paying attention. "Come on, Damone."

They were both juniors, and both lived in Ridgemont Hills, but Ratner and Damone were nothing alike. Mark "The

Rat" Ratner, a pale kid with dark hair that tilted to one side like the Leaning Tower of Pisa, had lived in Ridgemont all his life. He had grown up in the same house and gone to all the same neighborhood schools, of which Ridgemont High was one. Ratner was even born in University Hospital, just across the street from his house.

Mike Damone was darker, with longish black hair parted down the middle and a wide, knowing smile. He was a transfer from Philadelphia, "where women are fast and life is cheap." Damone and The Rat had a perfect relationship. Damone talked, and The Rat listened.

"All right," said Damone. "All right." He straddled a chair in his room facing The Rat. "Tell me all about it."

"Okay," said The Rat. "It started out just a typical day. I had to go to the A.S.B. office to get my student I.D. I was thinking about other things, you know, and then I saw her. She was incredible! She was so beautiful! She's a cross between Cindy Carr . . . and Cheryl Ladd! And she works right in the A.S.B. office!" The Rat shook his head in awe. "This is going to be such a great year!"

Damone sat listening to the story, waiting for more. There was no more.

"Is that it?" said Damone. "You didn't get her name or anything?"

"No. It's too soon."

"It's never too soon," said Damone. "Girls decide how far to let you go in the first *five* minutes. Didn't you know that?"

"What do you want me to do? Go up to this strange girl and say, 'Hello! I'd like you to take your clothes off and jump on me!'"

Damone shook his head. "I would, yeah."

"Fuck you."

"I can see it all now," said Damone. "This is going to be just like the girl you fell in love with at Fotomat. All you did was go buy fuckin' film; you didn't even talk to her."

"What do you do, Mike? Tell me. You're in a public place, and you see a girl that you really like. Do you just stand there and give her the eye? Or do you go up to her and make a joke or something? I mean you're a good-looking guy, you know these things."

"Okay. Okay." Damone sighed, but he loved it. "Here's what I do." He got up and began pacing his room, an orderly little cubicle with one huge speaker, a large poster of Pat Benatar, and a newspaper photo of a mortician's utensils. "Usually I don't talk to the girl. I put out a *vibe*. I let her *know*. I use my face. I use my body. I use everything. It's all in the twitch of an eye. You just send the vibe out to them. And I have personally found that girls do respond. Something happens."

"Yeah, Damone, but you put the vibe out to thirty million girls. You know *something's* gonna happen.'

"That's the idea," said Mike Damone. "That's The Attitude."

You hear about it under a multitude of names. The Knack. The Ability. The Moves. The Attitude. In any language it is the same special talent for attracting the opposite sex, and Mike Damone appeared to have it.

They met at Marine World, the famous marine amusement park outside of Orange County. Ratner had gone in, applied for a job, and they had given him Dining Area Duty, an auspicious-sounding responsibility that consisted of scraping the birdshit off the plastic outdoor tables. He didn't think it was that bad, though. It was fun for Ratner at Marine World, and there was a real spirit among the young workers. All the employees got together for functions like beer-keg parties and softball games, and everything would be just fine until someone asked The Rat what *his* department was.

"Hi. I'm Leslie from the Killer Whale Pavilion. Who are you?"

"I'm Mark from Dining Area Duty."

"Oh." And the same look would inevitably come over the other Marine World employee's face, a look that said, *so you're the guy they got.* "Well, Mark, uh, I'll see you over there sometime. Bye!"

The Rat always had trouble recovering after that. Making new friends, it seemed, was not his particular forte. Girls had been out of the question most of his life.

It seemed to The Rat a matter of fate when Marine World personnel dropped Mike Damone into Dining Area Duty as his new partner. On the first day, The Rat didn't speak to Damone and Damone didn't speak to him. On the second day, The Rat broke the ice.

"Hot day today."

Damone looked up from the table he was scrubbing and smiled. "Sure is."

Then his eyes glazed over. He opened his mouth to say something but nothing came out. Damone turned pale and fell over backward, landing on a lawn area. He appeared to go into shock, beating his head on the grass and making tongueless noises with his mouth. Several customers gathered around.

"Someone do something!"

"He's having a fit!"

"Can anyone help that boy?"

Ten more Marine World visitors arrived to gawk at the young worker flailing on the ground. The Rat rushed over to Damone's side and bend down to ask how he could help. And then, just when Damone had a huge audience, he popped back up again. He was the picture of complacency.

"I'm just not myself today," he said. It was Damone's special stunt.

Damone was fired after only three weeks at Marine World, but not before he had made fast friends with Mark Ratner. To The Rat, Damone was a one-of-a-kind character. But it was beyond the Twitching Man acts that Damone used on occasion to rip up whole restaurants and shopping malls. To The Rat, Damone was someone to study. He was a guy with a flair for living life *his* way, and that particularly fascinated Mark Ratner.

What was his secret?

"I'll tell you what it is," Damone said. "It's The Attitude. The Attitude dictates that you don't care if she comes, stays, lays, or *prays*. Whatever happens, your toes'll still be tappin'. When you are the coolest and the cruelest, *then* you have The Attitude."

To Mike Damone of Philadelphia, everything was a matter of attitude. Fitting into a California school was no problem for him. Once you had The Attitude, Damone said, success was never again a matter of luck. It was simply a question of whether or not you behaved as if it were yours already.

The Attitude. The Rat and Damone had been sitting in fourth-period biology a couple of days into the new school year. Damone leaned over. "Aren't you hungry?"

"Starved," said The Rat.

"Wouldn't you love a pizza right now?"

"Don't torture me."

A few minutes later, there was a knock at the front door of the classroom. Mr. Vargas had been giving a lecture. He paused to answer the door.

"Who ordered the pizza?" asked an impatient delivery man for Mr. Pizza.

Damone waved his hand. "We did back here."

The class watched in amazement as the delivery man took his steaming pizza to the back of the class and set in on Damone's desk. Damone paid for it, even pressed fifty cents into the delivery man's hand. "This is for you," he said.

Mr. Vargas looked on, bewildered, while Damone and The Rat began eating pizza.

"Am I the only one who thinks this is strange?" Mr. Vargas asked.

The Attitude.

Damone had put on a classic display of Attitude the day after hearing of The Rat's dream girl at the A.S.B. counter. Ratner chose to watch from behind the bushes on Luna Street while Damone cruised by for an official check-out.

He had meant only to look, but Damone went right up and said hello to the girl. The Rat's girl. She and Damone had a three-minute conversation that The Rat couldn't hear. Then Damone had tapped his hand on the A.S.B. counter once and turned to leave. He walked back over to The Rat.

"She's cute," said Damone, "but she doesn't look like Cheryl Ladd."

"Fuck you, Damone."

"Her name is Stacy Hamilton," he said. "She's a sophomore, and she's in Beginning Journalism. What more do you need to know?"

"She just told you that?"

"Sure."

"I'll tell you something," said The Rat. "I really think something could *happen* between this girl and me."

"You ought to meet her first, you wuss."

("Wussy" was a particularly expressive word that had sprung up in Paul Revere Junior High and taken a foothold in the Ridgemont lexicon. It was the handy combination of *wimp* and *pussy*.)

The next day The Rat had it all planned. He waited until the period he knew she would be working at the A.S.B. office. He walked slowly over to the 200 Building, down the hall to the corner office. It was a green counter, with a glass window in front.

And there she was! Stacy Hamilton. Both she and Mike Brock, the football jock, were finishing up with two students. There was only one other kid in front of The Rat. It was a fifty-fifty chance. A crap shoot!

Mike Brock finished first, and the other student went to his window. *Fantastic*, The Rat thought. Then Stacy Hamilton finished and looked at him.

"Next."

But just as The Rat stepped up, Stacy Hamilton's A.S.B. phone rang. She picked up the receiver and held a single finger up to Ratner. It was a call from the front office, and the conversation stretched on. The third attendance bell rang, but The Rat stayed.

Mike Brock finished with the other student. "Over here," he said.

And what could The Rat say? *No, you thick asshole. No, you stupid jock. I'm already being helped, you penis breath.* No. The Rat didn't say any of those things. He chose the *wussy* way out.

The Rat shrugged and went over to Mike Brock. He asked Brock something ludicrous, some lame thing off the top of his head.

"I was wondering where the Spirit Club meets," he mumbled.

"I don't know;" said Brock. "You oughta look on the big bulletin board."

"Thanks," said The Rat.

He turned to go.

"Oh, *sir?*" She had gotten off the phone and called out to him. "I think the Spirit Club meets on Tuesday after school in room 400."

"Thanks," said The Rat. He turned around again. "See *you* later."

She called me sir! He was overjoyed. The way The Rat figured it, she would never have done that if she wasn't interested in him.

Mike Damone shook his head sadly as he heard the whole story, incident by incident, over Cheetos on lunch court. "Is that it?"

"It's better than yesterday."

"Yeah, Rat, but you just opened the door a little bit. And then you let it slam back shut again. You gotta *talk* to the girl."

"Tomorrow!"

"You can't do it tomorrow," said Damone. "Tomorrow makes you look too eager."

"I know," said The Rat. "I know. I've got to have The *Attitude.*"

But for a guy like The Rat, the idea of waiting another two days was criminal. He felt there was nothing he could possibly do to fill up the dead time. What was good enough on TV? What was interesting enough down at Town Center Mall? What record or book could ever be interesting enough to take his mind off *her?*

In Spanish class the next day, someone offered The Rat a vocabulary lab listening headset. He was a zombie.

"You know what?" said The Rat. "I don't give a *shit* what happens to Carlos y Maria."

I Don't Know

Mr. Hand began dropping test papers on desks as if they were pieces of manure. "C . . . D . . . F . . . F . . . D . . ." He looked up. "What are you people? On dope?"

He continued, sadly, as he passed out more papers. "What is so difficult about this material? All week we've dealt with the Grenville Program. We have not even reached the American Revolution yet, and you people can't tell me what the *Stamp Act* is. How hard is . . ."

Then Mr. Hand looked up suddenly, interrupting even himself. "Where is Jeff Spicoli?"

Silence.

"I saw him on campus earlier today. Where is he now?"

Silence.

"Anyone?"

There was always one, of course. Always one kid willing to sell his soul for a shot at Mr. Hand's good graces. Or better yet, a shot out the classroom door.

"I saw him," said William Desmond, the wrestler-columnist. "I saw him out by the fruit machines."

"Me too," said Mike Brock, the football jock.

"How long ago?"

"Ten minutes. Just before class, sir."

Hand snapped his fingers, McGarrett-style. "Okay. Bring him in."

Desmond and Brock hustled out the door, and Mr. Hand continued his tirade over the Stamp Act. Five minutes later, a red-eyed Spicoli walked into the class with the Desmond-Brock posse.

"Hey," said Spicoli. "This is a frame! There's no *birthday party* for me here!"

"Thank you Mr. Desmond, Mr. Brock . . ." said Hand. "You can sit down now."

Mr. Hand left Spicoli in front of the class, for show.

"What's the reason for your tardiness?"

"I couldn't make it in time." Spicoli's bloodshot eyes told the story.

"You mean you couldn't," said Hand, "or you *wouldn't?*" It was a vintage "Five-O" line.

"I don't know."

"Why are you continually late for this class, Mr. Spicoli? Why do you shamelessly waste my time like this?"

"I don't know," said Spicoli.

Hand appeared mesmerized by the words. Then he turned and walked to the board. He wrote in long large letters as he slammed the helpless chalk into the green board: I DON'T KNOW.

"I like that," said Hand. "I don't know. That's nice. 'Mr. Hand, will I pass this class?' Gee, Jeff, I DON'T KNOW. 'Mr. Hand, when is the test?' Gee, I . . . DON'T . . . KNOW. I like that, Mr. Spicoli. I'll have to use that one myself."

Mr. Hand left special instructions that the words *I Don't Know* remain in front of the class all week. People began stopping Spicoli in the hallway.

"Hey," they'd say, "aren't you the I Don't Know guy?"

A Bad Day at the Fryer

There was a mirror in the boys' locker room that was perhaps the finest Brad Hamilton had ever used. Well lit, the perfect height, it was just *superb.* The kind of mirror that showed a guy for what he *was.*

On first-period P.E. days Brad spent his mirror time luxuriously. Pass the mirror test, he figured, and you were good for the entire day.

He caught himself—hi!—from several angles, and then ran through all the basic facial movements. Brad whistling. Brad happy. Brad sad. Brad macho. Then—Jesus!—he noticed a small blackhead at the base of his left nostril. Brad remembered someone had once told him that any time you popped a zit below your eyes and above your mouth it would leave a big crater in your face after the age of twenty-five. Brad weighed the dilemma in his mind. The same guy had once told him Colgate toothpaste was an aphrodisiac, so what did he know. Brad decided to eliminate the one tiny flaw.

Now. Brad stepped back and looked at the entire portrait. People were always saying he looked like a young Ronald Reagan, and Brad didn't mind that a bit. Why, he could even see some moustache action coming in over his lip! And he was more trim now than at his best football weight. This was it, Brad thought. The Lean and Hungry Look.

The tone was set for a great day. Brad bounded through his classes, went home for an hour, and then drove to work at Carl's.

Brad got along pretty well with his boss, Dennis Taylor. Dennis Taylor had been the assistant manager (the real manager had a desk job at the big Carl's building downtown) for as long as Brad had been there. Taylor was thirty-three and still lived in his family's guest room. He was obsessively clean. His Datsun was absolutely immaculate; he washed and waxed it constantly. Dennis would even walk around Carl's with a Windex bottle. Sometimes Brad got the idea that Dennis bolted out of bed in the middle of the night wondering if he might have missed double-checking the shake machine.

A lot of people made jokes about Dennis around Carl's. But those were the people whose hours he'd hacked, or the people who just didn't know Dennis. You had to know Dennis, the way Brad looked at it, to realize that he was a pretty simple guy. He was just a franchise man, all the way. He was the type of guy born to wear plastic pen holders and carry bundles of keys. Don't get him in trouble and he loved you.

Dennis Taylor was in a bad mood that night when Brad showed up. It was a Tuesday night, slow night, and just the guys were on duty. No Lisa at the intercom. There was a problem with the carbonation, and Dennis got more and more upset trying to fix it himself. He didn't like calling in another franchise man.

There was also the matter of new uniforms—brown-and-white country-style uniforms for Bar-B-Cue Beef months. Girls were required to wear bandanas. Boys were asked to wear string ties.

"A string tie?" Brad balked. He hated wearing a tie unless it was something like prom or Grad Nite.

"We get older clientele in here, too, Hamilton. They like to feel they're getting something special. Something they don't get at home."

"Hey," said Brad. "Why not. I *love* looking like a golf caddie." He turned to his buddies with the wild grin of a kid who doesn't often think of such lines until two, three days later. "I love it!"

Dennis Taylor spun off to the back office, where assistant managers like to stay until they hear their title called for.

To any fast-food employee, an irate customer was an I.C. There were usually about two I.C.'s a night, at least on Brad's shift. Brad had a philosophy about I.C.'s. It was all ego. Everybody was trying to impress someone. Everyone has to be a big man *somewhere,* and an I.C. was someone who had no better place to do it than in a fast-food restaurant, at the expense of some kid behind the counter.

The first I.C. of this night came into Carl's Jr. at 9:30 P.M. Brad knew she was an I.C. the minute she started to inspect the food before paying. She was an older woman with a silver-gray wig. She tried the fries last.

"These fries taste like metal," she announced.

"I'm sorry," said David Lemon, the clerk, following the customer-is-always-right party line. "I'll get you some new ones."

"No," said the woman. "No. They tasted the same yesterday. They'll taste the same tomorrow. I want to speak to the manager!"

Bingo. Dennis Taylor was out of the back office like a nine ball.

"What's the problem, ma'am?" Even the irate customer was always right, Dennis liked to say. He would do anything to keep a complaint from reaching the franchise office downtown. One complaint and they called Dennis himself on the carpet.

"I *said* these fries taste like metal."

Taylor looked at Brad, who had the duty of frying the potatoes. "Did you drain the grease yesterday before you started work?"

"Yes."

"Have you changed it since you came in, on the hour?"

Brad was getting indignant. It wasn't just ordinary frying, it was his specialty. "I change it," he said, "*every* hour. And I *always* make sure that the potatoes are fried in new grease. I can tell by the color."

Hamilton turned to the woman. "May I taste?"

The woman recoiled with her white-and-yellow Carl's Specialty sack. "Are you calling me a liar? I'll go to the head of the company if I have to."

She had pushed a button with Dennis "Mr. Franchise" Taylor. The words *go to the head of the company* struck him at the very marrow of his corporate aspirations.

"Ma'am," said Dennis through a Carl's Jr. smile. He rang open the register and scooped out the exact change. "Here's your money, ma'am, and I'm sorry you had a problem. The whole meal's on us!" Dennis laughed, as if it were party time, but the I.C. was still shaking her head.

"No," she said. "No, that won't do. That's not enough. I want that boy fired for calling me a liar. That boy right there."

She was pointing at Brad.

"I'm sorry, ma'am," said Dennis Taylor, "but Brad Hamilton is one of our best employees."

Brad was impressed. He found himself saying, "Thanks."

"Brad Hamilton," said the I.C. She reached for her purse. "Brad Hamilton." She rummaged through it until she found a pen. "Brad Hamilton." And a piece of paper. "Brad Hamilton." Then she wrote his name down. "Brad Hamilton."

Now the odds that the I.C. would actually write the letter were slim at best, everybody knew that. Most people were happy to have gotten a little attention; they usually forgot the hassle before they even arrived home. But the threat, even the *threat* of a letter, and the thought of having that letter sitting in *his* franchise file . . . well, you could see it ring up on Dennis Taylor's face like a big No Sale sign.

"Hamilton," he barked. "Go clean up the bathroom."

It was an insult, sure, but that's how Dennis Taylor worked these things out. Brad knew it was no big problem. Dennis took over the fryer. In five minutes he would beg Brad to come back and work it.

"I'm really sorry," Brad said, and grabbed a scrubbrush. He went to attack the new graffiti: I Eat Big Hairy Pussy.

Life, Brad marveled there in the john, is like a chain reaction. Someone gets pissed and then takes it out on the next guy down the ladder. Everyone has to piss on somebody.

Later he went home, called Lisa, and broke up with her.

Child Development

One of Stacy Hamilton's interesting new classes at Ridgemont was Child Development. Child Development was a new-age tax-cut class that combined bachelor arts and home economics into one big jamboree, "attempting to guide young adults past the hurdles of adulthood." The class met in a double-sized room complete with fifteen miniature kitchens. The teacher was a fidgety woman named Mrs. Melon.

It was a typical contract class. On the first day Mrs. Melon divided all the students alphabetically into tables of four. She passed out purple mimeographed assignment sheets and signed each table to their contract of work.

Mrs. Melon had a nervous habit of rubbing her forearms while she talked. The more nervous she was, the redder her forearms. Today she was rubbing harder than usual.

"You are grownups," she said, "and you live in a grownup

world. Most of you already know we'll be going into forms of sexuality, birth control, domestic problems, and divorce in this class. I'm going to need these state-required forms filled out and signed by your parents."

She began dropping more piles of the purple sheets on the alphabetical tables. Most of the students had already received their parental consent forms, including the sex-ed forms, with the thick green Ridgemont High School Rulebook sent out in August. And the school gave out more of the same forms with the first-day registration papers. Now Mrs. Melon was rubbing her arms and passing out even more of them. Somewhere along the line a student could get the idea Ridgemont was nervous about sex education.

Mrs. Melon's class was out of control most of the time. Students came, students went. Everyone seemed to feel adequately developed as a child, so they used the class as a free-zone study hall. Most students simply brought in all their work from other classes and saved their evenings by doing it during Mrs. Melon's lectures.

This would be the third consecutive year that Stacy Hamilton would be taking a sex-ed class. She felt she had seen most of the films, looked at all the cutaway diagrams; she *knew* what went on. But even Stacy couldn't deny that it was valuable to run through sex ed one more time. There were always some kids getting it for the first time, and they were always entertaining to watch.

There had been a guy in the seventh grade whose mother told him women had teeth in their vagina. The boy must have believed it. He stood up in sex-ed class one day—Stacy was there—and asked, "Do very many men get their penises cut off?"

The kid quickly got himself the nickname Jaws, and, didn't come back to Paul Revere Junior High the next year. Someone called his home and was referred to a number in Alabama.

Stacy herself had learned about sex from her mother, in a supermarket, in the feminine-hygiene section. "There is a certain thing that adults do after they are married," Mrs. H. told her. "The purpose is to have children." She went on to explain the sexual process in such cold clinical terms that Stacy's first question was, "Does a doctor perform the operation?"

"No," said Mrs. H., "your father and I did it ourselves."

In the years that followed, Mrs. Hamilton never mentioned the subject again. Not even a word. Stacy's mother seemed to consider sex an unmentionable obligation performed in unspeakable situations. Sometimes she'd say something like, "You watch out for boys with beer breath; you know what they want." And that was it. So Stacy was grateful for sex ed, even if it was old territory.

As Mrs. Melon droned on this afternoon, three weeks into the school year, Stacy decided the time was right to open the note from Linda Barrett that she had been saving since period break.

Stacy carefully unfolded the notebook page:

DEAR STACY,

HI STACE. HOW IS EVERYTHING GOING? WHAT'S NEW? ISN'T MY WRITING JUST WONDERFUL? ALL I HAVE IS THIS EYE-LINER PENCIL THAT I NEVER USE. (She switches here to a pen) SO HI! I HAVE REALLY GOT TO TALK WITH YOU. ABOUT SOME SERIOUS STUFF. STACY, I CAN'T BELIEVE THAT THE VET ACTUALLY CALLED YOUR HOUSE AND TALKED TO YOUR MOM!!! HOW DID YOU FEEL WHEN EVELYN GAVE YOU THE MESSAGE? PRETTY WEIRD, HUH? FIRST HE SENDS FLOWERS, THEN HE STARTS CALLING YOU UP. THIS GUY SOUNDS DANGEROUS. WE HAVE GOT TO TALK. WRITE ME AND TELL ME HOW MUCH YOU LIKE THIS GUY.

I WISH YOU WEREN'T WORKING EVERY SATURDAY! I WAS THINKING THAT IT WOULD BE NICE IF WE GOT TOGETHER THIS SATURDAY, BUT I GUESS WE CAN'T. UMMMMMM. . . . I GOTTA GO NOW. I'LL SEE YOU IN ABOUT 52 MINUTES. I HAVE TO REWRITE AN ESSAY NOW! BYE STACE! WRITE ME!

YOUR BUD, LINDA

Stacy withdrew a clean sheet of paper from her Pee-Chee folder. She wrote:

66

OH LINDA OH LINDA OH LINDA,

I DON'T KNOW WHAT TO DO. MOM IS OKAY. I NEVER
KNEW I COULD THINK OF SOMETHING SO FAST. SHE
GOES, "WHO IS THIS RON JOHNSON THAT CALLED YOU?
HE SOUNDS LIKE A MAN!" I'M NEARLY SHITTING, RIGHT,
BUT I GO, "HE'S JUST THIS GUY FROM SCHOOL WHO
WANTS A JOB AT SWENSON'S." SO THEN I ASK HER WHAT
SHE TOLD HIM, AND EVELYN GOES, "I TOLD HIM THAT
YOU HADN'T GOTTEN HOME FROM RIDGEMONT YET."
WHAT DO YOU THINK THE VET THINKS????? I TOLD HIM
ONCE I WAS GOING TO JUNIOR COLLEGE. AND THAT I
WAS 19. HE'S PROBABLY SO MAD AT ME! I LIKE HIM. I
FEEL KIND OF SECURE WITH HIM. I THINK WE SHOULD
GO OUT SOME MORE! BUT I SHOULD TELL HIM THE
TRUTH ABOUT HOW OLD I AM. WHAT DO YOU THINK?

YOUR BUD, STACY

About ten minutes before the end of Child Development, while Mrs. Melon was working her way around the room with enchilada recipes, Stacy noticed the class disrupted by the appearance of a buxom young office worker in a tight red dress.

She had come to give Mrs. Melon a mimeographed office memo, but the simple act became a much larger production in the hands of this girl. She *swung* through the doorway and scanned the room with two mighty whips of her head. She took a long while to separate the top sheet from her stack of other mimeographs pausing once to shake out her hair. Then she swung back out again. Somebody applauded.

The bell rang, and Stacy found Linda Barrett on her way to the next class.

"Here," said Stacy, handing her the note. "Write me back next period."

The next period, Stacy received this reply from Linda:

STACE,

DON'T YOU DARE TELL HIM THE TRUTH. YOU'LL NEVER
HEAR FROM THE GUY AGAIN. JUST TELL HIM THAT YOU
HAVE A LOT OF PEOPLE WHO LIKE TO USE THE PHONE,

AND UNTIL YOU GET YOUR OWN LINE PUT IN, YOU'LL CALL HIM! OKAY? SEE YOU AT LUNCH.

LINDA

Stacy thought about it all through her next period, and debated the subject further with Linda Barrett over lunch. She had to tell The Vet her true age, she said. She didn't want to have to keep thinking up and hiding more lies.

"You don't have to lie," said Linda. "Just don't talk about your age at all."

"But I already told him I was nineteen! I told him I was already out of high school! I totally lied!"

"Now it bothers you to lie," said Linda. "But it didn't bother you to sneak out your window at night."

"That's different."

"No it isn't."

"Yes it is."

And so it went. By the end of the school day, Stacy's mind was made up. She was going to tell The Vet how old she was, and she was going to do it in a grownup way. He would understand; and if he didn't, *forget him!* Right? After school Stacy took the H bus to Town Center Mall and picked out a card at the Hallmark Store.

She selected a middle-of-the-road cartoon card, nothing too wild. The face was a drawing of an intent astronomer, his telescope trained on the heavens. It said: "Don't dwell on all the mistakes of the past. Look to the future."

The card opened up to another drawing of the same astronomer, who had just realized the lens cap was still on his telescope: "And all the mistakes you can make, then."

Stacy decided to wait a day before she wrote The Vet anything on the inside of the card. Mrs. Melon was still preparing the class for sex ed, rubbing her forearms, while Stacy worked out the phrasing in Child Development the next day.

Dear Ron:

Thanks a lot for the flowers. I got the message that you called. I'm sorry I didn't call you back yet. I admit I have been pretty quiet, but I have to admit a few things, like I am only 15! But that's the *only* lie I told you! I hope we can still be friends! Good luck at the clinic, and I hope we can talk very soon.

Love, Stacy

After school, Stacy walked to the nearby mailbox and dropped her Hallmark card into the slot. Days, then weeks passed. She heard nothing from The Vet. He didn't call, didn't write, didn't come into Swenson's.

"Stacy," said Linda Barrett one late night on the telephone, "it doesn't look good for the relationship."

The Lear Jet Is Waiting

Two days had passed and The Rat awoke, bathed in The Attitude. Today was the day. He knew it.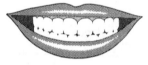

The first three periods of the day flew by. By now he was getting to know Stacy Hamilton's whole schedule. The last bell rang, and The Rat strode out the door of Spanish class, down the halls to the A.S.B. office.

And there she was. Except she was talking with *five* other guys. They were all standing around, leaning over the counter, smiling at her. The Rat took it in stride. He was all form. He took a swig from the nearby drinking fountain, very casual. They were still talking to her. She was smiling back.

Then it hit The Rat. What if a lot of guys asked her out? What if muscle-bound jocks hit on her all day long. Worse yet, what if she went out with Mike Brock? Maybe The Rat wasn't even good-looking enough to try.

He felt the cold fear of rejection spread through him. It sank The Attitude like a harpooned beach toy. The Rat turned and walked to his next class.

Later that week The Rat and Damone went to the first school dance of the year.

"Have you seen Stacy here yet?"

"I don't think she's coming," said The Rat. He kicked at the sawdust that was covering the gymnasium floor. "She's probably not the type who goes to dances."

The Rat had combed his hair into submission. Damone was carefully arranged so that he appeared ultracasual—tennis shoes and sweater. He leaned against the side of the bleachers, listening to the cheesy high school band performing their version of "Take It to the Limit."

A beautiful young Ridgemont girl walked by them. The Rat acted like he had been punched in the stomach. "Did you see that girl? Jesus."

"You are such a wussy with girls," said Damone. "Come on. They're just . . . *girls*."

"Yeah? You ought to hear my sister and her girlfriends talk sometime. You'd never call one a *girl* again. They talk like truck drivers."

Damone rolled his eyes and ignored the remark.

"That girl was so cute. Look at her over there!"

"Where?" said Damone.

"Over there by the metal chairs."

"Well *do* something about it," said Damone.

"Like what?"

"Just what I said, do something about it. You think she's cute? *Do something about it*." Pause. "You wussy."

The Rat stared at Damone. His eyes glazed over with a sense of purpose.

"Don't let them fool you," said Damone. "They come here for the same reason *we* do."

The Rat draped his fatigue jacket over his shoulder like a French film director. He began to swagger toward the girl.

"*Rat*," said Damone. "Ace the coat, okay?"

"Really?"

"Yeah. Give it to me." Damone took it. "Now you look okay."

The Rat walked straight over and sat down heavily on a

metal chair two feet away from the girl. She was watching the band.

"YOU," said The Rat. The girl turned around. "Sit." The Rat tapped the aluminum chair next to him with the palm of his hand. The Attitude.

The girl shivered as if the night air had given her a bad chill. She scurried over to some friends at the other end of the gymnasium.

Damone came over and sat in the chair. "It's a start," he said.

By Monday morning The Rat had a plan. Not another day was going to slip by without his meeting Stacy Hamilton. He sat grimly through all his classes, preparing for the attack. Then came fifth period, her A.S.B. period on Mondays. The Rat headed down to the A.S.B. counter.

She was all alone. Doing nothing.

"Hi," said Ratner.

"Hello."

"Listen," he said. "I have two question. I was curious . . ." He felt the beginnings of the same old cold panic, but barged through with his rap anyway. "What do you do with the old combination locks around here? I left mine on before we switched lockers . . ."

"We cut them off," said Stacy.

"So they're gone."

"Well, no," she said. She reached under the counter and pulled out a bucketful of old locks. "They're here."

"I'll never find it in there."

"Some people do."

"It's cool," said The Rat. "It'd take too much time." He chuckled to himself, like he had too much Attitude to be bothered with such small-time stuff as *locks*. He affected a look that said: The Lear Jet Is Waiting.

"Well, okay," she said. She returned the bucketful of locks under the counter.

"My second question," said The Rat, "is . . . what's your name?"

She smiled. "Stacy."

"Hi. I'm Mark." He stuck his hand through the glass hole in the window. "Nice to meet you, Stacy."

Spirit Bunnies

By the second month of the school year, Stacy Hamilton's favorite class was Beginning Journalism/School Newspaper. Not only was it her one class with Linda Barrett, but the atmosphere was always pleasantly chaotic. Time passed more quickly in this class than in any others on her sophomore schedule.

Today was assignment meeting day, and things usually got out of hand.

"I want to write about the rock group Van Halen," announced William Desmond, the wrestler-sports columnist. "I went to see them at the sports arena last Friday and they were disgusting."

"My *ass*," said Randy Eddo, campus ticket scalper and "advertiser" in the school newspaper. "They were tremendous."

Desmond turned and addressed Eddo. "Oh yeah? You like it when David Lee Roth sticks the microphone between his legs, don't you?"

"No, *you* like it," said Eddo. "That's why you remember it."

"There's too much rock in the newspaper as it is," interrupted *Reader* editor Angie Parisi. "Why doesn't anyone want to write about the foreign exchange students?"

Silence.

"All right, I'm just going to have to assign it." She looked around the room and settled her gaze on a curly haired young student sitting next to Stacy. "Why don't *you?*"

"Okay."

"What's your name?"

"Louis Crowley," he said, tugging at the blue down vest that was his trademark.

"Okay, I want you to interview the three students from India here this semester . . ."

The class's attention was diverted by the appearance of two cheerleaders at the door.

"Oh, *class*," said Mrs. Sheehan, the journalism teacher, from her back-of-the-room seat. "Dina Phillips and Cindy Carr wish to talk with us for just a few moments. Come on in, girls."

Head cheerleader Dina Phillips stepped forward to address the journalism class. At age seventeen, she was the best dresser in Ridgemont. She wore an expensive skirt-and-blouse ensemble that day. Her smile was a quintessential sosh production—the glimmer in the eyes, then the slight crinkle at the corners of her mouth, moving into the traditional broad teeth-baring smile. Even Cindy Carr stood back in silent deference as Dina spoke.

"I just want to say," said Dina, "that we are *not* Spirit Bunnies. Last year, all your articles in the school newspaper referred to us as Spirit Bunnies, and everybody started calling us that, and we just want to say that we've gotten the name changed this year to Commissioners of Spirit. We always hated the name Spirit Bunnies. It bugged the heck out of Cindy and myself."

"It's just such a put-down," said Cindy Carr.

"They don't call the Chess Club *Checker Champs* or something goofy like that," continued Dina Phillips. "We just want to be known as Varsity Commissioners of Spirit. We're going to go to everything this year, you guys. We're going to go to soccer, wrestling, and basketball. Not just football."

"We're going to do a lot of new and different things this year for spirit," said Cindy Carr. "Like, for instance, we're bringing back the Pep Club." She started to say something else, but Dina broke in.

"It takes a lot of guts to get up and do something that a lot of people will make fun of," she said. "Cheerleaders aren't some elite special little group in the clouds. We're not out to be better than the crowd. We just want the crowd to participate, and we want spirit from every little person in this entire school. We need your support."

There was no reaction, and the moment hung heavy in the air.

"Well, thank you, girls," said Mrs. Sheehan.

The former Spirit Bunnies were just about to leave journalism class when someone else appeared at the door. It was Vice-Principal Ray Connors, with a slip in his hand. He was grave and to the point. He didn't even ask Mrs. Sheehan if he could interrupt her class.

"May I speak with Louis Crowley, please?"

Crowley rose to his feet, unsure of what was about to transpire. It was an eerie sight. "Madman" Connors wrapped an arm around the boy's shoulder and walked him out of the class. By the next period, word had rocketed around campus. There had been an accident out on El Dorado Bridge. Two cars had been morning-racing across the structure, and one edged a third car out of the way. The third car had slammed up against the railing, caught its wheel on a turret, and had flown over the side and into the water below. The car had contained the father and sister of Louis Crowley.

Highway To Hell

The mood was somber around journalism class. Death—the idea of mortality—had struck close to home. Suddenly everyone was a close friend of Louis Crowley, had been talking to him *just that morning*. The word was he would be out of school for two to three weeks.

But two days later, there was Louis, back in journalism. Back at school. Blue down vest and all. It was amazing, and it was mystifying. A couple of students said something to Louis about how sorry they were, and Louis just kind of put his head down and nodded thanks. It was the quietest journalism class had been all year.

Then Jeff Spicoli showed up.

Spicoli bolted into journalism class holding the front page of the local newspaper. An amateur photographer had been loading his film, shooting pictures of the bridge, when he heard the crash, snapped his shutter a few more times, and caught a color photo of the Crowley car sailing off the El Dorado Bridge and into the ocean. The local paper had paid the photographer $500 for the shots and published the series on the front page in fire-blazing color.

"Look at these *bitchin'* photos of the crash," boomed Jeff Spicoli. "You can see the people inside and *everything*."

Everyone froze. No one spoke. Louis Crowley hung his head and began to sob. It would be another month before any-one spoke to Jeff Spicoli again.

To Spicoli, that rejection was just typical of high school kids. They were so serious, so hung up on their social status. The whole routine reminded Jeff Spicoli of a long climbing rope. All these soshes had been shimmying up that rope since grade school, and by the time they got to high school they were holding on for dear life. They wanted to be popular, at all costs, and maybe they would get voted Most Likely to Never Have to Shit in the annual. They were just dying to get to the top of that rope. Most of Spicoli's friends were still the junior high schoolers from Paul Revere. They knew how to have a good time.

Spicoli didn't consider himself a troublemaker. All he wanted in life, he said, was to wake up in the mornings to a decent buzz and six- to eight-foot breakers with good shape. He didn't care that most of the students around him were part of a fast-food world, talking about their hours and their assistant managers whenever they got half a chance. Spicoli was a surfer, proud to be the last of a dying breed around Ridgemont.

When Spicoli wasn't on the waves or playing pinball down at the mall or even going to school, he was usually in his

75

room. Spicoli's room was his castle; he could spend hours in there. Located at the top of the stairs in his family's split-level Ridgemont condo, Spicoli's room was another world from the rest of the wicker-decorated house. The walls were covered with posters, almost all of them naked centerspreads from *Playboy* and *Penthouse*. There were a few token surf action photos, and several headshop posters with calligraphy sayings like "Be with Me," "Come with Me, Now and Forever," and "Love and Ecstasy," but the room was mostly just a collage of fully nude women who confronted any visitor with a thousand melonous breasts. It was obvious that Jeff Spicoli's parents did not enter this room.

Spicoli's stepmother was a counselor at Clark Junior College, and his father owned a successful television repair business. Spicoli's real mother, a teacher, left her family several days after seeing the film *An Unmarried Woman*. Jeff didn't hold it against her, not as much as he held a grudge against his father for remarrying a woman with seven kids of her own. Jeff Spicoli carried on his self-imposed exile from inside his room. He didn't even know all the names of his stepbrothers and stepsisters. He didn't want to.

The only member of his family allowed into Jeff's room, in fact, was his only real brother, seven-year-old Curtis. Jeff liked Curtis. Any kid who could spend entire afternoons doing gymnastic flips into plastic garbage bags was okay by him.

Curtis burst into Spicoli's room early one morning, eight weeks into the school year. "Jeff, are you going to be taking a shower?" Curtis demanded of his brother's sleeping form. He threw the door open. There was a stale biological smell about Spicoli's inner sanctum.

"Ugh," said Spicoli. He'd been out late partying at the mall the night before.

"Jeffareyougoingtobetakingashower?"

Spicoli was half in, half out of the covers, his behind facing the door. He groaned and scratched his back ferociously.

"Why?"

" 'Cause I'm moving into the bathroom. I'm sleeping in the tub from now on."

"No you aren't."

"Dad *said.*"

"What if I turn the water on?"

"BETTER NOT!" Curtis shrieked, and left without shutting the door. "BETTER NOT, YOU BUTTHOLE!"

Spicoli got out of bed and kicked the door shut. He had been having a dream. A totally bitchin' dream.

He had been standing in a deep dark void. Then he detected a sliver of light in the distance. A cold hand pushed him toward the light. He was being led somewhere *important.* That much he knew.

As Jeff Spicoli drew closer, the curtains suddenly opened and a floodlit vision was revealed to him. It was a wildly cheering studio audience—for him!—and there, applauding from his "Tonight Show" desk, was *Johnny Carson.*

Because it was the right thing to do, and because it was a dream, anyway, Spicoli gave the band a signal and launched into a cocktail rendition of AC/DC's "Highway to Hell." When it was over, he took a seat next to Carson.

"How are ya," said Johnny, lightly touching Spicoli's arm.

"Bitchin', Johnny. Nice to be here. I feel great."

"I was going to say," said Carson, "your eyes look a little *red.*"

"I've been *swimming,* Johnny."

The audience laughed. It was a famous Spicoli line.

"Swimming? In the winter?"

"Yes," said Spicoli, "and may a swimming beaver make love to your masticating *sister.*"

That broke Johnny up. Spicoli recrossed his legs and smiled serenely. "Seriously, Johnny, business is good. I was thinking about picking up some hash this weekend, maybe go up to the mountains."

"I want to talk a little bit about school," said Carson.

"*School.*" Spicoli sighed. "School is no problem. All you have to do is go, to get the grades. And if you know anything, all you have to do is go about *half the time.*"

"How often do *you* go?"

"I don't go at all," said Spicoli.

The audience howled again. He is Carson's favorite guest.

"I hear you brought a film clip with you," said Carson. "Do you want to set it up for us?"

"Well, it pretty much speaks for itself," said Spicoli. "Freddy, you want to run with it."

The film clip begins. It is a mammoth wave cresting against the blue sky.

"Johnny," continues Spicoli, "this is the action down at Sunset Cliffs at about six in the morning."

"Amazing."

A tiny figure appears at the foot of the wave.

"That's me," said Spicoli.

The audience gasps.

"You're not going to *ride* that wave, are you Jeff?"

"You got it," said Spicoli.

He catches the perfect wave, and it hurtles him through a turquoise tube of water.

"What's going through your mind right here, Jeff? The danger of it all?"

"Johnny," said Spicoli, "I'm thinking here that I only have about four good hours of surfing left before all those little clowns from Paul Revere Junior High start showing up with their *boogie boards.*"

The audience howls once again, and then Spicoli's brother—that little fucker—woke him up.

Coach Ramirez

On a hot October afternoon twenty years earlier, the late great rock and roll star Ritchie Valens had stood at the very spot where biology lab was now and sung his two hits of the day, "La Bamba" and "Donna."

A local disc jockey had corralled Valens into making the personal appearance. Valens showed up at high noon on the day of the inaugural Ridgemont High School homecoming game against Lincoln. He brought no guitars or amplifiers. Valens simply stood outside on the hot concrete and sang a cappella.

"That's for the Ridgemont Raiders!" Valens shouted. "The best darn football team in the West!"

Ritchie Valens was killed four months later in the same tragic plane crash that took the lives of Buddy Holly and The Big Bopper.

It could be argued that in the twenty years of Ridgemont football played since that day, the Raiders had enjoyed an only slightly better fate than Ritchie Valens. Once, the football team had a season in which it won more than lost. That event's ten-year anniversary was coming up.

In recent years other sports had taken the spotlight at Ridgemont, particularly soccer. Ridgemont's soccer team had gone to the C.I.F. (California Interscholastic Federation) play-offs the year before, mostly owing to the spectacular efforts of junior Steve Shasta. Shasta had brought so much attention to himself, and to soccer, that Ridgemont football players went virtually ignored on campus. They thought it was a travesty! A kid grew up playing football, hoping, *expecting* some of that fabled high school f-ball glory. Then he got to Ridgemont and found he was lucky to be able to *meet* Steve Shasta.

At the helm of Ridgemont football these days were Mr. Vincent Ramirez and his assistant coach, Les Sexton. Ramirez spoke in sharp yelps. And he had a favorite phrase: "Take a lap." Depending on the inflection, it was alternately an insulting punishment or a symbol of his respect. If you were goofing off in class, talking with some girls, he might bark, "Take a lap, Casanova." Or if you had impressed him with a nice play on the football field, he might call for a command performance. "Take a *lap*, my friend."

Coach Vincent Ramirez knew he faced an uphill battle from the moment he arrived at the first budget meeting of the year. He had been placed last on the agenda.

He sat and waited while the head of the drill team argued for and won more school-purchased uniforms.

Coach Ramirez appeared supportive while the band teacher, Mr. Fletcher, presented a $387 request for new instruments. It was seconded. Fletcher then gratefully added that, to help repay the budget, he would sell mouthpieces to students for a dime profit. "And I thank you all."

Coach watched while Commissioner of Spirit Dina Phillips presented her report that the Sophomore Sockhop would require either a live disc jockey playing records ($125 an hour, but he supplies everything) or a band like Ridgemont's favorite, the T-Birds ($500 for the whole night). A budget was passed allotting $750 for the entire evening, to include entertainment and security. There were a few outraged whistles.

"Come on, now," said speech teacher Gina George. "The kids need to get out of the house."

"I think they manage just fine without our help," said Vice-Principal Ray Connors.

"There just isn't enough money in the till for all the worthy causes," said Mr. Haynes, a counselor.

"Come on, lighten up, Harold."

"I think Hal has a point," said Connors. "These kids already have the off-campus lunch, and they already have self-grading classes on campus, why *pamper* them any more?"

Through it all, watching his chances for a big killing with the board ebb, sat Head Coach Vincent "Take a Lap" Ramirez.

"You're next, Mr. Ramirez."

Coach stood.

Whenever he was off the field, people were always telling him to talk slower. Most of the time he did not pay attention to these people. It was enough, Ramirez thought privately, that he had learned English at all. English was a damn tough language. When Ramirez went home he still spoke rapid-fire Spanish.

"I'll tell you why we need money for the athletic department," Ramirez said slowly. "Because I'm out there every day watching our teams. I know the difference between the Raiders and a championship ball team." He paused, just as he had in practicing the night before. "The difference is $1,895."

More outraged whistles.

Ramirez whipped out a piece of paper. "We need new jerseys, nice red-and-yellow jerseys. They run $1,100 total. We also need helmets for these boys. I don't want any brain-damaged ball players. Not when I know we can replace the cracked plastic ones we have now for $300."

Coach Ramirez held his coat together and gestured with the other hand. "I think you all know it's dog-eat-dog in the C.I.F. And if we want to do *anything* at all, we need to keep up. We need what everybody else already *has.*"

He looked into the eyes of the board members.

"We need movie cameras," he said. "We need to take and review films like all the other teams in the C.I.F. Then we will be a complete *winning* football department. Don't we owe these kids that much?" Ramirez let his hands drop to his sides. For a moment it appeared that he had gotten through to his audience.

"Mr. Ramirez," said Vice-Principal Connors, "before we vote on this matter, I'd like to say something before this panel."

Ramirez nodded.

"I don't think I'm saying anything that isn't already on everyone's mind," he said. Connors passed a hand through his buzz cut. "We're already over our pay rate per season. Many of us are concerned about our own projects. We ask ourselves— Why more money for football? We just brought in Assistant Coach Sexton last year. Why the continued expense?"

"Mr. Connors," said Ramirez, placing his fingertips on the table before him, "you are forgetting our special weapon."

"And what is that, Mr. Ramirez?"

"I'll say only two words to you." It was a dramatic pause. "Charles Jefferson."

Ray Connors turned to the two teachers on either side of him. "That," he said, "I would like to see."

Charles Jefferson was a name spoken around Ridgemont with equal parts awe and fear. Jefferson was one of the few black kids who attended Ridgemont. He was just under six feet tall, quick on his feet, and blessed with those huge NFL shoulders that tended to make opponents take one look and think, *Fuck it.* At right end, he was by far the best football player Ridgemont High had.

Jefferson played on the Ridgemont varsity squad in his

sophomore year, two years ago. He was virtually unmatched in the California Interscholastic Federation. By his junior year, Jefferson, in spite of little support from his less-talented teammates, had attracted the attention of several colleges. There had been a sizable behind-the-scenes bidding war over the young athlete, and UCLA won out with the offer of a $40,000 scholarship. Shortly after accepting, Jefferson turned up at school with a cheery new blue Mustang. It became known among the students of Ridgemont as Jefferson's Scholarship Mustang, but no one really knew if UCLA had given him the car or not. Charles Jefferson didn't talk to anybody.

Charles Jefferson didn't want to be anybody's "black friend." His father was an insurance representative for Farmer's, and Jefferson always seemed more than a little on edge about the middle-class environment his family lived in. Jefferson stalked the hallways of Ridgemont High carrying his football duffle bag and wearing a wronged look on his face, and the hallways parted for him.

Toward the end of last year's football season, Charles Jefferson graffiti started springing up around school: Bonenose Jefferson Was Here. There it was, on the side of the gym, in the dugout, on the wall of the Mechanical Arts Building. Because the Charles Jefferson graffiti never appeared on any *desks*, it was presumed that Lincoln High was sneaking on campus after hours with their felt-tip markers and spray-paint cans. Jefferson himself made no comment, and stayed to himself as usual.

Then one day Jefferson walked into the 200 Building bathroom and saw scrawled on the mirror: Send Kunta Kinte Jefferson Back to Africa.

Jefferson went wild. He took off his belt and used the buckle to smash the big grooming mirror. (It was not replaced.) Jefferson walked off campus and decked the hall monitor, Willy Avila, who tried to stop him. Jefferson had been unreceptive to the many white administrators who tried to soothe him. He didn't apologize to Willy Avila, either.

Then, this year, Jefferson didn't show for summer football practices. Reached at home, he said he didn't feel inspired this season. He didn't feel comfortable in the school. Conferences with Coach Ramirez and Ray Connors hadn't much changed Jefferson's position. He attended two practices, and missed the first game of the season entirely. Many had given up on Jefferson when Coach Ramirez brought the name up in the year's first budget meeting.

"I want our student representatives here today to know," said Ray Connors, "that what I'm about to say I've said to Charles myself. Charles is probably the best end I've ever seen on a Ridgemont football team. But the vultures came right in and picked the boy clean. He has absolutely no ambition left at school, or on the field . . . he admits it himself. He told me he wasn't even sure he was going to UCLA."

"Oh, these kids do a lot of *talking*, Ray," said Mrs. George.

Connors continued. "Mr. Ramirez, members of the board, I do not question the jerseys or the helmets. What I want to know before we vote is this: How is a movie camera going to get Charles Jefferson or, for that matter, *anyone* to perform better on the field. Whatever happened to good old-fashioned *coaching?*"

"Mr. Connors," said Ramirez, "I can answer that question. This year I will deliver a championship team—whether you give these boys their equipment or not. That is our commitment to you. Now you show us *your* commitment to the Ridgemont Raiders."

The budget vote was put before the panel, and the committee slowly raised their hands of approval, one by one. It was as if no one dared diminish the institution known as high school football, not even Ray Connors. Coach Ramirez was granted the equipment, even the movie camera.

Charles Jefferson's car was in the shop for repairs, so he had taken the city bus to school that morning. Jefferson hated taking the city bus. The more the bus stopped, the more impatient he became. The more people who yanked on that little cord—*ding*—the angrier he got. All day long in classes Charles Jefferson was never far from the thought that he was going to have to take that lousy city bus back home again.

After school, Jefferson walked by football practice. He looked through the wire fence at the action on the field.

"I WANT YOUR BUTTS TO BOIL," Coach Ramirez was yelling. He had split the varsity team into two squads, each practicing pass-and-receive patterns on the still-yellowed field. Ramirez bolted in and out of the plays with his megaphone, complete with its own portable amplification system that hung from a shoulder harness in one hand and a movie camera clutched in the other. Charles Jefferson did not care for the megaphone, the little amplifier, the movie camera, or for Coach Ramirez.

Ramirez had come to Jefferson during Running Techniques and laid a whole line on him—this was the twentieth anniversary of the school, you're such a great player, bullshit bullshit bullshit. Jefferson knew Ramirez was just looking to save his own ass. Forget Ramirez, he thought, the man had been nice to him only after the first talent scout arrived last year. He stopped being nice when Jefferson stopped playing high school football. Now he was being nice again.

"GET IN FRONT OF HIM! WORK WITH ME WORK WITH ME WORK WITH ME! STICK TO HIM LIKE GLUE!!!"

84

Ramirez relished his job, anybody could see. When he spotted two small kids playing too close to the action on the sidelines, Ramirez simply stared at them with utter contempt and held the megaphone to his lips. He clicked it on to speak.

The kids scattered.

"NORTON! TAKE A LAP!"

Jefferson couldn't take any more. Without anyone ever noticing him watching through the wire fence, he turned and went to wait for the L bus heading downtown. Once on board, Charles lasted seven stops. He pulled a jacket over his arm and got up to speak to the bus driver.

"Driver," said Charles Jefferson, "take me home."

"Where do you live?"

"Belmont."

"We're getting closer. It's another twelve stops or so, son."

Charles Jefferson jabbed two jacket-draped fingers into the back of the bus driver's neck. "I want to go home. Now. To my *door*."

Charles Jefferson was driven to his door by the city bus, while a busload of amazed passengers looked on. As he was getting off the bus in front of his house, Jefferson turned to the driver.

"Now that wasn't very far out of your way, was it?"

Charles had barely set his books down, of course, when he was visited by two members of the Ridgemont Police Department. Jefferson denied the entire incident, but charges were still filed by the city bus company. He was barred from every RTD service, but that was just fine with Jefferson anyway.

The next day an office worker appeared at the door of Jefferson's English class with an office slip. When an office worker appeared at the door it could mean anything. It could mean a telephone call, it could mean an emergency, a referral, a rich uncle who died and left you a ton of money. It could mean anything, or it could mean *you*.

Of all office slips, the worst was a green slip. It meant that a student was headed directly to the front office, room 409, to see Vice-Principal Ray Connors. This was serious shit. A yellow slip meant Principal Gray wanted to see you—big deal, he was retiring at the end of year—and a blue slip was a phone message. It didn't even get you out of class.

"Okay," said Mrs. George, the English teacher. "Oh, my goodness, it's a green slip. Charles Jefferson, you need to go to the front office to see Mr. Connors right now. Here, take this with you."

Jefferson rose from his seat and calmly walked the quarter mile down the halls to room 409. The halls full of white kids definitely *parted* when they saw him coming. He liked that. Jefferson put his head down and studied the floor tiles along the way. Light green. Dark green. Light green. Dark green.

Charles was ushered into the office of Ray Connors.

"Charles," Connors announced, "I give up on you. I know you too well. I throw my hands up. So what we're going to do today is take you on a little walk to meet someone new. I believe you've heard we have a new dean of discipline . . ."

Jefferson nodded.

"I'd like to introduce you to him."

He led Charles Jefferson down the halls to the office of Lt. Lawrence "Larry" Flowers.

"Lieutenant Flowers . . . this is Charles Jefferson."

There were two posters on the office wall. One was of a waterfall, with white calligraphy: "You do your thing/And I do mine/And when we meet/It's beautiful." The other was of a cat hanging upside down from a steel baton. It said: "Hang in There, Baby."

And in the middle was Flowers himself. He had mellowed a bit from his first days at the school. Flowers had at first ripped into Ridgemont like a hungry dog. He sealed up the hole in the fence behind the baseball field, even tried to seal off the Point. Kids had ripped the access hole right back open with wire cutters, but the fact still remained fresh in many minds— *He tried to seal up the Point.*

Worse yet, Flowers had reinstated a Ridgemont policy that had gone out of practice in the sixties, presumably when students still retaliated with Molotov cocktails. Flowers had brought back The Student Parking Ticket. Student parking tickets, while not a valid city ordinance, still cost a kid money.

If you came back to your secret parking spot and saw an S.P.T. flapping on your windshield, that was still two bucks you had to hand over to Ridgemont. Lieutenant Flowers gave out 75 parking tickets in his first month at the school.

Lieutenant Flowers sat there now in front of Charles Jefferson, wearing a brown paisley shirt, brown polyester pants, and a light yellow sweater. Pinned on the sweater was the ever-present gold badge.

"Hello, Charles," said Lt. Flowers.

Charles Jefferson nodded.

"I want you to know, Charles that I am not a disciplinarian. I'm an independent man. I don't call parents. I just like kids coming to me, opening up and sharing what's going on. Letting me know how I can help them. I really don't like being known as a disciplinarian."

Flowers got up and closed his office door.

"I feel I can be open with you," he said. "I know about drugs, Charles, and violence and the street. I know about being black. I worked at a junior high school in Chicago for seven years. I may *look* mean, but I am not a mean man."

Charles Jefferson nodded.

"I feel the bottom line with any problem student—if I may be frank—is 'I love you.' We all want to feel love. Very few of us, Charles, are getting as much as we want. We're all beggars, and our cups are *empty*, Charles. Maybe there's only a few coins rattling around at the bottom ... but that is *it*, baby."

Charles stared straight ahead.

"Baby, you are kissing that scholarship goodbye! And for what? To get a city bus to give you a ride home? Charles, we all have restrictions and taboos keeping us from getting what we want, and it's the same thing. We're all human beings, alive and magnificent ... you are a magnificent student, and ball player ... and *baby*, you're about to kiss that scholarship goodbye! Now what do you have to say to *that*?"

"Fuck you," said Charles Jefferson.

High Noon at Carl's

Brad Hamilton reported for work as usual on Monday night at Carl's Jr. He knew instantly that something was wrong.

"Hamilton," said Dennis Taylor, "I need to speak with you about something."

"Yo." Brad had been setting up his fryer.

Dennis Taylor's voice was neither friendly nor accusing. "Brad," he said, "there was some money taken during your shift last night. A hundred-and-twenty-five dollars. We don't know where it's gone, but we do know this. We know who took it . . . and there was a witness. Do you know anything about this?"

"I don't know anything about it, Dennis."

There was a long pause.

"Jesus," said Brad, "don't look at *me*."

But they were looking at him. There was a small cluster of the other employees, his golf-cap buddies, watching silently.

"Let me ask you this," said Dennis Taylor.

"I don't know anything about it."

"Hamilton," said Dennis Taylor, "Carl's has the voluntary program of a polygraph test. Would you be willing to submit to one of those tests and have this same conversation with me at that office?"

"You mean a *lie detector* test?"

"Yes."

"You *bet*," said Hamilton. "We *all* would take a test."

"Okay," said Taylor. "We'll make an appointment for you tomorrow at the Harris Detective Agency, the agency that Carl's uses in these cases; it's located down at Third and Central. I'll give you the card, and I'll see you there tomorrow at, say, *four*."

Hamilton looked at his friends. To his horror, they, too,

were neither friendly nor accusing. They were more like a crowd of people across the street from a car wreck. They said nothing. Not David Lemon. Not Gary Myers. Not Richard Masuta. Not even Lisa. Brad felt it first as nausea. He was so angry, so confused, that only later would he try to remember who looked the guiltiest of the bunch. Who could have been a *witness* to his robbing Carl's? *Carl's*—his own turf?

"Aren't you guys gonna say anything?"

They said nothing. None of them.

"You think I took that money, Dennis? You think I took that money?" Brad yanked off his Carl's hat and apron and the country-style string tie. "Then you can SUCK SHIT because I QUIT!"

Dennis Taylor swung open the door built into the metal counter at Carl's. "You can leave right now, Hamilton."

Brad walked out of the top-of-Ridgemont-Drive Carl's Jr., straight to The Cruising Vessel. He roared out of the parking lot.

Two days later, Brad heard that Dennis Taylor had discovered the money hidden in a paper sack in a dumpster behind the kitchen. When nobody called Brad to offer his old job back, he knew what had happened. Dennis Taylor had set him up. The I.C. had probably written a letter to the franchise, demanding Brad be fired. When the franchise called Dennis Taylor, well, that was where Taylor's loyalty would end. He had promised to fire Brad, but was too spineless to do it outright. So he had set up a frame.

It was all beside the point, as far as Brad was concerned. He wouldn't take their job back if they begged him. Pleaded with him. He didn't care about Carl's. He didn't care about getting even with Dennis Taylor. He didn't care about his *friends* who kept their mouths shut when crunch came. He didn't even want to eat lunch with them anymore. Screw them. He'd find another job.

A Night at the Mall

It was a boring school night. Jeff Spicoli decided to head up to Town Center Mall and check out the action. He passed through the living room unnoticed by his father, who was engrossed in television. He even made it past the kitchen, where his stepmother didn't nab him for any chores. Spicoli made it out to the street with no interference.

He reached Rock City, the mall's pinball arcade, just after 8:30. He recognized only one face, an eighth grader, a little black kid he knew named L.C. L.C. was playing Space Invaders.

"What's going on?" asked Jeff.

L.C. stole a look and returned to the game. "What's going on."

After Space Invaders, they went out to the alley behind Rock City and smoked a couple bongfuls of Colombian.

"Well," said L.C., "I've got a car tonight. Let's go cruise. See if there's any ladies happening."

"You can't drive."

"Then you drive."

"Whose car is it?"

"My brother's." L.C.'s real name was Richard. They called him L.C., short for Little Charles, because his brother was Charles Jefferson.

"Where is your brother?"

"At a running clinic in Yuma, Arizona. He ain't comin' back until tomorrow morning."

The desire flickered in Spicoli's eyes. "Let's go check the car out."

They went out to the parking lot to inspect the car—a nice Mustang with a tape deck.

"Look at the tires," said L.C. "*Smoooooooooooth.*"

"I think the word is *bald.*"

"Well," said L.C., "you want to cruise or not?"

Spicoli's California driver's license had been revoked two months after his fifteenth birthday. Spicoli had decided one night to shake loose a cop who'd thrown a light on him. The chase had ended in a cul-de-sac, where Spicoli had tried to get away by driving up onto the pavement around what were by then three police cars. He had ruined a row of lawns and two station wagons.

"Let's cruise," said Spicoli.

They pulled out of the TCM lot, to Mesa De Oro Liquor, where L.C. hopped out and returned a few minutes later with an eight-pack of Budweiser. L.C. handed Spicoli one.

"Guy in there told me about a party out in Laguna. Two kegs. I got the directions and everything."

"We're out of here," said Spicoli.

They took Interstate 5 up the coast.

"See the new *Playboy*?" asked L.C.

"Naw. Any good?"

"Suzanne Somer's tits."

"All right."

"I like sex," said L.C. He said it like he had just figured it all out the day before.

They were headed for the Laguna kegger, down a lengthy stretch of road, listening to the tape deck, when a pair of headlights appeared half a mile behind them.

"Hold your beer down. I think it's a cop."

Spicoli slowed down; the car behind slowed down. They continued like this for another two miles. Then the car behind them pulled closer, within "busting distance."

"This is definitely a cop," said Spicoli.

Then the high beams of the car behind them switched on.

"What the fuck is this guy doing?"

The car behind them advanced to the point where it was

almost touching the back of Charles Jefferson's scholarship Mustang.

"What the FUCK is this guy doing?"

The car behind bumped the back of the car.

"He's gonna scratch my brother's car!"

The phantom car pulled back a moment, then passed Spicoli and L.C. on the left. It was a carload of laughing jocks in a Granada.

"A bunch of jocks!"

"They're just fuckin' with us!"

The drivers of the two cars eyed each other, both with heads tilted to the right. The classic competition pose. With an imperceptible nod of the head, Spicoli accepted the challenge. Both cars roared down Plymouth Road, toward the party.

"DIE, GRANADA JOCKS!"

"L.C.," Spicoli yelled in the heat of the race, "you wanna roll up your window?"

"Why?"

"It messes your hair up," said Spicoli, "to have one window down."

"I like the air. Why don't you roll yours down. Then you'll get a crosswind . . ."

Spicoli shrugged and rolled down his window.

The Mustang tipped eighty and passed the Granada, even passed the exit for the party.

"EAT MY DUST!" Spicoli was grinning. He turned to L.C. "You know the thing I love about Mustangs? The steering wheel." He fingered the bubbles in the wheel. "You can negotiate a hairpin turn with *ease*, my man."

On the word *ease*, Spicoli had intended to show his further driving prowess behind the wheel of Charles Jefferson's car. He curled a finger into one of the Mustang wheel bubbles and whipped it clockwise. The car screeched off Plymouth Road, onto a side street. The idea had been turn around and go back to the party.

But at the moment of the hairpin turn, L.C. had been attempting to switch the tape in the tape deck. He was thrown against Spicoli, who crooked his finger farther into the bubble than he expected. The car swung in a complete circle. Their path also included a fire hydrant, which ripped the side of the car open like a can of tuna.

"Are you okay?"

"   . . . . . "

The Granada jocks flew past them, laughing.

"Are you okay?"

"My brother," said L.C., "is going to KILL you."

"It's your fault, too."

"MY BROTHER IS GOING TO KILL YOU."

"Just be glad you're all right, you little wimp."

"MY BROTHER IS GONNA SHIT."

"Make up your mind," said Spicoli. "Is he gonna *shit*, or is he gonna kill us?"

"First he's gonna shit, *then* he's gonna kill us."

It was another one of Spicoli's dark moments, the kind that were getting all too familiar to him in his high school days. Sitting there in the battered car of the noted mauler Charles Jefferson, he waited for the screams of the police sirens.

But there was no screaming siren. The bashed Mustang started again with a death rattle. Then Spicoli and L.C. puttered back into the Ridgemont hills, where Spicoli put his mind to work.

He came up with a beauty. All he needed was a little help from L.C., and some of the soldering tools in his dad's television repair kit. Once they had the car back up at Ridgemont High School, it took exactly twenty minutes to perform the entire deed.

The next morning, students were met with yet another curious sight. The steel letters were still gone from the green brick vanguard, but this was something else. Charles Jefferson's Mustang had been wrecked and welded to the front flagpole. Spray-painted on the side: LINCOLN SURF NAZIS.

The next morning Charles Jefferson was insane. Beyond insane. By afternoon he was still wandering around lunch court speaking in half-sentences. "Someone will die . . . I had to fill out forms . . . I will find out who . . . someone will *die*."

It was Homecoming Week. Ridgemont tradition held that the school spent this week getting psyched for the game against their rival, Lincoln High. In past years the students had viewed Homecoming Week as just another high school custom established by adults. This year was different. No one had counted on the kind of incentive that came when Charles Jefferson saw his smashed Mustang. By late afternoon he had joined the Ridgemont football squad. For Ridgemont, this was more activity during football season than they'd seen in twenty years.

It took exactly two days for Kenneth Quan, the A.S.B. president, who had campaigned on the slogan Bring Back Crazy Ridgemont Spirit, to figure out a way to take advantage of it. Quan proposed a closed student council meeting in which he would discuss the details of his special plan for Homecoming Week—a little thing called TOLO.

Leave it to Quan. TOLO began as a tease campaign in the school newspaper. "TOLO is coming." Then signs went up around school. "Watch out for TOLO." "TOLO is almost here."

Rumors flew as to what TOLO actually was. TOLO was a big local band that would play at lunch. Or maybe TOLO was a secret bomb to unleash on the Lincoln Surf Nazis. Bootleg TOLO signs went up: "TOLO has been kidnapped." "TOLO changed his mind."

Then, finally, a mandatory assembly was called. There

were some brief preliminary announcements about the mural being painted on the auditorium walls (From Chaplin to Travolta), then Quan took the podium for the big announcement.

Kenneth Quan was frenzied. Kenneth Quan was always frenzied. Campaigning for A.S.B. president at the end of last year, he had given about a million speeches about the importance of spirit and enthusiasm. Quan, the former boyfriend of Cindy Carr, gave you the impression that air raids were not out of the question when it came to school spirit.

"I have detected this year," said Quan, speaking from the school podium in a high pitch, "a lot of students who want to see some spirit here at Ridgemont High. A lot of people are really anxious to get in there and do something for the school. But maybe they feel restrained, or that they aren't cool enough. Maybe they are afraid they might draw attention to themselves."

"Well, the A.S.B. has responded this year by decreeing next week TOLO."

Boos. Hisses.

"Many people have asked, 'Just what is TOLO?' " Quan gestured wildly with both hands. "TOLO . . . stands for Totally Outrageous. We're all going to act Totally Outrageous. And starting this Monday, it's TOLO Week!"

Quan had a whole schedule printed up in the next morning's bulletin. The idea was that you geared up all week for the big homecoming game, the game where Charles Jefferson would attempt to avenge his Mustang. Quan had even made a program of dress, so that everyone could show total spirit during TOLO Week:

> Monday—Tourist Day
> Tuesday—Li'l Abner Day
> Wednesday—Hollywood Day
> Thursday—Red and Yellow Day
> Friday—Punk or Disco Day

There were other activities during TOLO Week. Pie fights (in which twenty-five cents bought you a smock and small tin filled with whipped cream). Water balloon fights. A band at lunch. Quan had gotten it all approved by Principal Gray, to promote spirit on the week leading up to homecoming.

The hardcore surfers stood around the parking lot and grumbled all week. An amazing thing was happening to their school. The students were actually going along with TOLO. By Friday things had worked up to such a pitch, that most students, even the same people who swore they would never go along with pep and spirit and all that garbage, were dressed up like punks and gold-chained disco lizards.

Friday was also election day for Homecoming King and Queen.

Outside the gym, where voting took place at lunch time, the pie fight spilled out of its special ring. Jeff Spicoli told everyone he was going to nail Mr. Hand with a pie. He went out of the preordained pie-fight circle and went to stand by Hand, who was talking to another student. Everyone began to gather, waiting for the moment Spicoli would smash Hand with a pie.

Spicoli moved in slowly for the kill, holding the pie behind his back. He prepared for the perfect angle of attack. But something went wrong. Too many people knew. Another student got impatient and nailed someone else on the edge of the pie-fight circle. A small mele broke out. Pies everywhere. It was a TOLO free-for-all, and Hand strode out of lunch court in disgust before a drop of whipped cream could touch him.

The trash would sit for days afterward. "The A.S.B. thinks they run this school," said the head janitor, Art Hertz. "Let *them* clean it up."

In the gymnasium, voting was going on for Homecoming King and Queen. The winners would be announced during half time at the Lincoln game. The king and queen were to be crowned in the middle of the field, in front of the wildly cheering spectators, and then driven around the running track in a limousine.

On the ballot that Friday were eight nominees, four specimens each sex of quintessential maturity and adulthood:

—There was Cindy Carr, who would probably win Homecoming Queen because she had worked so hard for it in her two years at Ridgemont. She smiled at any- and everyone, and knew all their names.

—Then there was Betsy Rollins, who had come back from vacation this year with a nose job. And a new hairdo. Everything about her was now voluptuous and perfect. A late but strong challenger.

—Kip Davis was not to be discounted. She was the ultimate sun-kissed blonde, straight out of a Beach Boys song. That in itself carried a block vote, but Kip had also personally gone with half the senior class. Kip was the spoiler candidate of this race.

—But who could forget Sue Bailey, the black girl who dated only white boys. She had made a lot of friends this year, attracted a lot of attention, and had come on strong in the final moments.

The field for Homecoming King was even wider:

—Best bet was A.S.B. President Kenneth Quan. He was so full of spirit you almost couldn't give it to anybody else. Every day, every lunch period, he was out there pressing the flesh, listening to students and appearing presidential.

—If sosh-dom was a small body of water, Chris Brody was the Pacific Ocean. He was a curly headed kid, always drying his squeaky-clean, lemon-tinted hair. He would walk down a hallway, chest puffed out, waiting for any girl he could bear hug until she screamed. Then he would ask her to loan him a dollar.

—Vincent Mathias . . . who knew how he had ended up on the list? He was a low-level football player, pompous as hell by reputation. He was always talking about how secret the Raiders' plays were, then explaining exactly what they were and how they worked for *him*. He was always talking about getting out of school, but was the type who would never graduate.

—Gregg Adams had a shot. As Ridgemont's biggest drama star and, of course, current boyfriend of Cindy Carr, he was a high-profile character. He emceed all the school events.

He was at every football game. The guy really believed in living high school to the max.

After considering all the options, Jeff Spicoli voted for himself.

By homecoming game time, the only seats left in the Ridgemont bleachers were at the far left end. Linda Barrett and Stacy Hamilton climbed up and took the last two seats, next to Mr. Vargas, Vice-Principal Connors, and Mr. Hand.

"Grade my test yet, Mr. Hand?" Stacy asked.

"Yes," said Hand, without taking his eyes from the field. He was dressed, she thought, rather disappointingly in a bright red Pendleton jacket.

The Homecoming Game.

Jumping and leaping in front of the stands were the Ridgemont cheerleaders. Up front watching the spectacle were the sophomores and ninth graders from Paul Revere. Their mouths hung open as they watched the high school cheerleaders.

Behind them, gathered in the same general area like good cheerleader husbands, were the boyfriends of the "Spirit Bunnies." Most had already graduated—it was a classic syndrome. They had risen to the top of their heap, they had shimmied to the top of the rope, and they weren't about to let go now.

The Ridgemont cheerleaders were big on spelling. Everything had to get the full spell-out treatment. Players' names. Positions. You name, it, they spelled it. And while all this was going on, you had Richie Raider, a male cheerleader in a warrior headdress, jumping around. Every year the cheerleaders voted in a new Richie Raider. This year it was a senior friend of A.S.B. President Kenneth Quan's. His name was David Santos. Santos was said to have six toes.

Across the field, Lincoln was warming up for the game. Lincoln liked to intimidate, and one of their finer points of psychological warfare was their school band. The Lincoln High band had their own special stands, uniforms, and pulsating repertoire of sporty music ripped right from the heart of "Wide Wide World of Sports." On any given moment, when their opponent's ragtag combo might be playing the traditional

"Charge," Lincoln, for example, would be blasting out a bombastic version of "Get Down Tonight."

The Ridgemont High Raiders had won their last two games. All the games, in fact, since Charles Jefferson discovered his car welded to the flagpole. He had heard that Steven Miko had done it. Miko was a Lincoln student, a slender kid with wild eyes and no hesitation for pulling a brutal prank. A couple of years back, Miko had personally hoisted and painted a Ridgemont Raider on one side of the gym to look like Frank Zappa. Later he was fired from Jack-in-the-Box—a lowly fate—and told friends he was going to rip the place off. And he did just that—he ripped off the big plastic *Jack*. The sawed-off clown figure sat in his backyard for over a year.

This year, Miko had taken the Ridgemont steel letters. It was a proven fact. People had been to Miko's house and had actually seen the letters. There, in steel, on his bedroom wall, the letters spelled CLITS.

So everyone assumed it had to be Miko who had wrecked Charles Jefferson's car.

The Ridgemont Death Squad—Mike Brock and a few others from the football team—had taken care of the immediate retaliation. They had drenched the Miko house in large farm-stale eggs, and they had phoned in two bomb threats on Mr. Miko's Chinese Cuisine. But the best move came the night the death squad visited Miko's yellow Datsun pickup truck, parked outside the house. Poor Steven Miko should have known better than to leave his car door open. They had filled the cab with fertilizer . . . and live mice.

The Twentieth Annual Ridgemont-Lincoln Homecoming Game began. Within a few minutes of the game's first quarter, Charles Jefferson had already started to pick apart the Lincoln defense. At peak form, Jefferson could remind an entire team that they were still high school amateurs and he was *headed pro*. You could hear Coach Ramirez on the sidelines, performing for his movie camera.

"THERE YOU GO. THERE YOU GO. H.Q.A. HELLFIRE! QUICKNESS! ABILITY!"

That was his new one: H.Q.A. Before the cameras were

ordered it was always just "Take a Lap." Now he thought he was Vince Lombardi.

Lincoln, a tough football team with a tough band, refused to give in easily. At the sound of the half-time gun, Ridgemont held the edge, 13–12.

All cheerleaders not nominated for the homecoming court scurried into the bleachers to sit with their boyfriends and watch the homecoming coronation. But first A.S.B. President Kenneth Quan announced an R.O.T.C. demonstration. The two teams of R.O.T.C. trainees charged onto the field and demonstrated their strictly choreographed maneuvers.

"I don't *believe* they're dragging this out so long," said Stacy.

"It's like this every year," said Linda.

At last, the time arrived. They were all there seated on a stage at the center of the field, waiting while A.S.B. Advisor Joseph Burke handed the envelope to last year's Homecoming Queen, Beth Schumacher.

"And the winners are ... *Cindy Carr* and *Kenneth Quan.*"

His mouth dropped open. She screamed. *"I can't believe this is really happening."* They took their places on the back of a long black limousine, and the car began its slow parade around the running track of the stadium.

As soon as the procession moved in front of Lincoln's bleachers, the attack began. Eggs and paper cups filled with soda and ice came flying from every direction. Onto the field. Toward the car. Toward the Ridgemont bleachers. When a rock hit the windshield of the limo, the driver instinctively sped off. Kenneth Quan and Cindy Carr—the newly crowned king and queen of Ridgemont's Twentieth Annual Homecoming—slid off the back of the limo and into the dirt where they were pelted with more eggs.

Lieutenant Lawrence "Larry" Flowers was on the field in an instant. He had gotten information that the instigator of Lincoln's shenanigans was Steven Miko—the troublemaker who was also, as it turned out, school photographer for the Lincoln annual that year. As soon as the mayhem broke out,

Lt. Flowers spotted a photographer, wrestled him to the ground, handcuffed him, and hauled him to juvenile detention.

"We've got Miko," he reported into his walkie-talkie. The word spread—they had Miko.

They did not, however, have Miko. They had just beaten and apprehended Arthur Chubb, the photographer for the *Ridgemont Reader.*

It was a hard-fought second half. Still 13–12 midway in the fourth, Lincoln drove to Ridgemont's ten yard line. But instead of going for the obvious field goal, Lincoln elected to try for the first down. They were stopped inches short, and Richie Raider started whooping it up on the sidelines. He began hugging the other cheerleaders.

In the stands, the cheerleaders' boyfriends watched his every move. *Did that guy just grab Dina's tit?*

The Ridgemont Raiders, in retaliation, began grinding out the yardage. Their chief opponent was now the clock. Finally, with less than two minutes on the clock, the Raiders brought the ball to the Lincoln five yard line.

Steve Shasta, soccer star and Ridgemont's ace place kicker, began preparing himself to kick the winning field goal. He began walking out onto the field. But Coach Ramirez called him back. He waved for Charles Jefferson to come in from the sidelines.

"Jefferson," he said, the new movie camera whirring, "I'm gonna give you a big shot. We win or lose on the next play."

Jefferson nodded. "I'll take it in."

The next play was a pitch out to Jefferson, and Lincoln anticipated it. Jefferson grabbed the ball and ran into two defensive players waiting for him. From the stands it appeared he was a goner, stopped just feet short of the touchdown.

But however Charles Jefferson summoned to do what he did, it probably had something to do with his battered Mustang. Jefferson plowed right through his tacklers, up and over them, into the end zone. The two Lincoln tacklers lay motionless on the field.

In the stands, Jeff Spicoli turned to L.C. "I think we may have gotten away clean," he said.

It was a much-celebrated Ridgemont victory. Ridgemont residents could hear the hum of the car horns from two miles away.

The homecoming dance, an informal affair being held at Jack Benny Hall, was about to begin. But it was much, much too early to go there yet. For the victorious football players, there was another ritual to attend to. All the squad members picked up six-packs of beer at Mesa De Oro Liquor and drove out to the Alpine Information Tower at the foot of Ridgemont Drive to discuss the game.

Later, only later, when the time was right and the dance was almost over, did the team make their calculated entrance en masse. They were applauded, and a crush of girls who'd been sitting on the hardwood floor watching the band now gravitated to the celestial Ridgemont Raiders.

"Well," Steve Shasta whispered to a friend, "here's the dilemma—seek it or stroke it."

An adoring girl rushed up to him. "Here," she said, "I saved this for you." She surrendered a warm beer to Shasta.

Shasta took a sip and handed it back. "Thanks," he said. "I hear they drink it like this in Germany."

Linda Barrett and Stacy Hamilton, meanwhile, stood in the girls' bathroom and listened to the talk at the mirror.

"We were sitting in the bleachers," a girl was saying as she brushed her hair in long, savage strokes, "and he *really* had a boner. I was embarrassed 'cause you could see it and *everything*."

"Are you talking about Dave Carpel?"

"Yes."

"He walks around with a boner *all the time*."

"I think your tits are getting bigger," said another girl.

Three girls turned around and said, "Mine?"

"So, *anyway*," continued the brusher. "I thought it was going to *bust* out of his pants."

"What did you do?"

"Well, Mr. Burke *shined the flashlight* on us. And David just *wilted*. And I got out of there quick." She paused. "This school is so insane."

"Did you know," offered yet another girl at the mirror, "that Steve Shasta brought in booze."

"That boy is *such* a good kisser."

"You kissed Steve?"

"That boy is a fox and he *knows* it."

"I know, but he's nice."

"I know," commented the brusher. "It's such a shame, isn't it?"

The Shame About Steve Shasta

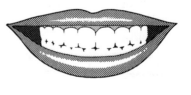

Steve Shasta walked into Child Development wearing his customary wraparound Vuarnet sunglasses. Cindy Carr was working in one of the mini-kitchens, making guacamole dip.

"What's for dinner, snookums," said Shasta, grabbing her waist from behind.

Cindy jumped slightly and pounded Shasta with little fists: "Steve," she said. "There's someone here to see you."

Shasta turned around to see his visitor, a man in his late twenties, holding a notebook. Reporter.

"Hi, Steve," said the visitor. "I'm Jim Roberts from the *Herald*. I found out at the office that you had a free period and might be here. I wonder if we could talk for an article I'm writing about high school soccer."

Shasta didn't flinch. He checked his watch and slipped into Steve Shasta mode. "Sure, Jim. I've got about twenty minutes. Want to do it in the cafeteria?"

It was not an uncommon sight on Ridgemont campus,

Shasta walking across the commons with the media in tow. Local print and TV reporters flocked to him, and he had the media personality that they loved.

"You know, Jim, the thing I like best about soccer is that it's not a *collisional* sport. You know what I mean? It's very physical, but the emphasis is on ball handling. Nothing against the game of football, of course . . ."

Shasta could dish it right up. When most of the other kids were down at Town Center Mall, Shasta was indoors watching soccer games down on the far end of the TV dial. He loved the sport, and had it added to the athletic program at Paul Revere Junior High. He had developed strategies that would probably be in use at RHS long after he, or even Coach Ramirez, left. The All-Out Crush Offense? Forget it—that was Shasta. The Dogmeat Five, in which five players converged on a single opponent by surprise? That was Shasta's, too.

Shasta was also a left-footed player, which made him doubly dangerous. He was nearly impossible to guard. He practiced his shots until dusk after school and all hours on weekends.

Last year he had been voted Most Valuable Soccer Player in the C.I.F. Shasta carried himself with a sort of disheveled dignity. He had those sloe-eyed just-woke-up looks. He wore shades almost all the time.

As he spoke with the reporter, Steve Shasta positioned himself with his back against the windows of the cafeteria. He was facing only the clock on the back cafeteria wall. Behind Shasta, Jim Roberts could see a small cluster of girls begin to gather, peeking and craning for looks through the cafeteria window behind him.

"I think last year it just kind of *clicked* as to what it was all about for me," Shasta was saying, tipping back in his metal chair and tugging at his green shirt. "That's why I started playing soccer better. All of a sudden I felt that confidence. Before that, I was just an average player—my coaches would tell you that. It was just *one day* it all popped into my mind what it was all about. On the soccer field it all seemed like everything was happening twice as slow. I've felt on top of the world ever since."

It was a stock Shasta rap, already published in the *Herald*.

"You practice quite a bit. Do you have time for friends, and girls?"

"Those things," said Shasta, "are of little or no importance to me. At all."

"Do you date at all?"

"Definitely." Shasta grinned. "Definitely." Shasta eyed the reporter carefully, as if to decide if he was okay or not, and then continued. "This is off the record, all right? My theory on girls—I've gone out with countless girls, and my motto is Don't get involved or you get yourself in trouble. You know it's true. As long as you don't think it's serious and you don't let them think it's serious, it's a hell of a lot of fun. But these people who go out for two years and *propose* . . ." He spit out an imaginary chaw.

Shasta leaned toward the reporter, and his tone became even more confidential. "See those chicks behind me? They follow me everywhere. See that one chick with the permed-out brown hair?" Shasta didn't even have to turn around to know she was there.

"I see her."

"I'll tell you, Jim. Girls are more aggressive than guys at this school. I went out with that girl *once*. She's followed me around ever since. And her friends, too. I never even went out with any of them! I'll tell you, Jim, these girls are all the same. They just want someone to go out with. You spend time with one of them, and it's all around the school the next day.

"They call me all the time. There's only one Shasta in the Ridgemont phone book so they know . . ." He sang it, like Sammy Davis, Jr.: "It's gotta be me!" Shasta checked the clock. "And when I don't go out with them, they start telling me off! It's amazing.

"But what else do you want to know about soccer?"

Steve Shasta had an ingenious way of solving his abundant problems with high school girls. He had used a convenient tool, the biggest gossip at Ridgemont, his sister Mia. Anything he told her was immediately dispatched to a large network of girls who regularly pumped her for information.

One night last year Shasta had a talk with his sister.

"I feel something terrible happening," Shasta had said.

"What do you think it is, Steve?"

"Well," said Shasta, "it's not really one thing . . . it's all the girls that I want to go out with. I don't know, Mia, I just think it's all gotten in the way of *soccer*. And when I don't have my soccer confidence . . ." Shasta looked at his sister woefully. "I don't feel like I'm worth *anything*."

"Wow."

"So I've made a decision."

"What's that?" She was eating it up.

"I'm becoming celibate."

"Are you *kidding?*" asked Mia.

There was a long silence. "Do you know what that is?" asked Steve.

"Are you becoming bisexual or something?"

"Fuck you, Mia, I'm not becoming a *fag!* I'm just abstaining from sex. It's called being celibate, and Mrs. George says more and more people are doing it. It's just . . . something I have to do. I'm going to be celibate during soccer season."

"But you're always saying that soccer is a year-round sport."

Shasta let his head fall into his hands.

The word had spread quickly and efficiently. Steve Shasta alone was responsible for the word *celibate* becoming part of the standard vocabulary of Ridgemont girls. It placed him at a distance from all the little boppers, he figured, and at the same time it made them want him more.

"Steve Shasta doesn't sleep with girls," they buzzed. "What a *shame* about Steve Shasta."

But it was a plan for which Steve Shasta considered himself a genius. It allowed him to be selective, and, as he once explained to the guys in his P.E. class, "I get a lot of blow jobs, too."

Changing

It had finally happened. Mark Ratner had gotten a C. Up until ninth grade he had a perfect A record. Then a few Bs had crept in. His mother had  warned him when he took the job at Marine World, "If you let your grades slip, it'll be on your record *forever*. No college wants an *average* student."

Then, last week, the mimeographed copy of first-quarter grades came in the mail. Mr. Vargas had dealt The Rat a cruel blow. He'd given him a C in biology. Mr. and Mrs. Ratner were more surprised than anybody. They wanted to know what was wrong with their son. All year long, they said, he'd been changing . . . and The Rat had to agree.

Mark Ratner had always wanted to be an entomologist, a bug scientist. All throughout junior high at Paul Revere, he was the kid who brought insects to school in a jar. For years, little glass display cases full of stuffed-and-tacked specimens hung on the walls of The Rat's room.

A few nights earlier, The Rat had come home, and it had all looked pretty ridiculous to him. He unhinged the display cases and stashed them in the garage. *Now what do I want up there?* The Rat replaced them later that night with about a hundred empty Elvis Costello album covers he'd fished out of the trash bins behind Tower Records.

"All year long you've been changing." The words rang in his ears.

"I don't know," Ratner reasoned later to his friend Mike Damone at one of their after-school sessions. "The more they start talking about the romanticism of Beowulf and Milton . . . Jesus, I just go to sleep, you know. I can't wait to get out of there. That stuff is so *boring*. It just doesn't enter into anything. I don't see why they try to get up all this respect for the

107

fourteenth century. Does the guy at the checkout stand at Safeway go, 'Hey, before I give you this food, you'll have to tell me about the metaphorical content of fourteenth-century literature in the Romantic Age'?"

"I think teachers get a bang out of it," said Damone. "It's just like mandatory P.E. I once asked Ramirez why we had mandatory P.E. He said, 'What would we do with all the out-of-work coaches?'"

"I guess I'm just depressed," said The Rat.

"Why are you depressed?" asked Damone, holding up his Tia Maria and cream. "I thought you were in *loooooooooove*."

"I'm totally depressed," said The Rat. Today, he had almost considered having a tall one himself. "Every time I go by the A.S.B. office she's talking to guys. Today I went there and she looked right through me."

"It's her loss."

"I don't know. I start out real confident, and then I see her and I feel chickenshit all over. It just kind of creeps up all over me. Especially when she doesn't even say hello." He paused, listening to the Lou Reed album blasting over the Damone family stereo. "I guess I shouldn't expect her to just go *wild* whenever she sees me."

"I would," said Mike Damone. "So tell me. Do you still like her?"

"Are you kidding? She's the only girl worth going for this year."

"Then just start talking to her," said Damone. "Just go up to her and ask her out. If she can't *smell* your qualifications, forget her! Who needs her! But that won't happen. Just go up there and ask her if she wants to go get a burger. That one has worked for me, personally."

"What if she's a vegetarian?"

Damone looked at his friend with scorn. The Rat just wouldn't learn.

"I know. I know. We've been through this before."

"About a million times," said Damone.

Braking Point

It was always a special treat for Stacy to round the corner of the 200 Building and see the blinds drawn in Health and Safety class. It meant that Mrs. Beeson was showing a *film*. It meant a break from the regular clock-watching routine.

The next question, of course, was *how long is this film?* And that was answered easily enough on this day with one look at the spool. Today's film was popping off the end, it was so full.

"Let's all settle down quickly," said Mrs. Beeson. "This is a long driver's-ed film. It's been a few years since we had it on campus. It's called *Braking Point.* Carl? Would you get the lights, please?"

Mrs. Beeson had gone through almost every title in every audio-visual catalog. She had seen them all, several times, and once she got a film rolling in her class, Mrs. Beeson usually spent the period in her cubicle at the back of the room.

More than a few students in Health and Safety had mastered the technique of checking the film spool, waiting for Mrs. Beeson to retreat into her cubicle, then slipping out the door only to return minutes before the film ended. Mrs. Beeson would be happy—her class was always refreshed and invigorated when the lights came back on after a film.

Sometimes even the hardcore truants stayed in class if the film was interesting enough to them. The last Health and Safety film had been a vintage antidrug movie narrated by Sonny and Cher. It was called *Why Do You Think They Call It Dope?* In the dramatic high point of the film, Sonny and Cher appeared as themselves and addressed the camera.

"You think marijuana is harmless?" asked Sonny Bono, as the camera picture grew fuzzy and nondescript. "How would you like it if your *doctor* took a smoke before operating on you? How would you like it if your *mechanic* smoked a joint before working on your car? How harmless is it then?"

When the lights came back on, a few guys from Auto Shop were deeply affected.

"Hey," one of them said, "Sonny had a *damn* good point."

Braking Point, like so many public service films for high school students, had a celebrity narrator. Desi Arnaz. The film began with a typical suburban street scene, as seen through the front window of a slowly-traveling car.

"Driving is an important part of each and every one of our daily lives," Desi began in his Latin accent. The car in the film accelerated. "It's a responsibility like no other, and it's a matter of life and . . ."

A ball came bounding out onto the street. The driver in the film braked, but failed to turn his wheel to the right. The film freeze-framed the face of the terrified child about to be splattered.

". . . death."

There was a swell of music. It was somehow hard to take seriously a driver's-ed film hosted by Ricky Ricardo.

"They have found The Braking Point."

Back to the serenity of a quiet suburban street scene.

"The driver here," continued the narration, "has had just two drinks. Just *two* drinks at a home of a friend."

"He's *fucked up*, Ricky," someone shouted.

"Get him out of the car! He's a fuckin' drunk!"

Continued the narration: ". . . And although this driver thinks he's driving well, he may be doing okay, but he forgets to perceive what's really going on . . ."

In the film, another car came barreling in from the left, running a stop sign and exploding into the side of the two-drink goner.

"ADIOS MUCHACHOS!"

Braking Point continued in this ascending-scale-of-blood-shed fashion so popular in driver's-ed films. The class got row-

110

dier and rowdier. When an entire family was maimed and a woman decapitated, the audience reached a peak.

"SO GROSS!"

"FUCK IT. I DON'T WANT TO DRIVE!"

"HELP! RICKY!"

Mrs. Beeson emerged from her cubicle at the back of the classroom. "Carl," she said, "do you want to get the lights, please? I think we've all had enough today . . ."

The lights came back on in Mrs. Beeson's Health and Safety class. As usual, a quarter of the class had sneaked out.

"Where is Stacy Hamilton?" asked Mrs. Beeson. "And where is Chuck Stillson? What happened to Tony Brendis? Where did all these people go? And where is . . ."

Happy Thanksgiving, Welcome to Jack-in-the-Box

So Brad Hamilton had to work on Thanksgiving. That wasn't the worst part. The worst part was having to say, "Hello, Happy Thanksgiving, welcome to Jack-in-the-Box, may I have your order, please?" Again and again and again. Not only did they want you to work on holidays, but they also never wanted you to forget exactly which major holiday it was.

Brad was working mornings. Decent hours, just a bad time of day. He had taken to getting up before daylight, which wasn't so bad, being alone on the highway in The Cruising Vessel and all, then going to school.

School. *Right.* School. He didn't think much about school these days. School was full of his so-called friends—all the people who were really sorry about what had happened at

Carl's. All the people whom Brad had trained for their jobs, and who still had them. They couldn't understand why he didn't come back and visit sometime.

It was a school night, an early winter evening. This was the time he was usually heading for work at Carl's. Now that he worked a morning shift he was free to do whatever he wanted. It was great!

Brad was sitting by the Hamilton pool, staring off into space. The joyboy days on lunch court were over, he was thinking. Times were going to be rough, but it would be *good* for him. Hey, he was probably riding too high. He was a different guy now, a *better* guy.

Brad started thinking about Lisa.

Mrs. George, the speech teacher, said in class that sometimes when you're thinking about someone a lot—all of a sudden—it was possible that a sensitive person was just picking up on the feelings of the other person. He could see Lisa right now, sitting in her room. She was probably thinking about him, too. Probably at that very moment.

Brad decided to take The Cruising Vessel out for a ride. Forget calling her; he would go right over there. It was only five minutes.

He pulled the LTD up around the side of the house. The light in Lisa's room was still on. He knew she would be home! He got out of the car and padded across the wet lawn to her window. He could hear the TV on inside, behind the curtain.

Brad Hamilton tapped on the window with the edge of a key—this was their special sign. No one tapped on the window with a key except Brad. Inside, he heard the TV sound lower. He waited, nothing. He tapped again.

No Lisa.

"Hey *Lisa*," he whispered. "It's me. Big B."

No Lisa.

"Hey *come on*, Lisa."

Brad hopped in his car, slammed the door, and tore home. At home he picked up the phone and dialed Lisa's number. It was the first time he'd spoken to her since The Incident.

112

He didn't care what time it was or who he woke up at Lisa's house.

"Hello?" Lisa answered in a hushed voice.

"You knew that was me outside your window!"

"What?"

"What the hell is going on? You hid from me. You knew that was me!"

"I'm sorry, Brad." Her voice was small, a million miles away. "I don't know why I didn't say anything."

"What's going on, Lisa? You want to break up? Is that it?"

"I thought we did break up."

"Come *on.*" He cleared his throat. "I love you. I've never said that to any other girl. You know that." Silence. "I know you love me, too."

"I don't know . . ." Her voice was getting smaller.

"You don't know?" Brad waited a second, then slammed the phone down.

He waited for her to call back. She didn't. He tried her number. Busy. He tried it again a minute later. Busy. He decided to drive back to her house. He had to talk to her in person.

Lisa was sitting on the curb outside her house. Not crying, just sitting, with her knees bundled up to her chest.

Brad sat down beside her on the curb.

"I'm sorry," he said. "Everything's changing. . . . I used to feel like I knew what it was all about. I just let myself get out of control, I guess. I didn't really mean it when we broke up before. I'm sorry." He kissed her forehead. "I don't want to break up with you. I know you don't want to, either."

Lisa said nothing.

"Can we get back together, Lisa?"

"I don't think so, Brad."

"There's another guy!"

"There's no other guy." She almost sounded sorry about it. "I'm just not interested in getting back together, Brad. I just don't feel the same way anymore."

"Why not?"

She shook her head. "I just don't feel the same way anymore. It's not easy for me to tell you, Brad. I've been trying to let you know for a while."

Brad couldn't believe it. He pointed to his chest and talked loud enough to wake up the neighbors. He didn't care. "DO YOU HEAR THAT, LISA? THAT'S THE SOUND OF MY HEART BREAKING, LISA. THAT'S WHAT IT SOUNDS LIKE!"

"Brad, please be quiet." And if that wasn't enough, she had to add the wretched phrase that would haunt him the rest of the school year. "I still want to keep you as a *friend*."

Two Dudes from Richards Bay

The last football game of the regular season was to be played against Patrick Henry High School. It would be a tough game. If the Raiders won, it meant the first play-off berth in the school's twenty-year history. Two days before the game, most of the players were already too nervous to go out and party. Not Charles Jefferson. He went out, partied, and broke into a Radio Shack with two men he'd met earlier that evening near the Richards Bay Information Tower. The police arrested Charles Jefferson later that night.

"Who were your accomplices?"

"I just went along with these two dudes! I didn't know what they were going to do."

"Two dudes? Can you identify them?"

"No."

"Do you know where they might be?"

"No. They were just some brothers. I thought we'd go get Colt and . . ."

Charles Jefferson was sent to juvenile detention camp to await trial. He lost his scholarship. Ridgemont lost the game against Patrick Henry. Teachers quit calling Jefferson's name for roll call. It was like he never existed.

"Charles Jefferson was an enigma," wrote Louis Crowley in the *Ridgemont Reader*. "He passed through our lives like a shot in the dark."

"Louis," said Mrs. Sheehan, "don't mix your metaphors."

The Rat Moves In

A student could mark his time by certain events that passed during the school year. First there was homecoming, then the World Series, then Hallo-
ween, and Thanksgiving, all working up to that coveted fourteen-day Christmas vacation. Like any other school, Ridgemont High made a big deal of the Christmas season. The classrooms were decorated in tinsel, the windows frosted with spray snow. Some teachers brought in trees. It all meant two things. First, it was a season to rejoice. Second, the race to vacation was on.

The Rat sat in biology watching the clock. Only three more periods until Christmas vacation; three more classes until Mark Ratner was sure Stacy would be lost forever. He made the decision sitting in Youth and Law. Today was the day.

After class, Ratner walked by the A.S.B. office and there she was, working side by side with Mike Brock. As usual.

Her eyes. She had the greatest *eyes*. And her hair! It was just great the way it fell onto her shoulders . . .

Stacy finished up. "Next," she said.

"Hi," The Rat mumbled.

"*Hello*. How are you doing today?"

"Pretty good," said Ratner. His glance turned directly downward. It was as if nothing, nothing in the world could get him to look up at this girl with confidence. "I was wondering when basketball tryouts started. I missed it in the bulletins."

"Let me check," said Stacy cheerfully. She shuffled through some papers. "*Monday.* They start Monday in the gym."

"During vacation?"

"I guess," said Stacy. "Are you going away?"

Ratner looked up. "Maybe," he said. It was a well-known fact that Cool People never hung around during Christmas vacation. "How about you?"

Stacy gave a sour look. "I don't know," she said. "I think I have to stay here in yuk-town."

If ever there had come a time for The Attitude, Rat figured, it was now. "Hey," he said. "How about if I give you a call over Christmas vacation?"

"Sure," said Stacy. "That would be fine."

"Great," said The Rat. He watched as she tore off a piece of an envelope, wrote her phone number on it, and pushed it through the hole in the window. He silently coached himself. *Take it slow.*

"Good luck with tryouts," she said.

"Thanks," said The Rat, all Attitude. "And maybe I'll talk to you over vacation."

The Rat nodded a cool goodbye, turned the corner, and banged into a trash can.

The 100% Guaranteed Breakfast

Well, Brad Hamilton thought, Jack-in-the-Box wasn't that bad in itself. At least they'd taken down all the little clowns—the plastic Jacks that kids would always make jokes about over the intercom. Jokes like, ". . . and after you give me that turnover you can tell *Jack off* ha ha ha."

No, working at Jack's wasn't as bad as Brad Hamilton thought. Pay was okay; he started at $3.10 an hour. He'd get a raise soon, no problem. But he was beginning to hate his new hours.

Brad had daybreak hours now, which meant a different atmosphere and mood altogether. Rarely did any kids his own age come into the place in the mornings. It was mostly the harried businessmen, on their way to work and hauling ass. *And how long will that take, please?* A morning man at Jack's got to hate the way they said "please" most of all.

Jack-in-the-Box spent a lot of money advertising their specialty items. They had a mushy steak sandwich that took Brad one entire minute to make. They had a chicken sandwich he wouldn't even talk about. Worst of all the specialty items, however, was the 100% Guaranteed Breakfast.

Even though it was a big publicity campaign for Jack-in-the-Box, a customer could only order the celebrated 100% Guaranteed Breakfast between the hours of 7:30 and 10:00 A.M. It took about eight minutes to microwave the complete pancake-and-syrup-scrambled-egg-and-English-muffin breakfast. *And how long will that take, PLEASE?* For the same amount of money you would think that the businessman would say "Screw it! I'll have a Breakfast Jack! They're already prepared and just sitting there!"

But the businessmen rarely backed off. During Brad's new

shift, from 8:00 to 10:15 A.M. (he was on independent work study for the first two periods), the businessmen stood and waited right there, with sweaty hands on the metal counter. *And how long will that be? Please!!*

The third week of work, the place was pretty empty. Just Brad at the fryer. David, the other morning man, was at the register. And the new assistant manager, an older man who'd transferred from a pep Boys in Santa Monica. Brad hadn't had a chance to talk much with him.

One morning David had turned to Brad and said, "I gotta whiz, will you just cover me at the register for a minute?"

Although anybody in fast food pretty much knew how to work a register, it was an unspoken rule that you didn't do it unless your assistant manager designated it as one of your responsibilities. Brad hadn't gotten that far; he was happy enough to be working the fryer.

But hell, here was David, a decent guy. They had to work together every morning. The assistant manager was in the back room. There was only one businessman in the place, and he already had his breakfast.

"Sure," said Brad, "take off."

It was like "The Twilight Zone." As soon as David disappeared into the bathroom, the one businessman in the place got up and returned to the counter.

"May I help you?" Brad asked nervously.

"Yes," said the businessman. He had short curly brown hair and spoke in a whine, the kind Brad hated. "This is *not* the best breakfast I ever ate . . ."

The man pointed to the huge cardboard display—Try Our 100% Guaranteed Breakfast.

". . . and I want my money back."

"Well, I believe you have to fill out a form," said Brad. He started looking beneath the counter for the pad of refund forms.

"No," said the man, "I get my money back right now."

"Well, that's not the way it works, really. And you ate most of your food already, too . . ."

"See that sign?" said the businessman. "It says, 100% Money-Back Guarantee. Do you know the meaning of the

118

word *guarantee?* Do they teach you that here? *Give me my money back.*"

"I can't do that," said Brad. "But if you wait a minute . . ."

"Look," said the businessman. He started talking to Brad in the tone of a kindergarten teacher. "Just *put* your little *hand* back in the cash register and give me my $2.75 back. Okay?" He looked at the name tag. "Please, Brad?"

"I'm sorry, sir. Just let me find the forms here."

"I am so tired," said the businessman. "I am so tired of dealing with *morons.* How hard is it to . . ."

Moron. That was a new one, Brad thought. Most irate customers just stuck to bitching. This guy not only had eaten most of his breakfast, he wanted his money back *now.* And he was calling Brad a *moron.* Brad didn't have to take that from anyone.

"Mister," said Brad Hamilton, "if you don't shut up I'm gonna kick 100% of your ASS."

"*MANAGER!!*"

Bam. The assistant manager came shooting out of the back. "Can I help you, sir? Is there a problem?"

"You *bet* there's a problem," said the businessman. He really put on the hurt act. "Your employee used profanity and threatened me with violence. I'm shocked, frankly. I've eaten here many times, and I've always enjoyed the service—until today. All I wanted was my money back for this breakfast. It was a little overcooked. And this young man *threatened* me. Now I plan to write a letter! I plan to . . ."

The assistant manager wheeled around to Brad. "Did you threaten this man or use profanity in any way?"

"He insulted me first. He called me a moron."

"Did you threaten this man or use profanity in any way?"

"Yes, sir."

"You're fired," said the assistant manager. He opened the steel door for Brad. "I'm very sorry this happened to you, sir."

"Thank you very much," said the businessman.

Brad stood there, stunned. Fired. Out of another job. He unhooked his fryer's apron and threw it on the counter.

The Five-Point Plan

The Rat had immediately come home and tacked Stacy Hamilton's phone number to his wall so he could look at it every day of Christmas vacation. *She actually gave me her phone number.* After two days his elation gave way to dread. The phone number challenged him every time he glanced at it. *Stacy*—555-6735. It's your move, the number said, what are you gonna do about it?

Ratner and Damone had been walking through Town Center Mall one Saturday afternoon during vacation.

"Damone," said The Rat, "what do I say to her?"

"Whatever you want." Damone stopped to flash a million dollar smile at a middle-aged housewife.

"I don't even know her, though."

Damone turned and looked at his friend.

"What you need, Rat, is my special five-point plan for scoring with girls of all ages."

As he talked, Damone passed a Country Farms shop. He plucked a free sample of cheese and sausage and moved on.

"All right," said The Rat, "what's your special five-point plan for scoring with girls of all ages?"

"I'm glad you asked," said Damone. "Men had *died* trying to obtain this information, you know. I will give it to you for free."

They continued walking past Rock City, which was packed with junior high schoolers, long-ashed cigarettes dangling from their mouths. Damone nodded to Jeff Spicoli, who was holding court by the Space Invaders machines.

"So come on," pressed The Rat. "Tell me. What's the five-point plan?"

"Okay," said Damone. "Pay attention."

The Rat nodded, always the student, as they passed

Tower Records. Damone stopped in front of a life-sized card-board cutout of Deborah Harry, the alluring singer from the group Blondie. She was just about his size.

Damone turned to The Rat. "First of all, Rat, you *never* let on how much you like a girl." He turned back to the card-board cutout of Deborah Harry to demonstrate. "Oh," he said disinterestedly, "hi." He turned to The Rat.

"Two. Always call the shots." He looked back at Deborah Harry. "You and me are going to the Charthouse, and then you're coming with me to the *movies*."

"Three. Act like wherever you are, that's the place to be." He returned to Debbie. "Will you *quit* telling me this is the most fun you've ever had."

"Four. When ordering food, find out what she wants, and then order for both of you. It's a classy move." To Debbie. "The *lady* will have . . ."

"Five. And this is *most* important. When you get down to making out, whenever possible put on the first side of *Led Zeppelin IV*." He turned to Deborah Harry one last time. "Why don't you put this tape on?" Damone put his arm around the cutout. "It sounds great in the back of my van . . . why don't we listen from there?"

Through it all, Deborah Harry looked back with the same intrigued cardboard smile.

"See what I mean?" said Damone. *"That* is how you talk to a girl, Rat. *Voila.* You can't miss."

"Gee," said The Rat after a long while. "Why can't I just be myself?"

"Later you can be yourself," said Damone. "What you want is for her to decide she likes you, no matter what. You know what else is good if you're not a *totally* popular guy? This has worked for *me*. You just kind of mention to the girl that you don't have a lot of friends in high school, that most of the people are worthless, but you like *her*. That makes her feel special. And you still have The Attitude."

The Rat nodded, taking it all in. They walked on through the mass of Christmas shoppers, past Thearles Music, where a friend of Damone's was demonstrating an organ out front.

"That's McCauley," explained Damone. "He likes it

when you talk to him like a Negro. His best friend is this black guy, Paul Norris, and Paul Norris acts like he's Gomer Pyle. It's bizarre."

Ratner grabbed Damone's arm. "Look at that girl. Look at that girl over there."

"You like that girl?" asked Damone. "You watch."

Damone positioned himself by the front of a shoe store and waited for the girl to pass. Then he pounced.

"Joyce!"

She looked at him strangely.

"Oh," said Damone. "I'm sorry. You looked like this girl in my abnormal psych class."

"I have that class," said the girl. "Do you go to State?"

Damone grinned. "Do you have that book where the guy . . . well, it's the one with the picture of the man with a spoke in his head? The man was walking down the street, and a spoke fell in his head. They left it there, right, because if they pulled it out they didn't know what would happen . . ."

"*Yes*," she laughed. "That's the book."

"What's your name?"

"I'm Karen."

"I'm Mike Damone. This is Mark Ratner."

Big smile from Karen. "Maybe I'll see you sometime at State!"

"See you later, Karen."

She walked on.

"Now *that's* how you talk to a girl," said Damone.

"You lie to her?"

"No, you wuss. One person says something to another, and it starts."

The Rat came back to Mike Damone's house. Damone's parents had left for the day to visit his grandparents in Riverside. The Rat didn't like to use things as a crutch, but on Damone's advice he downed a Colt 45. He made Damone leave the bedroom. Then he picked up the phone and dialed Stacy's number.

"Hello?"

"Hi. Is Stacy there?"

"This is Stacy."

"Hi, this is Mark Ratner."

"Oh, hi!"

They talked for a while, one of those conversations with lots of long silences. They decided they didn't know each other too well. Then The Rat popped the question.

"Stacy, would you like to go to the movies with me this Friday?"

"I can't." He knew it. *She had a boyfriend.*

"Okay ..." Then, an afterthought. "How about Saturday?"

"Saturday would be great."

A Date with Stacy

Mark Ratner had borrowed his sister's car. It was the result of an intricate negotiation process involving several past and many future favors, but the final factor had been Mark's holding over his sister's head her sex quiz answers in old copies of *Cosmopolitan.* That won him the car.

The Rat arrived to pick Stacy Hamilton up at the prescribed time, by the mailbox. *Led Zeppelin IV* was on the cassette machine.

"Thanks for coming to get me," she said.

"Sure thing."

Now what else would he say for the next four hours? The Rat sure didn't know. All he knew was that their next stop was the Charthouse Restaurant, and after that they were going to the Strand Theatre to see *Phantasm.*

"I hear this movie's pretty good," said The Rat. "They were talking about it in English today."

"Do you have Mrs. George?"

"Yeah. She's pretty good."

"Yeah. She's pretty good."

They drove along in silence until they reached the Charthouse Restaurant. The Rat's boss at Marine World had recommended it.

"I hear this is a pretty good restaurant," said The Rat.

"Yeah. Me too."

They took a seat at a table with a view of the ocean. A waitress handed them each a large wooden menu.

Damone's Rule Number Four, said a voice inside The Rat's brain: *When ordering food, find out what she wants, and then order for both of you.*

"What do you feel like eating?" asked The Rat.

"Well," said Stacy, "I think I'm going to have the Seafood Salad Special."

"That should be pretty good," said The Rat. He was starting to feel in control now. He was starting to feel like this could be the place, the very place. The lights were low. The view was good. The prices were . . .

Oh, my God.

The Rat reached back and checked his pants pocket. Then, casually, his jacket pockets. Empty. He had left his wallet at home on the dresser.

Jesus.

Cool. Cool was the name of the game. The Rat sat there, enjoying the view, smiling at Stacy. Inside he was dying a slow and miserable death. Stay cool.

"Do you mind," said Mark, "if I excuse myself for a moment?"

"Not at all."

The waitress bustled up to the table. "Are you ready to order?"

"Sure," said The Rat. "She will have the Seafood Salad Special."

"Okay. How about you?"

The Rat stared at her blankly. Of *course*. He had to eat too.

"I'll have the same."

"Okay. Anything to drink with that?"

"Sure. I'll have a Coke."

124

"How about for the girl?"

"Iced tea, please."

The waitress left the table. The Rat got up to make his phone call.

"Yo?"

"Damone. It's Mark."

"*Mark.* What happened to your date?"

"It's happening right now," said The Rat. "I'm here at the Charthouse. Everything's fine, except . . . I left my wallet at home."

"Did you go home and get it?"

"No. It's too late. The food is coming and everything. Damone, I've gotta ask you this favor, and I'll never ask you for anything again in this lifetime or any other. Will you *please* go by my house, get my wallet, and meet me back here?"

Silence.

"Hello, Damone? Are you there?"

"Just be glad I'm your bud," said Damone with a world-weary sigh.

Ten minutes later there was a page. "Telephone call for Mr. Ratner."

"Excuse me," said The Rat. "I'll just take this call and be right back."

The Rat picked up the phone at the front desk. "Hello?"

"Rat. It's not on your dresser."

"Did you look in the bathroom; that's where I was last."

"Hold on."

"Okay, I'll hold," said The Rat. The maitre d' gave him a nasty look.

"Okay. I found it."

"Okay. Thanks, Mike. I'll see you here."

"You owe me your life."

"Okay. Thanks, Mike. I'll see you here."

Mike Damone strolled into the Charthouse forty-five minutes later. Stacy and The Rat were still picking at their dinners and trying to make conversation out of life at Ridge-mont High.

"Hey Ratner! Is that you?"

"Damone! What are you doing here?"

"Hey, you know what, Mark? I found your *wallet* the other day. You want it back?"

"Wow. What a coincidence. I've been looking for that thing!"

The evening was a complete disaster. Only a few sentences passed between them after the wallet incident. They had gone to the theatre. The kid right in front of them hauled off and puked right toward the beginning of *Phantasm*. It smelled up the whole row.

By the time the movie was over, The Rat was wondering if he should even try the next step of the game plan—maneuvering her to the Point, where he would slip on the first side of *Led Zeppelin IV*.

They reached the car again. Something was wrong. The Rat had remembered locking his door. The Rat opened Stacy's side of the of the car, then she leaned over to open his and found it . . . already open. The Rat knew something was wrong. He looked at the dashboard of his sister's car.

The tape deck was missing. In its place was the steel bolting ensemble. The machine was gone.

The Rat turned pale, didn't mention it to Stacy. He drove her straight home, without even asking her about the Point.

He pulled up in front of Stacy's house. "I had a really nice time," he said like a zombie.

"Me too," said Stacy. "Do you want to come inside?"

"Aren't your parents asleep?"

"No, they're away for the weekend. Brad and I are watching the house."

It's midnight and she wants me to come inside.

"Okay," said The Rat sullenly. "Sure."

He followed her inside.

"Where's your brother?"

"I don't know. Probably out." She set down her purse. "Want something to drink?"

"No. That's okay."

"Well, I'm going to change real quick. I hope you don't mind."

"Naw. I don't mind."

She turned her back and pulled up her hair. "Will you unzip me?"

This can't be what it seems.

He unzipped her, past the bra and down to the small of her back. It was the first time The Rat had ever done that.

"Thanks."

Stacy walked down the hall to her room, easing out of her dress as she walked. She left the door to her room open. "You can come in if you want."

She wouldn't be doing this if she hated me.

He followed her into her room, his heart pounding in his throat. He turned the corner and stepped into the room. She stood there in her bedroom in a diaphanous white house dress. He pretended not to notice the difference.

"So . . . pretty nice house you got here."

"Thanks. What do you want to do?"

Damone's Rule Number Two: Always call the shots.

"I don't know," said The Rat.

"Do you want to see some pictures? I have all these pictures and stuff from Paul Revere. I kept a whole scrapbook! How stupid!"

"Sure."

She fished the old Paul Revere scrapbook out of her closet, and they sat together on her bed looking at the photos of mutual friends and acquaintances. Her knee grazed his.

She definitely expects something.

For twenty minutes, Mark carried on two conversations. The one with Stacy about her scrapbook and the one in his head. There was a scoreboard in his mind, and the odds seemed to be racking up in his favor. He debated all the signs. She had brought him inside, they were alone, she had changed. He had unzipped her.

But what if he tried to kiss her and she screamed or something? He would feel like Jack the Ripper. No, he wouldn't. Or maybe he would. What a wuss.

Then it occurred to The Rat. It wasn't one of Damone's

big rules, but he had given Rat the special advice just the same: *Tell her you don't hang around many high school people; make her feel special.* He decided to use the tip, but it came out like this:

"Not too many people like me in high school."

Stacy looked at him oddly. "That's too bad," she said.

More silence. He watched her pull her hair up and let it fall back down again. Another sign?

After a while it all got to be too much for The Rat.

"Well," said Mark, "I've got to go."

"Really?"

He got up off the bed and stood up.

Beg me to stay.

"Do you really have to go?"

"It's getting pretty late."

Beg me to stay just a little.

"Well . . . if you've got to." She stood up, too. "I'll walk you to the door."

The Rat gave her a quick kiss on the cheek and ducked out of the front door.

He walked down the steps of the Hamilton house. He wanted to turn around, to go back and tell her that he didn't want to leave. He wanted to violate all the rules of The Attitude and tell her how much he liked her.

And she, of course, she would tell him that she wanted him to stay, that she was glad he came back. And that this was just the beginning for them. And she would hug him and press up against him and . . .

Just as The Rat was heading back up the stairs, he saw Stacy's bedroom light shut off. He stopped in his tracks. It hit him like an enormous gong. It was as if the words were a Cecil B. De Mille production written in the nighttime sky, just for The Rat: YOU BLEW IT, ASSHOLE!

Bob Savage

Early in January, just after classes were back in session after Christmas vacation, Ridgemont High held a traditional mandatory assembly. The subject was ordering the school yearbook, the *Rapier*, and class rings.

A.S.B. President Kenneth Quan kicked the assembly off with a brief pep talk about spirit and rivalry as a *substitute* for violence and vandalism. It was a direct reference to the spray-paint job done on the school over vacation. The usual culprits had hopped the locked steel fence leading into the Ridgemont campus. When students returned from the Christmas break they found the black spray-paint insignia over everything: LINCOLN SURF NAZIS! It was the biggest green job for the janitors yet. Forty buckets. The school had smelled like paint all year long.

Kenneth Quan introduced the editor and two members of the *Rapier* staff. They gave a quick progress report and dropped a juicy news item—this year's *Rapier* would be black. They were off in a hurry.

Everyone was waiting for the main attraction. His name was Bob Savage. A young man in his late twenties, Savage was well known to many of the students. If you had no desire whatsoever to own or wear a class ring, you were digging for the money after ten minutes of listening to Bob Savage.

Bob Savage had the kind of shaped hairstyle that could only belong to (a) one of the Bee Gees or (b) a werewolf. It was reddish brown, and came back in a wide sweep that seemed to be held in position by laws defying nature.

Savage began his presentation with a slide show. "High school is a time for living and learning," narrated Savage, "and being young." His timing was well practiced, as it should have been; he had been making the same spiel for at least seven years. "It wasn't that long ago that *I* was sitting in class. Boy, did I want to get out . . ."

Polite laughter. He switched to a shot of kids in cars leaving their campus parking lot.

"But I have strong memories of high school. The cars. The fun . . ."

Switch to a shot of an attractive student couple walking down the hallway, hand in hand.

". . . The romance."

Switch to a shot of a gymnasium dance and lots of swinging teenagers in ten-year-old formals.

"And the prom. It didn't matter how you felt about going to the prom. You went. I went. I thought I'd go all the way with high school. I'd go to the prom. I'd take my best girl, and I'd even order a class ring."

Switch to a student admiring his new class ring.

"Some of my friends told me, 'You're not in sports, you're going to graduate soon, you don't need one.' I told them I was going to get mine anyway. I laughed at the time. 'Maybe it'll be worth something someday.' "

Switch to shot of drag racers at night.

"Racing was my thing," continued Bob Savage. "And it was on prom night that I made a real *bonehead* move. I know a lot of you may have heard about it. I played a little game called chicken on a blind curve. I didn't swerve in time to avoid the oncoming car. My girlfriend was killed. The other family had some injuries, but they're recovered now. But my legs are still severed."

A shocked silence settled over the assembly.

"A lot of people ask me why I do this—how I can still talk about it. I tell them it's the only way I *can* bear that accident. I think about it every day of my life. During my many months in the hospital we were unsure whether the grafting might take. My family and friends were there constantly. But there were many more times when no one could be with me at all. All I had were my memories."

Switch to a class-ring close-up.

"And that's what getting into the spirit, getting a class

ring, is all about. I want you to call me at home—I live right here in Redondo—and talk about it. My number is in the *Reader* and in the phone book. I'm honored to be able to represent Contemporary Casuals Class Rings. And I'd be honored if you ordered one from me."

Bob Savage. He'd probably been a real jock at school, before the accident. But as he wheeled himself offstage in his motorized wheelchair, it was like he was a rock star. He'd reached them all.

Even Brad Hamilton, who had decided against it earlier, went ahead and ordered a class ring.

Even Jeff Spicoli stood and applauded. "That guy is tremendous," he said.

School Picture Day

There is a certain smell unique to high school gymnasiums. It's a difficult aroma to break down exactly, but certainly the three main ingredients are old socks, hardwood flooring, and English Leather cologne. Every year teams of janitors are paid to sanitize gyms everywhere. Still they smell the same.

Today was School Picture Day at Ridgemont. Students were herded in and out of the gymnasium all day long, by class and last names. A professional photographer on the front stage faced thousands of students on Picture Day. Over seventy percent had been cool coached by friends not to smile—*no matter what he says*—and by the end of the day the photographer would invariably have no voice.

"Smile, *please.*"

During first lunch, the Ridgemont courtyard was cleared of all trash. Room was made for the entire school. It was School Picture time, a photo of no small importance, and for this the professional photographer would have to step aside and make room for *Reader* photographer Arthur Chubb. Chubb relished the job. He got to get up on top of the Technical Arts Building with all his camera equipment and take The Big Picture of the entire school. It was the double-page color centerspread of the Ridgemont *Rapier* yearbook.

Before going out on the courtyard for The Big Picture, Mike Damone mentioned to The Rat an idea he had for a bet.

"How much will you bet me I won't take off my pants for this picture?"

"Nothing," said Ratner. "You'd do it anyway."

"I'm serious. How much will you give me to take off my pants? And *face the camera* while I'm doing it."

"And not cover your face?"

"And not cover my face," said Damone.

"A buck," said Ratner.

"But you have to *moon*."

"Me, moon?"

"It'll be great. You'll be immortalized and no one will know who it is."

"What about you?" asked Ratner.

"Chubb will just airbrush me out. He did it once before in junior high school."

The Rat thought about it for a second. "It's a deal."

Mick Jagger Gave Me This

A peculiar thing happened right about the middle of January. Students from all classes began to plot out a calendar in their heads. Homecoming. Christmas vacation. School Picture Day . . . all the good stuff had already happened. What else was there to look forward to? Why they'd even started talking about the *Rapier* and class rings and the prom.

It was the most insidious of diseases, not in any journal but as infamous in its many names as the common cold. It was called Senioritis, Graduation Fever, Terminus Attendus, The Apathy Bowl, The Adios Syndrome.

It was that gnawing feeling that all that stood in the way of graduation were a lot of deadhead months of needless paperwork. Even colleges, as the rumor went, only looked up to your *seventh* semester. Even *they* knew about Senioritis.

One of the best gauges as to just how much Senioritis had set in was usually Mrs. Gina George's Public Speaking class. Mrs. George prided herself in the personal attention she gave to her speech students. She believed in their intrinsic good, which was either her greatest asset or fatal flaw, depending upon which side of the faculty lounge door you ate your lunch.

Students called her Mrs. G. She even let them grade themselves. All a student had to do was justify the grade in front of the class—and it was interesting how brutal the class could be at times—but it was still a matter of students grading themselves. She was not a contract teacher, but her only assignment for the semester was a five-minute demonstrative or informative speech. The class was always packed at the beginning of a semester. Then a substantial number of students disappeared for months, only to reappear from the abyss for a quick demonstrative around grade time.

Mrs. George was a Texas-born woman in her late thirties. She still spoke in the wild, excitable accent of her youth, and still wore her hair long like a schoolgirl's. She was divorced, the mother of two children who had grown up and moved back to Texas. She was the kind of teacher who had students over to her house and loaned them money. Few ever pushed Mrs. George to her limits.

Jeff Spicoli was one student who never seemed to accord Mrs. George the proper respect. He had to be forced, one week after report cards went out, to give his five-minute demonstrative speech and replace the incomplete that Mrs. George had given him instead of an F.

Spicoli stood before the class, leaning hunchback over the podium. The years of marijuana use had taken their toll on Spicoli. His speech had become slower and thicker, and he had the classic surfer affliction of dropping the ends off all his words.

He grabbed a hunk of his stringy hair and whipped it back over his head. He had no idea what to say.

"Jeff, you ought to try standing away from the podium."

He wandered just to the left of the podium. Then, in a burst of inspiration, he reached into his sock and withdrew his steel marijuana-smoking apparatus. He held it high, for all to see.

"I wanna tell you about *bongs*," said Jeff Spicoli.

Students stole anxious looks at Mrs. George to check her reaction. *We went through this phase in junior high.* Mrs. G. sat at the back of the class, expressionless.

"Bongs," said Spicoli, "I personally like better than smoking through papers. Because you can just put in how much you want to smoke and . . ." He shrugged. "That's it."

Mrs. George interrupted him. "Jeff? Do you like two bowls or three?"

The class laughed, and Spicoli seemed unsure exactly who was being laughed at.

"Jeff?"

"Well . . . it depends, really."

"Have you ever tried bonging through wine?" asked Mrs. George.

"Uh . . . no."

"I've heard you haven't lived until you've bonged through *wine.*"

The class was definitely laughing at *him*, Spicoli had decided. His face now taking on a distinct red tint, he responded by plucking a medallion off his chest. He then launched into the most incredible Jeff Spicoli story anyone could remember.

"See this necklace?" Spicoli said, looking to all parts of his audience. "MICK JAGGER gave me this necklace."

Pause.

"It's true. Mick Jagger gave it to me himself at the Anaheim Rolling Stones concert. You know? I was walking around behind the stage, you know, and I . . . I just saw Mick standing there. And he had some white stuff on his nose, and I said, 'Mick, you've been snorting coke!' And Mick said, 'Yeah, I've been snorting coke, man. You're right!' And he kind of laughed and said, 'What's your name?' "

"I said, 'Jeff Spicoli.' He goes, 'Nice to meet you, man,' very gentlemanly. Then he asks me if I want to do some coke with him."

Spicoli cleared his throat. He had them now.

"I figured, Mick Jagger? 'Sure.' I don't do coke, but I'd do some with him. So he pulled out a vial and we sat down. And Mick Jagger asked, 'Do you have a coke spoon?' And I said, 'No! Are you crazy?' So he goes, 'I know what, we'll use this necklace to do the coke!' And he took *this necklace* off and we got high and then . . . he *gave* me the necklace."

Spicoli held it high again. "And I won't sell it. Not for ten thousand dollars."

There was a pause, after which someone said loudly, "Bullshit."

Spicoli thrust out his hand. "Any amount of money. *Any* amount of money."

"Okay, Jeff. What grade do you think you deserve in this class? My book shows you missing twenty-three times last semester."

"Well," said Spicoli, "I think I deserve an A because I really used all the basics that you taught me in this class. I use them in real life." He pointed out the window, to Luna Street.

Silence. There was no majority of hands from the class.

"All right," said Spicoli, "a . . . B."

No hands.

"Hey, come on . . . get 'em up."

No hands.

"Okay. Okay. I guess I could take a C."

No hands.

"I won't take a D."

Hands.

"Thanks," said Spicoli, "I'll remember all of you."

College Orientation Week

The third week in February was College Orientation Week. For five days, representatives from city, state, and junior colleges came to the Ridgemont campus to speak to the students. Afternoon assemblies were held in the gym, mandatory for seniors and optional for underclassmen.

Brad Hamilton filed into the Thursday assembly entitled "The Advantages of Higher Education," sponsored by University of Southern California. He took a seat in the bleachers with the rest of his period-four English Composition class, and watched as David Lemon, one of his old Carl's buddies, tested the podium microphones.

All year long Brad Hamilton had delayed making any decisions about his life beyond senior year, though somehow he knew he would end up in college. To him the thought was like a dentist's appointment or a visit to a crotchety relative—he could always put it off another month. This, after all, was to be his Cruise Year, and he had intended to consider life beyond high school only after he had a maximum amount of fun. Now everyone was going around talking about college applications and essay questions, and Brad hadn't even gotten his cruise year into gear. College Orientation Week made him nervous.

The presentation began with Principal Gray. "Now, I realize," he began, "that it's getting near prom time and the end of the year . . ." The audience of seniors laughed and cheered, interrupting his prepared speech, and Brad joined in. Somehow Principal Gray had uttered the magic words *prom time* and *end of the year.*

Principal Gray smiled and acknowledged the cheers. "High school *is* about having fun," he continued, "but it's also about preparing yourselves for the crossroads of life . . ."

The laughs and cheers died out.

One thing about Principal Gray, Brad thought, he sure knew how to kill a good time. He talked for several minutes about the importance of college, and mentioned that many students, like Cindy Carr and Steve Shasta, had already been accepted by the college of their choice.

Then Coach Ramirez took the podium and, looking like he had been lobotomized for the afternoon, said that "even big-time sports takes a back seat to big-time education."

Halfway down the bleachers from Brad, a group of guys started laughing and nudging each other. Brad knew them from Mechanical Arts. They were another group from the out-skirts of lunch court, the construction workers. They drove Datsun pickups, and their common refrain was, Construction is where the bucks are. You could bet they weren't headed for "big-time education," Brad thought.

The main speaker of the afternoon was a red-haired woman, fortyish, wearing a smart, peach-colored suit. She was the head career counselor from University of Southern California, and the first thing she said was, "Don't believe the jargon about Ph.D.'s driving taxis—a great education will get you a great job.

"It's easy," she went on, "to ignore the issue of college while you're having fun in high school. But going to college, especially a school like USC, is like making a big investment. There's a lot of work involved, but the dividends you reap are enormous. And who's to say we can't make college fun for you, too . . ."

Brad Hamilton sat there, listening, and in the back of his mind he realized what was bothering him about College Orientation Week. It was one long parade of adults, and the thrust of all their presentations was, *Yeah, we know high school's one big party, but now it's time to get serious.* Didn't they understand how tough it was to work, to go to school, deal with teachers, and then with assistant managers, with parents, and with customers, and then with the lunch-court crowd, too? Hey, he felt like saying, who's having *fun?* Life isn't like "Happy Days."

"The important thing," the woman from USC concluded, "is to fall in love with your work. There's always room at the top for the best. You'll suffer for your vocation, but you'll be happy."

Now that made Brad feel better. He was already several weeks into a new job, and even though it wasn't the *best* location in Ridgemont, it was at least a job that gave him fryer duty. That was his specialty. That was what he *did*. He was a fryer, and he was the best!

Still, after College Orientation Week, Brad Hamilton began to get a nagging image in his mind. In it he was forty years old, wearing an apron and working in a burger stand. He was surrounded by junior high school kids, telling him his fries were still the best.

Frisbee Champs

The first Friday of every month in Public Speaking class was Expert Day. Mrs. G. had an expert address the class on his or her field. They were usually the best-attended classes of the year.

Several members of the class were chosen at the beginning of the year to assist Mrs. G. in talent coordination for Expert Day. They had sent letters to everyone—to Ted Nugent and Henry Kissinger. To Jack Nicholson and Pete Townshend. From Bo Derek to G. Gordon Liddy. To Budweiser and the FBI. They even sent a letter to Charles Manson, just to see if he'd write back. (He did—saying to invite him again when he was due for parole, in 470 years.)

Once a demolition chief showed up on Expert Day. A meek-looking man in an old brown suit, he calmly showed the class how to make an explodable bomb out of household materials. Another time two members of the Gay Liberation Front showed up and explained the homosexual act in great detail.

"Now *boys*," said Mrs. G. cheerfully. "We didn't send out slips to the parents on you two, so let's clean it up a little."

One day a letter came to the speech class. It read:

Dear Mrs. George and all members of the exciting Public Speaking class at Ridgemont University:

We are pleased and delighted that you have requested our special World Class Frisbee Champion Presentation, featuring two (2) World Class Frisbee Champions. Should your college campus be available to them on the twentieth of January, and a room can be reserved for the 10–3 P.M. time frame, please let us know. We will be glad to provide you with our World Class Frisbee Champion Demonstration.

Very truly yours,

Rick Slutzah
Frisbee Champion Liaison

A call was put through to Rick Slutzah at Frisbee headquarters. No, it wasn't a college, the Expert Day coordinators told him. It was a *high school.* No problem, said Mr. Slutzah. Wham-O was happy to accommodate their interest. The date was set for the twentieth, fourth period, at 11:20. The two champions would be there, said Mr. Slutzah. They always arrived one-half hour ahead of presentation time.

By the end of third period on the twentieth, Mrs. G.'s room was packed with sun-bleached surfers. Kids who hadn't been around Ridgemont since the first week of school. It was as if they had traveled across the burning desert to lay a wreath at the foot of the demigod. They were in Mrs. G.'s class to pay homage to a hero. Here was someone who had *beaten the game.* Here were guys paid to travel around and throw a Frisbee around. It was *inspiring,* man.

At twenty minutes after eleven, a white El Camino pickup screeched into the Ridgemont parking lot. Two men leaped out like a couple of SWAT team members. The hall monitor brought them into the room filled with admirers.

"Introduce yourself, boys," said Mrs. G., "and I won't write you up for being tardy."

It was a typical teacher's joke, the kind anybody with a heart at least gave a courtesy laugh to. But the Frisbee champs did not. They stood there, humorless, looking like Laurel and Hardy after a few years under a sunlamp. They were holding bulky white plastic sacks.

"Uh, listen," said the taller of the two Frisbee champs. He spoke in a bewildered voice. "We thought this was a college."

Mrs. George spoke up. "We cleared all this with Mr. Slutzah, who said he'd tell you. He said there would be no complication."

The two champs looked at each other.

"*Slutzah*," said the taller Frisbee champ.

"Hey, we're happy to be here," said the shorter, swarthier of the two. He knew how to switch it on. "Hi everyone! I'm Kent Vanderjack. This is my brother Todd. As Senior World Class Frisbee Disc Champions we have a special slogan. His is Let It Fly, and mine is Fly with Me."

Then Kent Vanderjack's brother Todd reached into his white sack and began flicking three-inch mini-Frisbees to kids in the audience. Each Frisbee was meticulously inscribed with a champ's name and motto. They were Frisbee business cards! The surfers sat up in their seats.

"Hey, how do you get to be a champ, man?"

"Well," said Todd, "I broke the twenty-four–hour disc-throwing record in Australia. I threw in Europe for a while, then came back here for the season a few years ago and just stayed. I won eighteen out of the twenty-one qualifying tournaments leading up to the big Disc Championship at the Rose Bowl every August."

"Who won it last year?"

"Some little wimp from Virginia," said Kent Vanderjack.

"How much is the prize?"

"Four thousand dollars."

"How much do you guys make a year?"

"About $15,000," said Todd.

There were whistles among the enraptured surfers.

"And Wham-O got hold of *us* and hired *us*."

The room was enthralled.

"How much do you practice?"

"Between four and eight hours a day," said Todd.

"But it's not all hanging out in the sun," said Kent. "It's a lot of hard work. When you're throwing the disc, your hobby is your job. And that takes a lot of effort."

"How long have you been throwing Frisbees?" came another question.

"Well, I've been throwing the *disc* for fifteen years. Todd for twelve."

The message was clear—it's called a *disc*—and thereafter no surfer at Ridgemont, no real hardcore, ever called it a Frisbee again.

It was a brief presentation, this World Class Demonstration, and the two champs ran through it by rote. They described the six basic disc holds, offered an explanation of how to join the International Frisbee Association as a lifetime member, and gave a brief "health report" on how disc throwing improved hand-to-eye coordination.

They made a dramatic exit, with upraised fists and a cry of "Circulate the disc!"

It was a great effect, ruined only slightly by the fact that the two champs then hung around the rest of the lunch period, *on* lunch court, and collected phone numbers from the very girls who had been so unattainable all year long to the surfers who idolized them.

A Late-Night Phone Conversation

Linda and Stacy had already been on the phone over an hour.

"Linda," asked Stacy, "what makes a great lover?"

"A style."

"Gentleness?"

"In some guys," said Linda. "That's Doug. Doug's

tender. He's very gentle. He really is. He goes for your neck and your mouth . . . you just go, 'Ohhhhhh.' "

"What other styles are there?"

"Aggressive. Like Bob, who used to work at Swenson's. Remember him? He attacked me in front of Jack in Jack's Camaro. He tried to get Doug mad by giving me a hickey."

"You never told me this."

"He never gave me the hickey."

"Did Betsy know about that?"

"Betsy doesn't know about half the shit Bob does."

"I don't know," sighed Stacy. "I think I want to find somebody funny. The guy's gotta have a sense of humor. And be well built . . ."

"And good in bed."

"You never can tell that."

"Hey," said Linda, "whatever happened to that Mark Ratner?"

"Nothing. He's around. He's real nice. His friend is pretty cute."

"High school boys," said Linda. "No matter what they look like, they're still high school boys."

Blow-Job Lessons

 A new girl from Phoenix, Arizona, had transferred into Stacy's Child Development class. She looked a little scared standing at the front of the class. When Mrs. Melon placed her at Stacy's table, Stacy decided to make friends with her.

Her name was Laurie Beckman. She was a doctor's daughter. She wanted to raise horses. She was a friendly girl, if a little shy, and she wore braces.

Stacy had introduced her to Linda Barrett, and the three had taken to eating lunch together. It wasn't long before

Laurie realized what a gold mine of sexual expertise was sitting before her every lunch period. Within two weeks she was already into the hard stuff.

"Did you see that movie *Carrie?*" asked Laurie. "Do you know when John Travolta gets that girl to give him a blow job?"

"Yeah."

"Yeah."

"Do *you* do that?"

Stacy looked at Linda.

"Of course," said Linda. "Don't you know how?"

"No. Not really." Pause. "They don't talk about it in sex ed."

"It's no big deal," said Linda. "Bring a banana to lunch tomorrow and I'll show you."

The next day, Laurie Beckman brought a banana to school. The three girls sat down together on the very outskirts of lunch court. Linda peeled the banana and handed it back to Laurie.

"Now, what you've got to do," she instructed, "is treat it firmly but carefully. Move up and down and hold it at the bottom."

"When am I supposed to do this?"

"Do it now."

"Give it a try," said Stacy, in fine deputy form.

Laurie looked casually to the right, then to the left. Then she mouthed the banana.

"Is that right?" she asked.

Her braces had created wide divots down the sides of the banana.

"You should try to be a *little* more careful," said Linda. She watched as Laurie tried again, with similar results.

"I have a question," said Laurie. "What happens?"

"What do you mean?"

"What happens . . . I mean, I've never asked anyone about this, right, and . . . and don't laugh at me, okay . . ."

"Just *say* it, Laurie."

"Okay, like when a guy has an orgasm . . ." Laurie sighed

143

heavily. "You know ... I've always wondered ... *how much comes out?*"

Linda leaned forward and stared Laurie in both eyes. "Quarts."

Laurie's eyes popped. "*Quarts?*"

Stacy slugged Linda. "Don't do that to her."

"Okay ... not that much," said Linda. "You shouldn't worry about it. Really."

Laurie looked relieved as she stared down at the peeled banana still in her hand. From the two opposite ends of lunch court, Steve Shasta and Mark Ratner watched the blow-job lesson. The Rat had no idea what was going on. Shasta had a wide grin on his face.

Cuba

Mr. Hand was going over Chapter Thirty-One of *Land of Truth and Liberty*. He was lecturing about Cuba.

"We gave Cuba independence in 1901," said Hand. "But with certain strings attached. The Platt Amendment dictated that the U.S. could interfere if they felt *compelled* ..."

Mr. Hand stopped. It was one of his favorite tactics. He'd be dutifully lecturing in his best McGarrett bark, then suddenly he'd just *stop*.

Anyone daring to whisper during the lecture naturally took an extra second to react and shut up. But in that second, an extra syllable might slip out of a talker's mouth, and Hand could always trace it right back to the culprit. All he needed was a syllable.

It was no big surprise to find Jeff Spicoli hanging from the extra-syllable noose today. Hand had put the brakes on his Cuba talk ... and plain as could be, Spicoli had let two whole words fill the crashing silence.

"... my *anus*."

Amid the barely stifled laughs, Hand moved in on Spicoli, just like McGarrett did every week when he finally found the schnook who was threatening the law and order of the fiftieth state.

"I'll see you after class, Spicoli. Right *here* at 2:11." Then Hand slammed the book he held open in his hand. "You know, Spicoli, you're a big *waste* of my time."

Spicoli cried out, "Aw, come on, Mr. Hand. I was listening!"

Hand looked at him and gritted his teeth. You could tell from his face he was about ready to say something about saving it for somebody *else's* class, some other class where the goof-off contract teacher lets *you babies flourish*. It wouldn't happen here. Not in U.S. History.

But Spicoli threw him a curve.

"Mr. *Hand*," said Spicoli in another tone entirely. It was a tone that said, Hey, we do this cops-and-robbers bit for the kids, but outside of that, between you and me, guy to guy, I gotta ask you this ... "Mr. Hand," said Spicoli, "how come you never *laugh*? How come your face is always like ..." Spicoli couldn't find the word. "I don't know," he said. "It's always like *that*."

Hand was standing there, in classic ice-man pose, with a sprig of Vitalized hair on his forehead.

It was a brilliant move on Spicoli's part. Somewhere within the resinous caverns of his mind *that* had come winging out, and it was just perfect. Hand was stunned.

"*Yes*," said a girl, the Vietnamese exchange student who always sat in front. "You never smile!"

Then Stacy Hamilton spoke up. "My brother," she said, "said Les Sexton saw you smiling once in the faculty lounge."

Mr. Hand glared at Stacy with laser eyes.

"I was never smiling in the faculty lounge," said Mr. Hand. "And since when does Les Sexton visit the faculty lounge, anyway?"

"I guess he saw through the window."

"I doubt it," said Hand. "I doubt it very seriously. And I'll *still* see you in detention, Spicoli."

And from there Mr. Hand resumed his Cuba lecture. But everyone knew they had nearly broken through to The Man. That alone was good enough for Spicoli, who showed up for detention in good cheer.

Late-Night Phone Conversation

Stacy called Linda Barrett just after dinner. "I found this book in my mother's drawer," she said. "It's called *Total Orgasm.*"

"What were you doing in your mother's drawer?" asked Linda.

"I can't remember," said Stacy. "Maybe looking for the extra set of keys or something. But I found this book."

"Did you look at it?"

"Of course I looked at it," said Stacy. "It had all these drawings of men and women getting down, in all kinds of positions. It was pretty funny. The point of it was that most women don't have orgasms unless they work real hard at it."

"Really?" Linda Barrett felt a slight competition with any other sex expert. "It says that?"

"Yes. It says most women derive pleasure, but don't have real orgasms."

"Hmmmmmm."

"Linda," said Stacy, "what *is* a total orgasm?"

"I'll tell you what a total orgasm is," said Linda Barrett. "A total orgasm is when I'm lying in bed early on a Saturday morning, and I hear this little knocking at the window. I open my eyes and it's Doug standing there. He knows and I know that my parents aren't up yet or anything, so I let him in through the window. Then I go brush my teeth, and he gets in

146

bed with me. Then we start getting it on, and I'm still kind of waking up. And it hurts a little bit at first, and then the hurt turns into a little itch. It's like I'm floating on a river, and I feel this little itch . . . and just as I'm about to scratch it, the boat takes me over the edge of the river . . . and I *don't care*. That's a total orgasm."

"Shit," said Stacy. "That's better than anything in the book."

"I still want to look at it, though," said Linda Barrett.

The Hamiltons' Jacuzzi

March arrived, and in rolled a rust-colored wave of killer smog, the worst in forty years. A blanket of dry heat hung over Ridgemont. Newspapers and announcers warned against unnecessary activity. At school, even the P.E. classes were called off.

Coach Ramirez and girls' P.E. teacher Anita Zix spent the day in the faculty lounge, having a grand time and visiting with faculty members they hadn't spoken with since the Christmas party.

After school, Stacy Hamilton went home and tested the water in her family's pool. Cold.

The phone rang inside the house. Stacy ran inside to pick it up. She waited the proper three rings.

"Hello?"

"Hel-lo." It was Linda Barrett. "Gee, Stacy. Why don't you invite me over to go swimming?"

"The water is pretty cold."

"I don't care."

"Okay. Let's go swimming. But I don't know if I'm getting all the way wet."

"I am!"

Linda arrived at Stacy's house a few minutes later. Just after she walked in the door, the phone rang again.

Three rings. "Hello?"

"Stacy?" The voice was low, male, and sounded as if a hand was cupped around the receiver. "Is that you, Stacy?"

"Who's *this*?"

"Stacy?" Pause for heavy breathing. "It's Mike Damone."

"Oh, hello Mike."

"Gee, Stacy, it's really hot outside, isn't it?"

"It's fairly warm," said Stacy.

"Gee, I wish I knew somebody who had a pool."

"Oh, really?"

"Yes," said Damone, " 'cause it sure is hot."

There was another click on the line, then Mark Ratner's voice. "Hey, sorry Mike. I didn't realize you were on the other phone. I was just going to call the weather bureau and find out how *hot* it is."

"I don't blame you," said Damone. "I'm curious how *hot* it is myself."

"It's pretty hot," agreed Stacy. "And I've got to go because my mom is coming home soon and Linda is over here and everything and we're about to go swimming! So thanks for calling!"

"Hey. Thanks for *answering*," said Damone. "On such a hot day."

Stacy replaced the receiver, laughing.

"Who was that?"

"Mike Damone and Mark Ratner. They wanted to come swimming."

"Did you invite them?"

"*No.* They were so obvious about wanting to come over. I just didn't want to give them the satisfaction. They'll probably call back."

The phone didn't ring.

"Which one is Mike Damone?" asked Linda.

"He's this friend of Mark Ratner's. He's in my English class this semester, with Mrs. George. He's the one who got Mark's wallet and brought it to the Charthouse."

"I think they're both virgins," said Linda.

A moment later the doorbell rang. Stacy opened the front door to find Mike Damone and Mark Ratner standing there in their bathing suits.

"Hey," said Damone, "thanks for inviting us over!"

"Yeah!" said The Rat.

"I don't believe you guys." Stacy looked at the floor, shook her head, and swung the door wide open. "Come on in. I can't keep you out."

"Oh," said Damone, "and I brought some Wisk, too."

One of the best reasons to swim in the Hamilton pool was their Jacuzzi. The pool was constructed in a huge S with a king-sized Jacuzzi attached to one end. The Jacuzzi (or "ja-cooz," as Brad called it) was separated from the rest of the pool by a tile wall. It was possible to flip from the Jacuzzi into the bigger portion of the pool, like a dolphin. Best of all, if you really had the hot tip on the Hamiltons' Jacuzzi, you brought a little detergent with you. Wisk for dishes was best. A little Wisk in the Hamiltons' ja-cooz and you had so much foam that the effect was one of a huge hot and cold bubble bath.

Brad Hamilton slumped in the doorway, home from school. He came out to the deck, took one look at the proceedings, and grimaced. He didn't mind Linda. The other two guys he didn't like on looks alone. Underclassmen. Brad went upstairs into his bedroom and slammed the door. He even shut the curtains to his bedroom window, which faced the pool.

"Poor Brad," said Linda Barrett.

"I know," said Stacy. "He hardly even talks anymore."

"Poor guy," said Damone.

"Really," said The Rat. There was a somber moment. Everybody knew the story, the sudden fast-food topple from inner lunch court of poor Brad Hamilton.

For The Rat this pool party was pure heaven. A great situation. Damone had become friendly with Stacy in his English class. And she and The Rat had begun to talk a little, even though things had never been on an even keel since the Atlantis. This was a much better situation, though. There was his best buddy Damone to make sure The Attitude was right. The Rat felt pretty good. Why, he even treaded water in the deep end and had a whole conversation with Linda Barrett, the older girl with the great bod.

At the other end of the pool Stacy was sitting in the Jacuzzi talking with Mike Damone. He was a nice guy, a funny guy. She kind of liked teasing him.

"Can I ask you a question?" she said, looking the other way.

"Sure."

"I heard you were a virgin."

"Where did you hear that?"

"I just heard."

"How much is it worth to you," said Damone, "to *know*?"

"Are you or aren't you?"

"What do you think?"

Stacy looked up at the sky. "I think you are."

"That's a pretty personal question, don't you think?"

"You are!"

Underneath the layers of Wisk bubbles Damone felt a cool hand on his thigh, moving upward. It stopped just short of his inner leg.

"You'll never know," said Damone coolly. But it came out strange. Like Burt Reynolds, but going through puberty. Under the calm Wisk bubbles Stacy could feel the vibrations in the water. She knew Damone's swimsuit was a tent.

"Mike!" cried Stacy, flipping back into the pool with a splash. "Why don't you get up and do a *dive!*"

"Yeah," said The Rat from the other side of the pool.

"Go ahead!" cried Linda. She hopped off the board.

"No," said Damone. "No, I don't think so."

"Come on," said Mark.

"Naw," said Damone. "I gotta go pretty soon."

"Me too," said Linda. She sunk a finger into her ear and began shaking vigorously. "My ears are really blocked. Hey Stacy, do you have any Q-tips?"

"God," said Stacy, "I don't think so. Why don't you try inside."

Linda Barrett strolled through the glass sliding doors of the Hamilton living room, dripping wet. She was wearing a maroon string bikini. Brad had seen her standing on the diving board through the curtain in his room, wet suit and all. Brad usually had one thing to say about Linda Barrett—she really had a bod. And she liked to show it off, too. First chance Linda got, it was always, "Let's go swimming." Her fiancé, Doug Stallworth, would just have to sit there while Linda, who was already wearing some little bathing suit underneath, ripped her shirt right off. She would always have on that bikini top. Guys went crazy. Doug just sat there, usually choosing that moment to start polishing his glasses.

Brad kneeled on the floor of his bathroom. His green t-shirt was on, his underwear in a pile on the floor behind him. His arm was pumping slowly.

A short film unreeled in his mind. This film featured Linda Barrett, just as she stood on the diving board a moment ago. She was gorgeous. Her breasts seemed even bigger than usual. Her nipples were hard, poking through the filmy maroon string bikini. Water rolled slowly down her cheeks into the corners of her mouth. Her lips were parted slightly. Her eyes were filled with desire.

"Hi, Brad," she said in the daydream, "you know how cute I always thought you were. I think you're so sexy. Will you come to me?"

In the daydream, Brad was wearing a nice shirt. His hair was combed back and looking great. He walked to Linda. She reached out and grabbed him for a kiss, pulling him close. Then she pushed him away so he could watch as she carefully unstrapped the top of her bathing suit. The incredible Linda Barrett breasts fell loose. She took Brad's hands and placed them on her as she began unbuttoning his shirt. They were just about to fall into passionate teenage love making when Brad heard . . .

"Hey Brad! Got any Q-ti . . ."

There was a swift knock at the bathroom door and then—Jesus—it just opened. The words *I'm in here* stalled in Brad's mouth.

There stood the real-life Linda Barrett, her top very much

still on. She was standing in the doorway, paralyzed by the sight before her. Poor Brad was kneeling on the bathroom floor, a sizable erection shriveling in his hand.

"Sorry," she said, "I didn't know anybody was in here." Linda Barrett pulled the door shut as if she wanted to forget what she saw as quickly as possible. They would never again discuss the incident.

Brad stared down into the toilet bowl, still not believing what had happened. It was funny how everything could just turn around on you in a matter of seconds.

Brad slammed the toilet bowl cover down. "Doesn't anyone fuckin' *knock* anymore?" he said.

The Talent Show

The Ridgemont High Talent Show was the last of the February blitz. It was held at 7:30 P.M. in the auditorium on the last Tuesday of the month. Some of the participants were chosen from auditions; the rest were doing it for a grade in English or speech class. The idea was to convince your parents not to go, go with your friends instead, and laugh at the contestants.

The talent show was the specialty of Gregg Adams, the drama whiz and boyfriend of Cindy Carr. He served as chief organizer, arranged the school band, wrote the show opening tune, wrote the material, and hosted the show with his own sidekick, David Leach. Gregg Adams owned the night.

Twenty minutes before showtime, as the school jazz band, led by Mick Stillson, played its boozy warm-up music, Gregg Adams was backstage getting ready, rushing here, rushing there. Are you okay? Great! Are we ready, Leach? You look *incredible!* Okay, let's *really* put on a show for 'em. Let's *go.*

The red velour Ridgemont auditorium curtains parted and out bounded Gregg Adams and David Leach. The school band switched to a jazzier, showtime tempo.

Adams and Leach grabbed microphones and hopped onto a pair of stools. Adams had written the whole bit.

"Hi, everybody! Welcome to the Twentieth Annual Ridgemont High School Talent Show." A few sophomore girls screamed. "I'm Gregg Adams!"

"And I'm David Leach!"

"And have we got a show for you!"

Gregg Adams then began singing his own show-opening tune, "Wild Feeling." He sang in a semicroon, semiyodel, switching verses with David. Then—and this was Adams's favorite part—he got to speak to the audience over the instrumental passage.

". . . And I've got a crazy feeling, David, that these people are in store for an incredible evening of entertainment!"

"Some great singing," said David.

"Some hot dancing!"

"And a monster surprise later on!"

They swung back into the last verse of the song, which revealed the wild feeling to be, of course, *looooo-ooooove*, and Adams finished up with a Tom Jones–style pump.

Gregg Adams was no fool. After the applause died down, he let David Leach tell the first joke.

Leach was different from Adams. A nice guy, but not *quite* as good looking as Adams and not *quite* as funny. His first joke was one he'd told before in Mechanical Arts.

"Why did the monkey fall out of the tree?"

"WHY, LEACH???" There were some rowdies sitting near the front.

"He was dead."

The rowdies unloaded on him. Threw programs at him. Cackled at him. Leach grinned. He loved the attention.

Adams introduced the first act. "First off," said Gregg, "is a good example of good entertainment." Poor Adams. He hadn't been in English class much this year. There was always a rehearsal or something. "We have a good singer who's not recognized 'cause she's not in a lot of the groups or anything. But it's ... it's Brenda Harrison, and she's singing a song called 'I Never Meant to Leave You.' Let's bring her out!"

Brenda Harrison, a pretty brown-haired girl with large Irish eyes, curtsied and launched right into the song. She was accompanied by a single piano, and after two normal notes she quickly headed for the point of no return, that Bermuda Triangle for amateur singers ... *the next register*. Would she make it?

Too bad.

It was easy to forgive if you were up on the behind-the-scenes info, as most of the students in the audience were. The song "I Never Meant to Leave You" was clearly for Brenda Harrison's adoring ex-boyfriend, Tim Copeland. Tim was a young-looking sophomore, known for always being seen with squeaky-clean hair, white-and-green-striped Nike tennis shoes, and Brenda Harrison. But Brenda had recently broken up with him, after two years, for a policeman she'd met one night at her job at Yum-Yum Donuts. Sorry, Tim! I never meant to leave you!

Brenda Harrison even grabbed herself for the final line— "I never meant to leave you/But one day you'll understand/That I love you forever/And I'll always be your friiiiiiieeeeeennnnnnd."

She leaned forward into the spotlight and whispered, "I love you, Tim."

In the audience Tim Copeland's friends slapped him on the back.

"She loves *me*," Tim said ruefully, "but she's jumping on some *cop*."

"Our next guests combine talent and beauty into a musical feast! Virginia Finch!"

Whooooooa.

"And Marla Buchanan."

Yeahhhh.

"And Janine Contreras on vocals and flute."

O-kaaaaay.

"And Mick Stillson on guitar!"

What a fox!

"And they're gonna play 'Landslide,' by Fleetwood Mac!"

The red spotlight hit Mick Stillson, school fox, as he sat on a stool with his guitar. He was wearing a red shirt and new Levi's. He began fingerpicking the introduction to the song, and there were gasps from the seniors.

"Landslide," still the most requested lyric for reprinting in school annuals and graduation presentations, is the stuff of which many elderclassmen's high school lives were lived by. When you got together, "Landslide" was on the radio. When you broke up, it still reminded you of him or her. They would probably graduate with "Landslide."

Janine sang the song in a quavering voice, barely audible out from behind the Ridgemont superstar backing.

> *Well I've been 'fraid of changing*
> *'Cause I've built my life around you.*
> *But time makes you bolder*
> *Even children get older*
> *And I'm getting older too.*

A strange beeping noise began at the back of the gymnasium.

Next up was the Girls' Dance Chorus, featuring Linda Barrett and new soloist Laurie Beckman. They fanned out across the stage, a row of young girls in red, white, and blue tights, singing "Boogie Wonderland." It went on a little too long.

"Okay," said Gregg Adams, "are you guys ready for something *radical?* David, are the special effects ready? They are! OKAY! We are almost ready for the fascinating Puuu-eee Balls Dance!"

"THE WHAT?"

"For you guys who don't know what that is," Leach announced with authority, "this is a Maui dance that originated in New Zealand and will be performed for you by the drill team!"

The stage was lit in dark fluorescent blue, the kind you

see in Tahitian restaurants where umbrellas come in the drinks. Then Day-Glo colored balls began to pitch about the stage. Faster and faster. It was the members of the drill team, hidden in the lighting, whirling these fluorescent balls around on twine. Incredible! A Puuu-eeeee Balls Dance! All right!

It was a big hit with the audience, and when the ovation finished Gregg Adams made like he was exhausted, even by watching.

"There's going to be a twenty-minute intermission."

"Don't you dare go away!"

"And there's PTA punch in the lobby!"

The school combo started blasting the jazz-rock Muzak again.

In the lobby, once nervous performers were now stars. They stood around with parents and relatives, luxuriously sipping PTA punch and considering futures in show business. Even Adams and Leach were in the lobby.

Adams was cross-examining Cindy Carr. "Did you come late? You came late, didn't you? You missed the *best* part. David and I came running out and sang part of this song and then talked over it like a couple of Broadway Joes. It was totally classy! And you *missed it*, didn't you?"

Back on stage for the second half, Gregg Adams was all pro. He led with a joke.

"I don't know about you," he said, "but I've been noticing Lieutenant Flowers. He's actually a nice person! I went to him the other day and said, 'Some sophomore looted my locker,' and he went and took care of it in the calmest way he knew how. He SHOT THE KID AT SUNRISE!"

Big laughs.

The second half of the Ridgemont Talent Show opened with a duet between Kathy Golson and Dave Kepler. They began at opposite ends of the stage and worked toward each other as they sang. It was another case of aspiring amateurs. For the first time all night, the rowdy contingent came alive.

Then came the noise again, an incessant little series of beeps, nearly impossible to trace to its holder. Jeff Spicoli was playing a pocket computer football game in the last row of the auditorium. Gregg Adams chose not to mention the noise from the stage.

Rex Huffman came out for a skateboard routine—all his best tricks, then Ernie Vincent did his balancing act, culminating in his balancing a wheelbarrow on his nose. No one knew he could balance until he auditioned for the show. (Interviewed in the school paper, he said, "It started two years ago with a broom, and the rest is history. . . .")

"Okay," said Gregg Adams, "now we have a special nonsinging nondancing act. We've got Rhonda Lewis, whom you've seen at the fair and at the Baton Twirling Championships at the sports arena. She's one of Redondo's biggest baton twirlers, and we are glad to have her with us here tonight! Rhonda Lewis!"

The music started—a scratched and crackling record that would have been better suited to a Tijuana strip joint—Rhonda Lewis, in a ballerina costume, flipped through her first few twirls with a self-assured cock of the head. It was just like her at school; she did not acknowledge anyone in the slightest.

Then she tried a high-kicking twirl . . . and dropped the baton. Parents gasped. She was upset, gave a snotty little stomp of her foot, and picked up the baton again.

Now, Spicoli had decided to give her all the breaks, but after that . . . well, there was no choice. He started in with the football game. He was merciless, beeping away while she dropped it two more times.

Gregg Adams and David Leach returned, continued with their all-showbiz philosophy of ignoring the casualties around them.

"Well, David, you know what time it is?"

"What time is it, Gregg?"

"It's time that we answer *your questions*. And you know what, David? It's funny, but every year we get asked the same question on talent show night."

"What's that, Gregg?"

"They ask, 'Where did you get those great tuxedos?' "

Boos.

"They sure do ask us that. And we always tell them . . ."

They sang in harmony, pointing thumbs at the huge clapboard signs that had been sitting on both sides of the stage all night.

"We got 'em at . . . Re-gis. REGIS FORMALWEAR, LADIES AND GENTLEMEN. A BIG HAND!!"

"You look like SHIT," someone yelled.

"Okay okay! The next number for you cannibals is . . . a slight deviation from the program. Originally it was to be Reginald Davis's Stevie Wonder medley. But he's sick, and he'll be replaced by Paul Norris, with his original composition, sung a cappella, "The World.""

A lot of people didn't know Paul Norris could sing, but sing he did. In a very loud voice.

"The wooo-hu-hu---hooooooorld . . ."

He sang every syllable as if his very life depended on the line.

"The woo-hu-hu-hooooooorld is a pa-laaaaaaaaaace of dooooo-uuuuuuu-ha-ha-ouuuuuut . . ."

He kind of *snapped* off the ends of his words.

"But *we* are Chilllll-dreeeeeen of the woooooooor ha-ha-ld."

Some thought he had finished and applauded, but Paul Norris was just getting warmed up.

"The woooorllll . . ."

In the audience, Jeff Spicoli's friends were goading him, challenging him. *Go ahead. Go ahead,* Spicoli.

"I say beeeeeeeeeeeeeeeeeeeeee-heeeeee. . . ."

Spicoli started tapping on the electronic game, *bip bip bip* . . . and right away Paul Norris started noticing it.

"I say *beca* . . ."

Paul was getting nervous.

"Because you *got to,* I say GOT TO take a chooooooo-iccc . . ."

It was a low-threshold night for Paul Norris. He probably didn't want to be there, but Reginald Davis had no doubt called and bottom-lined it. *Man, I'm just not up to that Stevie Wonder medley tonight. . . .* You could see something inside Paul Norris snap, his concentration shatter.

"KISS MY ASS!" he shouted.

He dropped the mike at his side and stomped backstage. There was silence, then embarrassed applause. Adams and Leach came bounding back out.

"*Okay* . . . we've reached that special part of the evening when we present THE BIG SURPRISE!"

The big finale of the Twentieth Annual Ridgemont High School Talent Show was pretty standard stuff. More fluorescent lights, another scratchy Polynesian record, and a big Tahitian dance featuring the entire football team in hula skirts.

It's Up To You, Mike

Stacy Hamilton caught up with Mike Damone on his way to the bus stop. "Can I walk you home?" she asked.

"I was going to take the bus."

"Let's walk."

"Okay," he said. Might as well give her a taste of the Damone charm, he thought.

They made some small talk about how all the sophomore guys blasted K-101, the lamest station in town. Then Damone just said it point blank.

"You know Mark Ratner really likes you, don't you?"

"I know," she said.

They walked on.

"Do you like him?" asked Damone.

They arrived at Stacy's house. "I like you," she said. "Do you want to come in for a second?"

"Do you have any iced tea?"

"I think we have some."

"Okay." He was just going inside for an iced tea, Damone told himself. "You know Mark's a really good guy."

They stood around in the kitchen while Stacy fixed two iced teas.

"I really like Mark, too," said Stacy, handing Damone the tea. "He's really a nice boy."

"He's a good guy," Damone said.

"You want to take a quick swim?"

"Well . . ."

"Come on. Brad probably has some trunks you can borrow. I'm going to my room to change!"

She's going to her room to change.

"I think I better go," said Damone.

"Don't go! You don't have to shout! You can come back here to my room!"

She's asking me into her room while she changes.

Stacy was standing there in her bikini.

"Let's go to the changing room and see if there are some trunks," she said.

"I think I better go," said Damone

"God," said Stacy, "you're just a tease!"

"I ain't no tease," said Damone.

"Good!" said Stacy. Things were working out just as she and Linda had planned.

They went into the changing room, and Stacy locked the door behind her. "Are you really a virgin?" she asked.

Damone could feel his legs starting to shake the slightest bit. "Come *on* . . ."

"It's okay." Stacy walked over and kissed him.

"I feel pretty strange here," said Damone. "Because Mark really likes you. He's my friend."

He kissed her anyway. Standing there, feeling Stacy in her bikini, feeling her kiss him, Damone felt some of his reservations slip away.

"You're a really good kisser," she said.

"So are you."

"Are you shaking?"

"No," said Damone. "Are you crazy?" But he was. The

last time Mr. Attitude had gone this far on the make-out scale with a girl had been with Carol back in Philadelphia. Carol had let him reach into her pants and touch her, *but just for a second.* That had been enough for back then. That had been enough to make him feel like he and his brother, Art, could really talk about *women.* But this . . . this was The Big One.

"Why don't you take your clothes off, Mike?"

"You first."

"How about both of us at the same time."

And as if that made it emotionally even, they both stripped at the same time. Stacy unhooked her top and stepped out of her bikini bottom. She went to sit down on the red couch in the changing room.

She watched Damone hopping on one leg, pulling first out of his pants, then his Jockey underwear. Then he caught the underwear on his erection, and it slapped back into his abdomen. He sat down next to Stacy, expressionless.

"Are you okay?"

"I'm okay," said Damone.

She reached over and grabbed his erection. She began pulling on it. The feeling of a penis was still new to her. She wanted to ask him about it. Why did it hurt if you just touched it one place, and not at all at another . . . but later she would ask him that. For now, she just yanked on it. Damone didn't seem to mind.

"I want you to know," said Stacy, "that it's *your* final decision if we should continue or not."

"Let's continue," said Damone.

As Mike Damone lost his virginity, his first thought was of his brother, Art. Art had said, "You gotta *overpower* a girl. Make her feel helpless."

Damone began pumping so hard, so fast—his eyes were shut tight—that he didn't notice he was banging the sofa, and Stacy's head, against the wall.

"Hey Mike," she whispered.

"What? Are you all right?"

"I think we're making a lot of noise."

"I'm sorry. I'm really sorry." He continued, slower.

What a considerate guy, Stacy thought. He was kind of loud and always joking around other people, but when you got him alone . . . he was so nice.

Then Damone stopped. He had a strange look on his face.

"What's wrong?"

"I think I came," said Damone. "Didn't you feel it?"

He had taken a minute and a half.

They were unusual feelings, these thoughts pooling in Mike Damone's head as he lay on the red couch with Stacy. He was a little embarrassed, a little guilty . . . mostly he just wanted to be alone. He wanted to get the hell out of there.

"I've got to go home," said Damone. "I've really got to go."

Stacy called Linda as soon as he left.

"Where did it happen?" Linda answered her phone.

"On the couch. In the changing room."

"Bizarre."

"I left it up to him, Linda. I could have made the final decision, but I left it up to him. I said, 'It's you, *you* make the final decision.' And he said, 'Why not?' "

"Did you talk afterwards?"

"A little. He said he was relieved."

"So are you guys boyfriend and girlfriend now?"

"I don't know," said Stacy in a singsong.

"How do you feel?"

"Guilty." She laughed.

"Did he call you yet?"

"Lin-da. He just left."

"You know, Stacy, that when someone asks him on his deathbed who he lost his virginity to, he'll have to say *you*. He'll remember you forever!"

A Late-Night Phone Conversation

"Linda," asked Stacy, "how long does Doug take?"

"Doug takes *forever.*"

"You told me once it was twenty to thirty minutes."

"I didn't say twenty to thirty. I thought I said ten to twenty."

"You were arguing with me 'cause I told you that The Vet took twelve. You were arguing with me . . ."

"I didn't say *twenty* to *thirty.*"

"You said at least twenty."

"Maybe I did," said Linda. "How long did Mike take?"

"A while."

"How long?"

"A long, long time."

"Not bad," said Linda. "Not bad for a *high school* boy."

A Surprise in the Shower

The A.S.B. Ball was coming up. Second only to the senior prom in overall stature, the ball was the one dress-up dance that sophomores could also attend.

Stacy had hoped Mike Damone would ask her to the A.S.B. Ball, and, for a few days, he was sure he would.

Then, just one week before the ball, Damone had been

taking his regular morning shower. He was singing along to a radio, washing himself, thinking about school, thinking about nothing, when he noticed—jeez—a small red pimple at the base of his penis. At first he thought nothing of it.

Then, slowly washing over him like the soap running down his back, came the memory of a million Health and Safety films. A red pimple. A sore near the genital area. Syphilis. Blindness. Infection. Death.

He had to call a doctor when he got to school. But he knew only one, old Dr. Morehead, the family's pediatrician. He had to call. And worse yet, Cindy Carr was sick today. Gregg Adams was on the pay phone every two periods. Finally Damone got the jump on the third bell in English II and beat feet down to the phone. Clear. He dialed the medical office.

"Dr. Morehead's line."

Well, Damone thought, what if it wasn't syphilis at all. Where would that put him? Where would he be the next time he came in with his parents for a physical? He could just hear it.

"*Yesssssss,*" old Dr. Morehead would say, "we were all very happy around here when your boy Mikey didn't have venereal disease."

Damone slowly replaced the phone on the receiver. Who else? Gregg Adams snapped it up behind him.

Damone decided to go visit Les Sexton, assistant P.E. coach. In the past Damone had made his share of Les Sexton jokes. The Sextons were one of *those* families who had a name, a great house, and about a million kids. You couldn't go anywhere in Ridgemont without running into a Sexton. They all had those classic master-race looks. Les was a real jock. He knew he was cool. But how cool was it, Damone always questioned, if you graduated Ridgemont High . . . and then came *back*. That was the feeling Mike Damone had about Les Sexton. Until now.

Les Sexton's office was in the boys' locker room. It was more like a cubicle, separated from the steamy shower area by a glass compartment. The glass was thick, the kind with wire mesh running through it.

164

Damone always figured it looked like a cage. Sitting inside this bulletproof enclosure, Les Sexton did his paperwork at his desk. To Damone, Sexton in his office was like a human in a zoo for aliens.

"Jock Working at a Desk," Damone figured the sign should read.

Mike tapped on the glass. Sexton looked up.

"Damone," he said. Everyone was a last name to Sexton. "Howyoudoin'." It was less a question than a single-word statement that meant—speak.

"Can I talk to you?"

"What's up?" Sexton immediately took a few books off the extra chair in his office. Already he sensed it was a Guy Problem.

"Well," said Damone. Gee, he thought, it wasn't that easy. It wasn't like you could just *sit down* in a guy's office and say, I think I have V.D.

"I mean, *really* talk to you, Mr. Sexton?"

"Sure, guy."

"Well . . . I was taking a shower the other day, and I noticed that . . ."

"Yeah?"

"*Well.* I noticed that I was starting to get athlete's foot. And remember when we used to have those dispensers in here? I just think you could install maybe *one* of them again." He looked at Sexton, who was waiting for more. "You know?"

"Well, Damone. You could bring some athlete's-foot powder from home—like some of the other guys—and keep it in your locker."

"I could do that," said Damone. "I could do that."

"I appreciate your mentioning it to me, though. I'll bring it up with Coach Ramirez. Okay?"

Damone leaned forward in his chair. "Mr. Sexton, I'm really worried. I think I have venereal disease."

Sexton snapped to like an anxious firedog. Now this was more like it. He scooted to the edge of his swivel chair and clasped his hands. "What makes you think that?"

"I noticed this sore at the base of my . . . penis." The word *penis* came out funny. He didn't often use the word.

Dick, crank, cock, wang, pud, pecker, schlong, weiner, or frank—they all came much more easily.

"Have you had sexual contact?"

"Yes."

"Do you know the girl?"

"Of *course* I know the girl."

"Have you talked to her about the problem."

"No. I thought I'd check first."

"You want to show it to me?"

"Not really," said Damone. But he dropped his pants just the same.

"Is she married?" asked Sexton.

At first Damone thought Sexton meant his dick. Then he realized he meant the *girl*. It was still a strange question.

"Naw."

"That lets my wife out," Sexton said. Then he laughed.

Gee, Damone thought, if I was looking at some guy's dick I sure wouldn't be making jokes about my wife. Especially if I thought he had syphilis.

"Hey," said Sexton, "I'm just trying to make you feel better. Now what this looks like to me is a normal chafing blister. But I wouldn't leave it at that. You gotta go to your doctor or the free clinic and get a test taken to be sure."

"Okay, *thanks* Mr. Sexton." Damone pulled his pants up. "Thanks a lot!"

"And it's between us," said Sexton.

A Late-Night Phone Conversation

"So," said Stacy Hamilton. "He says all these sweet and wonderful things to me when we're alone. But when anyone else is around, he's Mr. Cool."

"Did you talk to him last night?" asked Linda.

"Yeah."

"What did he say? Did he call you?"

"I called him. I just called him and said, 'Guess what?' He said, 'What?' I said, 'I'm reading our English assignment, and I just realized we're all going to *die* someday . . . we're all *dying.*' I said, 'Do you realize that, Mike?' And Mike goes, 'So what?' I said, 'Doesn't it bother you that even if the nuclear reactors don't react and kill us all, we're *still doing to die?* Doesn't that bother you?' He goes, 'No.' He says that pain is what bothers most people, not death. And pain doesn't even bother him. That's what he says."

"Wow," said Linda, "I didn't know he was that deep."

The Rat Finds Out

It was just a feeling that Mark Ratner got. There had been a bunch of them all sitting around at a cookout down on Richards Bay. It was a group that was forming—Stacy, Linda, Damone, Ratner, Doug Stallworth, Randy Eddo, and Laurie Beckman. They had been having a good time, but there were little hints that The Rat didn't quite understand.

Damone got up to leave. "I gotta get to work on some chemistry," he said. "Come on, Mark."

The Rat got up to leave with Damone. He heard an odd conversation behind him.

"That Damone sure works hard," cracked Randy Eddo.

"He gets to play a little, too," said Linda. "Doesn't he, *Stacy.*"

There were knowing giggles. Giggles that made Mark Ratner think. When he reached the car, he mentioned it to Damone.

"Hey, is there anything between you and Stacy?"

Damone shook his head. "No."

"Really?"

"No. Not really."

"What do you mean, not really?"

"Let me tell you something, Mark." Damone sighed. "Sometimes girls just go haywire. I went over to Stacy's house to go swimming once—I've been trying to think of a way to tell you ever since, 'cause you're my bud—and we started messing around and . . ." Damone shrugged. "Something happened. It's nothing serious, and it's all over."

The Rat said nothing.

"I don't like her as a girlfriend," said Damone.

The Rat said nothing.

"I don't even like her as a friend that much. She's pretty aggressive."

The Rat started shaking his head. "No, Damone. I don't understand."

"She wasn't really your girlfriend," mumbled Damone.

"Hey, FUCK YOU, Damone. There are a lot of girls out there, and you mess around with Stacy. I can't believe you. What have you got to PROVE?"

"I'm sorry," said Damone. "*Jesus.*"

"I always stick up for you," said The Rat. "I always stick up for you. Whenever people say, 'Aw that Damone is a *loudmouth*'—and they say that a lot—I say, 'You just don't know Damone.' When someone says you're an idiot, I tell them they just don't know you. Well, you know, Damone, maybe they DO know you pretty GOOD. And I'm just finding out . . ."

"Fine," said Damone. "Get lost."

Ratner walked away and vowed never to speak to Mike Damone again. It didn't make sense to him. For all the time The Rat had spent talking and dying over girls, he would never consider ruining his friendship with Damone over any one of them. Friendship—wasn't that what it was all about? Apparently not to Damone.

Ratner kept to himself at school for the next several weeks. His first social appearance since the Damone incident was a dance for Marine World workers held at a local hotel. The Rat wore his green army-fatigue jacket and sat in a corner.

Two Marine World coworkers stood at another part of the dance. "Where's Mark Ratner?" asked one.

"He's over there," said the other, "looking like he's going through Vietnam flashback or something."

Moustaches

Brad Hamilton had been sitting in Mechanical Arts, making a tape rack for his car. It was already March. As the year wore on and brought all its devastating twists and turns, Brad had realized something important. More than a lot of things, he liked his car. It made him feel responsible. It was a ticket to happiness. It *got* him places. It didn't let him down, not like girls and managers. The Cruising Vessel. It was his best friend.

Brad had been making custom items for The Cruising Vessel all year in Mechanical Arts. He'd made a tissue box, a special cover for the tape deck, and now he was almost finished with the tape rack. School, he figured, was good for some things.

Brad was just sanding down the tape rack when the buxom office worker came swinging into Mechanical Arts with a white slip. He looked at the girl, and the slip. Somehow he knew.

"Brad Hamilton?"

"Yo."

"You're to visit Mrs. Crawford in the front office."

A white slip was medium priority, so he went to the office after Mechanical Arts. He trudged down to the office and took a seat outside the counselor's department where Mrs. Crawford worked.

She poked her head out. "Brad Hamilton?"

"Yes."

"Hi, I'm Mrs. Crawford. Do you want to come in for a moment?"

"Sure."

"Brad, we've been reviewing the credits for most of the graduating seniors, something we do every year, and I have to ask you something. I'm afraid I don't see a credit for English Composition. Do you remember taking that class in tenth grade?"

"I think so."

"I see that you took English Grammar and English Lit., but never English Composition. It's taught here by Mrs. George."

"I had her for speech."

"So you never took English Composition?"

"I guess I didn't. Is there a big problem?"

"Well, it shows up on your SAT right now that you have a basic problem with your writing skills. But I think we can get you into a Contemporary Composition class real quick and sort this whole problem out."

"You're not really going to do that, are you? I work and everything. I go straight to school from work."

She studied his transcripts. "Well, your Mechanical Arts class is an elective. You can switch that with English Composition and not harm your workload at all!"

Brad looked down. "Damn it."

"It's for your own good."

Brad had a theory about that line. Every time someone told you something was for your own good, it meant you had to pay for it.

Brad Hamilton's Contemporary Composition class consisted of tenth graders and several foreign exchange students who were in the same leaky boat as Brad Hamilton. He was seated next to a Korean kid named Jim Kim. Mrs. George was always having Brad grade and correct Jim Kim's papers. The kid didn't know much English.

Today's assignment was to write about the pros and cons of moustaches.

"Okay, now switch papers," said Mrs. George toward the end of the class.

Jim Kim handed Brad his paper. It read:

170

I'm going to try to grow a moustache. Because it will be looks nice and more younger person. You grow moustache too. If you grow moustache, I think persons look at you for gentle man and more strong person and people can respect you better than right now. If you have moustahce, some people think about you like this, maybe they think you have nice personality and good knowledge. So you try to grow your moustache. I hope you will grow your moustache when I grow my moustache. I think secondly moustache will make you look more solemn. Because man must have solemn. It is a manner of man. If not man looks like woman. I think most women like solemn man. I think you should grow the moustache. It will probably improve your sex life and will also make you stand out.

Brad, who had already been trying to grow a moustache for some months, thought about writing: "You should learn English before you worry about moustaches." But he didn't. The guy didn't know any better, so Brad wrote: "Pretty good. B."

Jim Kim handed him back his paper. Brad had written a basic little essay about how he always wanted to grow a moustache and was going to this year.

"You don't answer the question," Jim had written. "So I give you D."

It was that kind of year for Brad Hamilton.

Mr. Six-and-a-Half

Of course The Rat was taking it hard. It was difficult falling out with your best friend in high school. Particularly when he was your *only* friend. He was down, depressed.

He stood at his P.E. locker, twirling the combination, and he could hear the thyroidal voice of fellow classmate Bob Tobin getting closer. Tobin was like a blue jay, always squawking about something. The only reason he got away with it, The Rat thought, was because he was so fucking tall, about 6'1"

"Ratner," said Bob Tobin. His voice naturally carried to all ears in the area. "Hello there, little man."

The Rat ignored him. But that just ignited Tobin, who got right up in The Rat's face and said, very loudly, the words that struck the solar plexus of the American male, however young: "Why is your dick so short?"

Ratner wriggled into his pants and tucked in his shirt. Things had been going bad enough without this guy.

"But why is your *dick* so short, Ratner?"

He took a long look at Tobin. The line just came out: "Sorry to *disappoint* you."

The Rat had Spanish next, and Mr. Valencia was going over subjects that might appear on the next quiz. The further conjugational adventures of Carlos y Maria. Aw, fuck it, The Rat just wasn't there.

No, now he was thinking about his dick.

Now he wasn't a guy who went around *looking* or anything, but The Rat knew this much—his dick wasn't any bigger or smaller than that of any of the other guys in the P.E. showers. But he had never thought much about it . . .

By the end of the day The Rat knew what had to be done.

"Want to go to the mall?" someone asked him.

"Naw," said The Rat, "I gotta study."

At home The Rat went straight for the garage and rummaged through the old magazines his dad kept in stacks. It had to be there somewhere! Somewhere with the *Playboys* . . . there it was! *Dr. Canby's Guide to Marital Bliss.*

Funny, it had the most official title, but this was the most hardcore book of all the ones in the stack. Pictures of all kinds of people, all wrapped around each other in pulpy color photos. There was even a guy in there who looked like Mr. Vargas.

And then Rat found it—the sex doctor's question-and-answer column. He flicked down the list of questions.

Q: DR. CANBY, HOW BIG IS THE AVERAGE PENIS SIZE? John Bilecky, Los Angeles, CA.

A: The average penis size is 6–7 inches when erect. When not erect, the penis can shrink so small as to be enveloped by the scrotum.

Six-to-seven inches! Well, there was no choice but to measure! So The Rat rummaged through the toolkit and came up with the best he could—a tape measure. He pocketed the tape measure and went back to his room.

He thought of Stacy. No, she was better than this! She was above a cheap tape-measure job.

He thought of Cindy Carr. Of Cheryl Ladd.

Slowly he peeled out the tape measure and laid it against his maligned dick.

Four. Only *four?* His heart sank.

Hold on! Two-and-a-half inches for the case! The case made him . . . six and a half. Normal! Better than normal!

"*All right,*" The Rat found himself saying. And he didn't even talk to himself.

"Mark? Are you home yet?"

"Yeah, Mom! Just going through the tools!"

War Games

There had been a poll taken in the *Reader* earlier in the year. The question had been, Would you be willing to go to war to defend American interests in the Middle East?

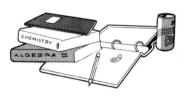

Overwhelmingly, from liberals to reactionaries, the basic student response was, No way. I wouldn't go to war unless America was attacked.

But you had to wonder just how sincere that was when Mr. Hand began his most popular class exercise, the five weeks in March and April when his class played War Games.

War Games was a Mr. Hand invention, built as a large-scale version of the popular home game of world domination, Risk. Each player-student was allotted a number of armies and countries. Turn by turn, the students were expected to defend and bombard each other until only one remained—the ruler of the world U.S. History class.

War Games brought out the maniac in some students. This was a time when the kids who carried briefcases to school reigned. They could barely wait until U.S. History, when the moves began again.

"How are you doing?"

"Okay. I've got Bulgaria. I'm going for the entire continent today."

"Are your armies in good shape?"

"Are you kidding? I'm going to blow their heads off, eat their flesh, and drink their blood!"

"Okay, Delbert, see you at lunch."

"Yeah."

Jeff Spicoli was, naturally, one of the first players to lose all his armies and sit drawing motorcycles for the rest of War Games.

"What is your problem?" Mr. Hand had demanded of him.

"Boredom," said Spicoli.

"Mr. Spicoli," said Mr. Hand, "the next world war will be fought out of boredom."

A Date with Linda

 Linda Barrett was standing in Child Development when she felt two hands on her waist. She turned to see herself in the reflector sunglasses of Steve Shasta.

"What's for dinner, snookums?" asked Shasta.

"You scared me, Steve."

"I hear you called me."

"I didn't call you."

They never called each other. Ever since their one make-out session in the bleachers of an eighth-grade Sadie Hawkins dance, nothing had sparked between Steve Shasta and Linda Barrett. There had been polite hellos in the hallways, a few words here and there on lunch court, but mostly Linda left the Shasta-watching to her girlfriends.

"Well, it doesn't matter if you called me or not," said Shasta. He tipped his shades. "I just want to say that you're looking real fine . . . You want to play some miniature golf this Friday night?"

Linda Barrett looked him up and down. He was cute, that much she had to say for Steve Shasta. And if she *were* going to go out with a high school boy, there wasn't a more sought-after or mysterious figure around Ridgemont.

"You know I'm engaged," she said.

"Sure," said Shasta. "Still Doug?"

Everyone always said that to her these days, even her mother. Sometimes Linda had nightmares in which she died and her unmarked tombstone read only: *Still* Doug.

"Of course, still Doug."

"Well, leave him at home."

He laughed. She would.

Shasta was a half-hour late to pick Linda up on Friday night. He had been out pursuing a favorite Shasta pastime after a tough soccer game—downing a six-pack of Miller within ninety minutes.

He had forgotten to write down the address, instead remembering it as the corner house at Avenida Western and Avenida Birch in the Valley View condominium development. Ah, but . . . which corner house?

They all looked the same. Shasta first tried the house on the northern corner.

"What do you want?" a voice challenged through the door. "I don't open the door past 8:30!"

"Does Linda Barrett live here?"

"No!"

"Do you know which house she lives in?"

"Absolutely not."

"Well fuck *you*, lady."

Shasta went back out into the street to regroup. He did not see her car; it must have been in the lousy garage. Which garage? He just could not remember. In fact, he was not remembering too much of anything.

He was, in further fact, really *blitzed*. Six beers on an empty stomach. If he didn't get some food soon, the spins would be there. He popped a mint into his mouth and thought about it some more.

Shasta tried the doorbell on the next-best-looking house. It was the one with a Martini flag hung outside the door.

"Does Linda Barrett live here?"

Linda stood in her room, listening at her door as Shasta entered the Barrett home. She knew what would happen. They would invite him in and, under good light, inspect him carefully. Then they would call her out of her room.

She hoped he hadn't been drinking.

"Hello, *Steve*," she heard her mother say. "Car trouble?"

She heard Shasta swallow a small alcoholic laugh. He was drunk, just like he'd been when they made out at that dance in eighth grade. *Asshole*.

"Are you all right, Steve?"

"Oh, yes, Mrs. Barrett."

"Congratulations on that game," said Mr. Barrett.

"May I have a glass of water, please?" Shasta asked.

"Look, Ben, look at the boy's *face*. It's *flushed*."

Listening behind the door, Linda winced.

"Look at him, Ben," her mother said. "Doesn't he look just like . . . just like *John Kennedy*?"

Linda heard them seating Shasta in the living room on the sofa. *Typical*. The sofa faced Mom's and Dad's chairs, the fireplace, and two mammoth department-store oil paintings that dominated the entire room. One of the paintings was of Linda and the other was of her brother, Jerome, The Brain.

"Do you know Jerome?" asked Mr. Barrett. "He used to go to Ridgemont. He goes to USC, now."

"I don't know him."

"Well," Mr. Barrett chuckled, "if you don't know math, he doesn't want to know *you!*"

"I see," said Shasta.

"Ben, where is Linda?" Her mother spoke in a real Taster's Choice testimonial voice. "Come out, honey, *Steve's* here."

Linda opened the door and came bounding out. "HI! Wanna go?"

"Sure," said Steve.

"Have a good time, kids!" Her mother patted them both on the head, like good kids.

They walked the forty feet to the car in silence.

"Is it too late to play golf?" asked Linda.

"We gotta get some food first," said Steve. "That's okay, isn't it?"

Shasta slammed the door of his car shut and turned the ignition key. The radio came on at a deafening volume. He turned it off. They pulled out onto the highway and lurched into overdrive.

"I get behind the wheel of a Corvair," said Shasta, "and I'm a *madman*." He laughed. "You know what I hate? I hate people who give their cars names."

Linda nodded. Her pickup was called Dino, after her first dog.

They went to a Swedish Smorgasbord, where Shasta knew a night cook named Walsh. The place was closing. Walsh kept it open.

Walsh, a freckled kid in a white smock, pointed to the limp remains of the day's Swedish Smorgasbord. "Go for it." Walsh even sat down with them at the table in his white smock and watched Shasta and Linda eat.

"How's it going?" Walsh's head bobbed constantly as he spoke.

"Pretty good. This is Linda Barrett."

"*Hi.*"

"Hi."

"So," Shasta said, "how's it going with you?"

177

Walsh's head kept bobbing. "Old people," he said, "Lots of old people. Man, they *flock* here. And they eat their brains out. They don't even talk to each other, they just *eat*. It's amazing."

"Really?" asked Shasta. "I heard there's a movie where people eat themselves to death."

"*Yeah*," said Walsh. "They probably filmed it at a Smorgasbord. It's most crowded on weekends, you know, and that's real funny 'cause on the weekends we get a lot of stuff from Denny's. They get their new food on Saturday mornings. They clean this stuff out on Friday afternoon. It's all *leftovers*."

Linda picked at the rest of her meal. It was Friday night.

After dinner at the Swedish Smorgasbord, Steve Shasta played his car radio and drove Linda Barrett directly to the Point.

"I really made a decision, you know," said Shasta. He brushed some hair out of his eyes and checked himself in the mirror. "I made a decision not to *pressure* myself." He looked at her, giving Linda the full eye. "Some girls I could really fall for . . ."

"Why don't you?" asked Linda innocently.

Shasta took a deep breath. "Well, because of *soccer* mostly. It takes the ultimate in concentration. It's not a *collisional* sport, you know. A lot of people don't realize the mental stress. Plus, I've always got guys out there on the field trying to mark me. Like last year. Just before the injury, I had . . ."

He hung his head.

"Been with a girl?"

"Yeah," said Shasta, "and she broke my heart, too. She didn't go to Ridgemont High, so you don't know her. But she took my mind off the game. And I don't want that to ever happen again. I'm really counting on getting that Yale scholarship." He paused. "College is really important to me. It may not be to everybody else, but it is to me."

Linda Barrett leaned over and kissed him.

"I really like you," said Shasta. "I always have. I just want to remember you after I graduate. Always."

"But Steve, it's only March."

Shasta reached out and crooked his hand around her neck. He pushed her head gently downward. And she went willingly. Like so many before her.

Test Answers

The next day was Tuesday, and that meant Stacy had first-period biology. She slept past the point her clock radio clicked on. Her mother had to wake her up at 7:20.

"You're late, Stacy!"

"Okay *okay*," Stacy yelled at the door.

"Don't yell at me, young lady!"

These days Stacy was always late. Running slow, running behind.

She was late for biology. Late for P.E., where it was Rape Protection Week and Ms. Zix was taking attendance all of a sudden. She was even late for the Child Development test-answers session in the 200 Building girls' bathroom.

Test-answers meetings had to move quickly, especially if you had the class before lunch. This meant you had exactly eight minutes to receive and memorize the answers.

Stacy arrived three minutes late.

". . . And she asks a lot of cooking terms," a girl was saying. "She asks about garnish and simmering . . . let's see, and sifting. And blending and basting."

"What's the definition of basting?"

"To moisten food, while cooking, with melted butter or pan drippings."

"What else?" asked Stacy. "What else?"

But the talk had already shifted to Tina Dellacorte.

"There's this picture of her in Graphic Arts," said one

girl. "Just her in her bikini underwear. And she's holding a hose with the water turned on. And she's got this *raunchy* look on her face, with the water running out of her mouth . . ."

"Who took the picture?"

"Greg Gardner."

"Greg Gardner!"

"Come on. Come on. Anything else for Child Development?"

"That's it, Stacy." Back to the story. "Now a girl like her, she knows when she goes *out* with a guy what she's gonna do. She's gonna get down. She just plans for it. That's part of the evening, and she always schedules it in. She's such a slut."

"Why," said Stacy, "because she gets *laid?*"

"I just think she's a slut for doing that." Pause. "Maybe *you* don't . . ."

"Why don't you just shut up," said Stacy. She walked out of the bathroom to Child Development.

She was sick of the school and the people in the school. She was sick of Mike Damone and his Mr. Stud routine. She was sick of work at Swenson's and getting up in the mornings and . . .

And if that wasn't enough, Stacy Hamilton began to let another thought take hold. It began as an itch in the back of her head. Sick in the mornings. Backaches. Why shouldn't her birth control pills, those wonderful Norinyl I Plus 50s, be like everything else—leaving her on the two-percent side of everything ninety-eight–percent effective.

She found Linda Barrett after class.

"Hey," she said, "I want to talk to you later."

"What's it about?"

"I'll call you tonight, okay?"

She called Linda later that evening.

"Linda," she said, "I think I want to go down to the free clinic and take one of those tests. I don't feel right."

"Did you remember to take your pills?"

"Sure." Pause. "I think so. Sure."

"It's easy to forget.'

"I'm sure I took them."

"Okay," said Linda, "let's go down there day after tomorrow, because tomorrow is swimming practice. Don't you *want* to go down there and check it out?"

"I don't think so, Linda."

Fridays were the free clinic's busiest day. There was an hour-and-a-half wait just to take a blood and urine test; to check pregnancy they had the girls sit through more lectures. More nurses parading more facts for you. More of those cutaway diagrams, like in Mrs. Melon's class. More of those meaningless statistics where every one girl in some low number got pregnant or contracted venereal disease. Or how 2,000 girls got pregnant *while you came in.*

Just give me the test, she thought.

They sat Stacy down with another nurse, who asked her more questions.

"How often do you have your periods? Regularly?"

"Yes."

"Have you ever used any form of birth control?"

"Yes."

"Do you remember the name?"

"Norinyl I Plus 50s."

"Have you ever been pregnant?"

"No."

Finally, they gave her the pregnancy test.

"You can call us on Monday morning for the results," said the nurse. "Have a nice weekend!"

A Late-Night Phone Conversation

"There's one thing you didn't tell me about guys," said Stacy Hamilton. "You didn't tell me that they can be so nice, so great ... but then you sleep with them, and they start acting like they're about *five years old.*"

"You're right," said Linda. "I didn't tell you about that."

The Abortion

"Good morning, Miss Hamilton," said the nurse's voice over the telephone. "We received your test results from the lab, and they show that you are pregnant."

"I *am* pregnant?"

"You *are* pregnant."

"Oh." Her head fell downward.

"Have you made plans for the baby?"

"Yes."

"What plans have you made?"

"I mean no. I haven't made plans for the baby."

"Did you want to get pregnant?"

"No. It was a mistake."

"Have you told your boyfriend?"

"No."

"Well, I'm sure he'll be very happy and excited about it." It sounded to Stacy like the nurse said that a lot.

She walked over to Linda's house in a daze.

"I can't believe it," Linda said. "Hadn't you been taking the pill?"

"I guess I forgot."

They sat in glum silence.

"I knew I was pregnant. They didn't even have to tell me. I felt all different. The thing is—when they first told me, I was happy that I could get pregnant, and that Mike could do it. I really was. I didn't think about it as an abortion until the nurse kept asking me about what *plans* I'd made."

"What plans *have* you made?"

"Well, I made an appointment. It's going to happen in a week."

"Wow. Debbie has never taken a pill and has never gotten pregnant. She's been with guys since she was twelve. She never had to have an abortion."

"Great. Debbie sleeps with half of the Western world and nothing happens. I sleep with my second guy, A VIRGIN, and *I* get pregnant."

"Do you crave things? Like pickles and things? Is that a stupid question?"

Stacy sighed. "Okay, you get cravings—and you really want to sleep in. You get cravings not for weird things, but things you like. I get cravings for fruit and potato chips and Tootsie Roll Pops."

"Yuk."

"I know."

"What are you going to tell Mike?"

"I'm not going to tell him. Are you crazy? And don't you tell anybody either. I don't want anybody finding out."

But the problem with high school, as Stacy Hamilton would soon find out, was that one still saw the same people every day. It wasn't hard for Stacy to miss Mike Damone whistling down the hallways, acting like Joe Stud. He should know! He should know he was a prick! He should know how it felt!

Within two days she knew she had to tell Mike Damone. She thought about it and came up with the best location to have The Big Conversation. It was away from everybody, and yet still at school. Stacy Hamilton walked out onto the field during Damone's P.E. period with Assistant Coach Les Sexton. Damone was timing runners on the football field.

"Hi, Mike," said Stacy.

"Stace. What's going *on?*"

"Mike, there's something that's been on my mind, and I have to tell you about it."

"What? Now?" He clicked off a time on a runner and then turned to her. "Why don't you call me?"

Stacy looked at him, and the feeling that came over her was, as she later told Linda, zero compassion. She took Mike Damone's hand and placed it on her stomach.

"I'm pregnant," she said.

Damone made a spitting sound with his mouth. "Give me a break. You're lying."

"I'm not lying. Why would I lie about it?"

Damone put his hand up to shield his eyes from the afternoon sun. "How do you know that it's mine?" he asked. "We only did it once."

"I know it's yours."

Damone switched tones entirely. Now he sounded whiny, like a child trying to talk his way out of a spanking. "You made me do it," he said. "You locked the door to your changing room." He paused, then said the words that hurt the most: "You wanted it more than me!"

She didn't flinch. She stood there and stared at Damone, waiting for him to take the words back.

"There's only one thing we can do," said Damone. He folded his hands across his yellow P.E. shirt. "We gotta ace it."

"What does that mean?" asked Stacy.

"We've got to get an abortion. My brother, Art, got his girlfriend one. It's no big thing."

She looked down at the ground. "It's already planned."

"Do you want me to pay for it?" asked Damone.

"No," said Stacy. Suddenly she felt like a character from one of Mrs. Melon's sex-ed lectures. "Just give me a ride downtown day after tomorrow."

"No problem," said Damone. "No problem."

It was strange how society set these things up, Stacy thought. She was upset. She was *scared.* And she was *hurt.* Hurt just to think that someone who cared about her so much could be so cruel. To think that *anybody* could be that cruel. But what could she say about it? They both went to the same school. She needed a ride.

Stacy waited out the week. She had P.E. first thing in the morning and had to get out there and run even though she felt sick most of the time. The day came for Damone to show and take her down to the free clinic in his Toyota.

Her abortion was set for three in the afternoon. Stacy followed her plan that night, contracting a phony twenty-four–hour flu that would keep her home the next day. She waited until the time Damone was supposed to show up at the mailbox—2:00 P.M. He didn't show.

She waited twenty minutes and walked back to her house. She dialed Damone's house.

"Hello?" Damone answered.

"I can't believe you're still home!"

"Oh, hi Stacy . . . oh shit, I *forgot* about today."

"*Forgot?*"

"Yeah, my mom wanted me to stay with the house. Some people are coming over to look at it. Can you reschedule it for another day?"

"I guess I could reschedule it. I'll call. I just don't want to be alone when I go. Will you please take me?"

"Just call me back and tell me when. I'll be right here."

She was a little relieved, happy to put it off for any length of time. She was told by the free clinic that it would be unwise to delay more than another week. They reset the date for the following Tuesday. Stacy called Damone back. He was almost nice, and for a few days it was almost easy to forget she was still pregnant.

Guys. She'd already had just about her fill. Why, in retrospect, Linda had pretty much been right down the line. High school boys. One part of them wanted to be in high school, and the other part wanted to be back at Paul Revere Junior High. The more the year wore on, the better The Vet, his slight *dorkiness* aside, looked.

One night Stacy decided to call him up. It had been seven months. He couldn't still be mad that she'd lied about her age.

"Hello?"

"Hi, is Ron there?"

"This is Ron. Who's this?"

"This . . . is Stacy! Remember me!"

"Oh, hi. What can I do for you?"

"Well . . . I just thought I'd call and say hello."

"Hello."

"Is something wrong?" asked Stacy.

"No. But if you'd like any further attention you can give me a ring at the office. Okie-dokie? Thanks." He hung up.

Stacy sat staring at the phone for many minutes afterward. She decided to forget about that, and remember him as he was. Under the fifty-watt lightbulb up at the Point.

Time always went quicker when you dreaded something, and Tuesday rolled right around again. It brought—*I can't believe it, Mom*—another twenty-four–hour flu. She waited around the house for the appointed time, then went to wait by the mailbox.

Five minutes away, Damone sat in his living room and waited for the phone to ring. He had finished a large tumbler of Tia Maria and cream. Lou Reed was blasting in the background.

Damone was paralyzed. All he wanted to do was go away, forget about this problem. Why wouldn't it just go away? Why did it fall on him? She'd had just as much fun as he; it was her responsibility, too. Things like this weren't supposed to happen when you had The Attitude.

Stacy waited. Finally, she went home and called Damone, forty-five minutes before the operation.

"I'm sorry," said Damone. "I gotta help my dad in the garage."

"You could have called!"

"I forgot."

"PRICK!" She hung up on him.

Stacy immediately called Linda. No answer. There was only one way to get downtown, now—waiting for the bus would take too long. Only one person would do it on such short notice.

"Hello?"

"Mark?"

"Stacy!"

"Hi. How are you?"

"I'm all right. How are you, Stacy?"

"Just great. Mark, you're going to think I'm crazy, but could you do me a big favor?"

"What's that? Are you okay?"

"Well . . . I'm really stuck for a ride downtown right now.

You know, the flea market. I have some girl's shopping to do . . ."

"Sure. I'll give you a ride."

The Rat pulled up in his sister's car and tooted the horn.

"Thanks for picking me up."

"Any time." She looked at him. If he only knew.

"God, Mark, you're the nicest guy I know."

"Just once," said The Rat, "I want to be dark and mysterious."

"Okay. You're dark and mysterious."

"Thanks," said The Rat. "Are you going to be needing a ride home?"

"No. I'll take a bus. It's all right."

They rounded the corner onto Broadway Street, passing on their right that big maroon building with FREE CLINIC painted on the side.

"There's the flea market over there!"

The initial examination took the most time of all. Blood pressure. More urine and blood samples. Flashlights in the eyes. It gave her plenty of time to get more scared. She wanted to scream, *Just get it over with!*

There were many other girls around, most of them with the same embarrassed look on their faces. Filling out forms. Taking samples. *Why didn't men have to go through this?*

Finally she was led to another room—the operating room—and seated on a steel table. Minutes passed. Another nurse came in and told her to wait just five more miniutes.

Ten minutes later, the doctor entered the room. He by-passed courtesy greetings. He by-passed conversation completely.

"If you'd like to change your mind, please say so now," he stated.

"No, thank you."

The nurse reentered the room. They did not speak to each other. The doctor turned his back and opened a metal cabinet. He selected from it a tube filled with an emerald-colored chemical, then took from the nurse a sealed packet. He ripped the packet open and withdrew *the biggest syringe* Stacy had ever seen.

She started to panic.

"Will I be able to have a child after this?"

"You should," said the doctor.

"Is this going to hurt?"

"Have you been taking the pills we gave you?"

"Yes."

"Well . . . those should help a lot. They'll reduce swelling and bleeding."

"But does it hurt a lot?"

"This is your first time, right?"

She nodded.

"Well," said the doctor, "you've felt pain before. It's over very quickly . . . is your boyfriend out there?"

"Yes," said Stacy. Out there somewhere, she thought.

The doctor watched as the nurse strapped Stacy's legs into stirrups. He inserted the syringe into her vagina.

"Squeeze me when you feel pain," said the nurse.

Stacy shivered as the cold rush of anesthetic swept through her lower torso. "I feel all cold," she said.

"It's normal."

The nurse inserted two metal tubes leading into a large glass jar that had been placed between her legs.

"I'll be with you after this is over," said the nurse. Then the suction noise began.

Stacy started to panic again. "Aren't you going to knock me out?"

"Oh, not for this," said the doctor. It was as if she was in the dentist's chair, and he was filling a quick cavity.

"I thought you were going to knock me out . . ."

"It will be over in a moment," said the doctor. "You're a good patient." The words seemed to hold no particular meaning for him.

A huge cramp pulled Stacy's stomach into a tight knot. Then she felt daggers of pain shooting into her solar plexus. She squeezed the nurse's hand until it was white.

"It'll be over in a moment. You're a good patient."

In one minute the jar had filled to the top with a purplish bloody membrane. She had most wanted to be knocked out so she wouldn't have to see . . . *it*. But it was not even an embryo. It was just a glob.

"Send that to the lab," the doctor directed. The tubes were withdrawn.

"Is it over?"

"Not yet. We have to do a little scraping."

"The papers didn't say anything about . . ."

"Just relax," the doctor said.

They had inserted two metal scraping devices. The doctor started probing and scratching her deep inside. She was bleeding heavily, all over her white gown.

"This hurts even worse than it looks."

"It'll be over in a second. You're a good patient."

"I wish men could experience this," Stacy said.

Her abortion had taken a total of ten minutes. The doctor patted her behind the neck. "You were a good patient," he said. "Is there anything you need while you're resting in the next room?"

"A box of tissues."

The nurse left the room to get the tissues, leaving only Stacy and the doctor.

"I have one question," said Stacy. "Does it hurt more to have a baby?"

"Yes," said the doctor. "But you mind it less."

She emerged from the resting room, her eyes a teary red, and sat down to complete the last of their forms. As she did, a girl and her boyfriend entered the same reception area. This girl was on her way in. Her boyfriend picked up a magazine and leafed through it.

The girl looked at Stacy. For a moment the two caught each other's eyes and locked in. What passed between them Stacy was not sure about, but she knew she would remember this a long, long time. The tubes. The jar. The doctor. And she would remember the look in that girl's eyes. They were like a deer's eyes, caught in headlights.

It was March twenty-first, and she would always remember the date, too, because it was her mother's birthday. Stacy Hamilton felt a lot older today.

"Nurse," she said, "I'm going to wait for my boyfriend downstairs."

The Tribute

Mrs. Paula Benson, the forty-two-year-old cafeteria manager of Ridgemont High School, had come to the end of the line with her job. It was her ninth year with the school, and still the administration hadn't favored her with a policy change. A decade ago, then Vice-Principal William Gray had decided that the cafeteria was the best training spot for retarded and handicapped students hoping to make an entrance into the mainstream. The idea caught on. For nine years Mrs. Benson had been helping the handicapped help themselves help her.

A next-door neighbor had planted a terrible thought in Mrs. Benson's head: "Paula, you are the same age now that Elvis Presley was when he *died*. You take care of yourself." Mrs. Benson looked in the mirror and saw a woman much older than her years. She decided to quit Ridgemont.

As she explained to Ray Connors on the Friday before Easter vacation, it was *not* that she minded working with the disabled. She was just tired of *all* the students, and it was about time that she "started keeping her own house clean."

Ray Connors took a look at this woman, this quiet soul who had summoned all her courage to make this decision, and rewarded her, typically, with a promotion to area manager. It was a job that involved her traveling to all the local schools and working with *all* the handicapped students in *all* the cafeterias. With the promise of a small raise to go along with the new title, a tired and wan Paula Benson reported to her last day at Ridgemont High School.

She had heard the loud screeching noises from as far away as the parking lot. As she drew closer, she realized with no small terror that all the racket was coming from—my God—the cafeteria.

She entered through the side door. It was an incredible sight—there had to be thirty young men in Afro hairdos or wigs, all carrying amplified guitars. Wearing scarves. They looked to her with hope.

"What's going on here?" she asked.

"We answered the ad," said one boy. A red scarf was tied around his thigh. "For the tribute."

"What ad?"

"Oh, *man*. You mean you don't know about it either?"

"I'm the cafeteria manager. I'm afraid I don't know about any of this. Who let you in here?"

Another boy produced a scrap of paper from the local *Reader*. "Look at this!"

It read: THIS MONDAY MORNING, 7:00 A.M., all-day auditions begin for HENDRIX, an Off-Broadway tribute to the greatest guitarist of all time. Big money commitment. Performances across the country. Must be able to look and perform like the great Jimi Hendrix. Report to cafeteria at Ridgemont High School. Be early!

"But there ain't nothing around here got to do with Hendrix," complained the kid.

Three more Hendrix lookalikes appeared at the doorway holding amplifiers. "This where the tribute is?"

Then it dawned on Mrs. Benson. The last time someone pulled a prank like this was about three years ago . . . to the day. April first.

"Gentlemen," said Mrs. Benson, "I think this is someone's idea of an April Fool's Day joke."

"Motherfu . . ."

"*Hey*," said another kid. "Jimi would have wanted us to play all day!"

"Let's get a P.A.in here!"

The Jimi Hendrix imitators set up camp in the cafeteria. More kept arriving all morning. They had jammed for an hour and a half before Lt. Flowers pulled the electricity switch. During lunch time he visited the various troublemakers of the school and grilled them as they bit into their sandwiches.

"Do you know who is responsible for this action in the cafeteria?"

"I don't know, Lt. Flowers. I heard it was Steven Miko."

That Little Prick

After the operation, Stacy took the bus to Linda Barrett's house. The two girls disappeared into Linda's room to discuss the experience. When Linda heard about Damone's standing her up a second time, about his leaving Stacy to find her own ride downtown, she did something uncharacteristic of her normally regal manner. She slammed her fist into the wall.

"That prick!" she said.

"I know. You told me about high school boys."

"Forget that," said Linda. "He's a LITTLE PRICK!"

"Calm down," said Stacy. "Your parents are in the living room."

Her mother knocked at the door. "Are you all right, Linda?"

"I'm okay!"

"We're all right, Mrs. Barrett."

"THAT LITTLE PRICK," shrieked Linda.

Stacy had gone home and gone to sleep. Linda went out later that night and found Mike Damone's smart new Toyota. Using a key, she had scratched three words along the driver's side: PRICK PRICK PRICK.

There had been only a brief confrontation between Damone and Stacy, and it happened in Public Speaking. On Expert Day. Mrs. J. had a Personal Growth Counselor from nearby City College come in and lecture on such consciousness-raising methods as Awareness Therapy. The counselor had selected Damone as a centerpiece. He asked several students around the room to comment on Damone's personality.

It was soon Stacy's turn.

Three weeks after the abortion, she was still disoriented at times. She still experienced the symptoms of pregnancy. Slowly her body adjusted to its loss. But the resentment deepened.

She still saw Mike on lunch court, in the hallways and in Speech class. His mood was mostly one of relief at having averted a near-disaster. He had even become jovial, wisecracking with her. She had come to feel like a notch on his Lynyrd Skynyrd belt buckle.

"I think Mike is always covering up," said Stacy. "Every time you see him he's got this *facade*. I just wonder what he's really like, what he was like back in Philadelphia."

Silence.

"Well, now *that* was insightful, wasn't it Mike," the counselor had said. "That young lady has given you a perspective on yourself that could have only come out of Awareness Therapy. There are other kinds of therapy . . ."

"What are you *talking* about?" added Damone. "You don't know me! You may think you know me, but you don't know me!"

"I know that you've got an act."

"You're just saying that," raged Damone, "because you wanted to be my girlfriend, and I didn't feel like having a girlfriend."

"Bullshit!"

"Bullshit!"

"Okay you two," said Mrs. George. "I think we've had enough Personal Growth for one day."

And of course there was the matter of rumors. Between Damone's PRICK PRICK PRICK Toyota, and the few friends he'd told about the abortion, and Linda and Laurie, it soon seemed that the only ones who hadn't heard the story were The Rat and Brad Hamilton. *Was it really true that Stacy Hamilton had a. . . . ?*

No one dared question Stacy. She was never around anymore. She had done the American thing about putting some distance between herself and the traumatic memory of March twenty-first. She had thrown herself into her work. There were new managers now at the Town Center Mall Swenson's, and they had given her some tough weekend hours to hostess. She worked them without a complaint, and the new managers made a big deal about it. They made her Employee of the Month. Some of the back kitchen girls even began to worry about their jobs.

Then came a further twist. Some of Damone's friends began to work at the Town Center Mall Swenson's. Damone, tired of his own janitorial job, resigned, and one day turned up on a job interview with the new managers of the mall Swenson's. Stacy did nothing to block his being hired as a busboy. A few weeks later, it was announced that Stacy Hamilton was new Weekend Nighttime Manager. This meant only a few hours, two days a week, but the title alone was awesome for a girl who was still fifteen years old and a sophomore at Ridgemont High School.

One weekend in early May, Swenson's was filled. Stacy was rushing here, rushing there, exercising her new authority.

"Damone," she said. "You want to clean off table 19? Or do I have to do it myself!"

And out of the back bustled Mike Damone—Mr. Attitude—in a peppermint shirt and a bow tie.

"Gimme a break! I'm coming! I'm coming!"

Danny

"Some people," said Mrs. George, "come to this school to learn."

She was red-eyed and shaking as she faced her morning speech class. Today was meant to be Debate Day, a period in which students like Damone and The Rat took the podium and argued such subjects as "The fifty-five–mile-per-hour speed Limit: Boon or Bust," but it was obvious there would be no speeches and no debates on this morning. This morning Mrs. George had been awakened with the news that one of her students had hanged himself.

His name was Danny Boyd, and to many students he had been a joke figure, another campus character. Danny Boyd had been a senior for two years, taking a couple of courses at a time, trying to improve his grades to get into a state college. He wasn't around school that much, but he always carried a big black briefcase with a double combination lock. Sometimes he stood around the parking lot, near Mrs. George's brown Monarch, talking with other members of the "briefcase preppy set." Like the surfers, they too had been pushed out onto the parking lot by the fast-food militia, but not even the briefcase set could really find room for Danny Boyd.

"Danny came to me two months ago," said Mrs. George, "and told me that nobody here would talk to him." She was a teacher of great enthusiasm, and nobody had quite heard such disgust in her voice before. "He felt that just because he studied more than the rest of you for College Boards, he made people feel uncomfortable. All of you knew he *had* to work harder, and still not one of you reached out to him. You were all too busy with yourselves." She sighed, examining her hand.

"Well. He was turned down again last week by every college he applied to. And it appeared to him he didn't have a single friend to help him through his disappointment. You were all too busy . . ."

In the nervous silence of the room, only the electric buzz of the clock was heard. Mrs. George looked up again.

"Sometimes I sit back there and listen to you talk amongst yourselves," said Mrs. George. "And it is absolutely amazing to me. You talk about your working hours, your adult lives and your *adult* emotions, yet you are *all* such children, really. You'd do yourselves well to remind yourselves of that from time to time."

And even though Mrs. George had not been particularly *close* to Danny Boyd, she made a point of admonishing each of her classes for their insensitivity toward the student. There was a special article on Danny ordered for the school paper, the yearbook staff made an announcement that they would keep him in with the senior class photos. Danny Boyd became a special cause for about two weeks, before the onrushing pace of high school events swept his memory into the past.

Fish and Chips

Brad's new job location was way down on Ridgemont Drive, in a green building between two office-supply stores. There was a huge off-purple drawing of a lobster out front. The sign read: Captain Kidd Fish and Chips. Brad himself couldn't really tell you how good the fish was. He didn't like fish.

But that wasn't the real problem. He could even deal with his new assistant manager, Harold, a guy Brad thought looked like that TV ventriloquist who worked the bitchy puppet named Madame. Harold was always asking Brad to run errands for him, and he expected Brad to love doing them. Harold was big on company pride.

Brad didn't even mind that so much. He was the new guy at Captain Kidd, so he went along with it.

The real problem, as Brad saw it, was the uniforms. Captain Kidd Fish and Chips demanded that all employees wear blue-and-white-striped buccaneer outfits. The uniforms came with hot, baggy pants and phony black plastic swords that an employee couldn't remove—"Where's your sword, Hamilton? You've got to wear the sword!"—and worst of all, a big floppy Ponce de León swashbuckler hat. Like a bunch of pirates. Behind the fryer, Brad felt, this got to be a bit much.

At least no one from Ridgemont High came into the place.

One day Brad was at the fryer, tossing some frozen cod into the oil. It was pretty amazing, Brad was thinking. Here was Redondo Beach, a warm-water port, and they still flew in this frozen fish from Alaska. It didn't make sense. But he didn't eat fish anyway, so he just cooked it up and didn't worry about it. Anyone who would come into a place with a big purple lobster on the sign out front, Brad figured, would probably love the stuff.

His thoughts were interrupted by the breathless appearance of Harold, the assistant manager. "Hamilton," he said, "I need you to run an order for me. I'll take over the fryer. Those boys over at IBM are really socked in, and I told them you would personally deliver their order within the hour. Can you just run it over in your car? I'll reimburse you for gas."

Brad dutifully unhooked his apron. "Okay. Just give me a minute."

Brad fried up fourteen boxes worth of frozen cod and stacked them by the counter. He loaded the boxes into The Cruising Vessel, then went back to get the bill from Harold. The last thing Brad did was take off the buccaneer outfit and change into Levi's for the drive to IBM. It was definitely worth leaving the fryer for a chance to take off that uniform.

Harold caught sight of him as he was leaving the Captain Kidd employees' restroom. "Hey Hamilton, what are you doing? What are you dressed like that for?"

"This," said Brad, "is how I dress all the time."

"Come on, Hamilton. You're going over to IBM to represent Captain Kidd Fish and Chips. I told them you would deliver those boxes *personally*. Part of our image, part of our *appeal* is in those uniforms!" He said it like he had nabbed Brad in the act of sabotaging the place. "You've got to be proud to work at Captain Kidd!"

"You really want me to change back?"

"Yes," said the assistant manager, "I think so. Why don't you change back." He paused. "Show some *pride*, Hamilton."

Now there was a time when Brad Hamilton might have said something, a time when he might have taken a stand. But those were the days, as he saw it, before the punching bag of life had come back to hit him in the face. His new policy was to shut up and make money. Gas was expensive. The Cruising Vessel didn't run on pride.

"Okay," Brad sighed. "I don't believe you're asking me to do this . . . but okay."

He changed back into the buccaneer outfit and walked woefully out the door. He got in his car and rode out onto the Interstate. People in other cars were giving him strange looks.

Brad was on the Interstate when he realized what he was doing. It was already the time he would have normally taken off for lunch. But now he was out running errands for the assistant manager, delivering fourteen boxes of fish and chips—and the place didn't even deliver. He was hungry.

Brad pried open one of the boxes and, so as not to disturb the careful order of the fish arrangement, grabbed a couple of fries. One thing he had to say: The fries were about twenty times better now that he was there. He had a few more.

He wondered how the fish tasted. It couldn't be *too* bad; he had fried it himself. Maybe since he was the fryer that had gotten better, too. He took a nibble off one of the fish pieces . . .

It was the worst-tasting piece of shit that had ever passed for food. And that was a compliment. What was he doing at this place?

Brad threw the piece of fish out the window, a symbolic move that made him feel damn good. Some IBM executive would get one less piece of frozen Catch-of-the-Day cod. It would probably save the guy's life, anyway.

In another car on the Interstate Brad saw a pretty girl looking at him. He smiled back at her, the winning Brad game-show-host-young-Ronald-Reagan-lean-and-hungry grin.

The girl started laughing.

The *uniform!* He forgot he was wearing that stupid uniform! And the swashbuckler hat! Shit! That girl had been laughing *at* him.

He whipped off the hat and tossed that out the window, too. And the plastic sword. And his little scarf. And even though Brad Hamilton knew it would cost him the last fryer job in town, he sailed right past the entrance for IBM.

Ritchie Blackmore's Birthday

April was a big month for school events. It was as if someone in the administration realized that unless a couple of jolts were thrown in early, the long slide toward June/Total Apathy might get mighty steep mighty quick.

There was the student-faculty basketball game, a heavy-pitched event that was the culmination of weeks of morning bulletin announcements on tryouts, practices, and challenges. The students won, and Steve Shasta took Coach Ramirez to the ground in one fight for the ball. Big news for two days.

April also brought PSAT exams, the Sophomore Circus, the Annual Lunch-Time Concert, the Chocolate Sale, college acceptance notices, and the first announcements for Grad Nite, coming in June.

Surely there was enough action there to touch on every Ridgemont student's interests, but none of these special April events meant a thing to Randy Eddo the ticket scalper. Eddo, the man on whom most of the high school depended for their concert tickets, had his own reason to celebrate in April. To Randy Eddo, fifteen, April could tolerate no holiday other than . . . Ritchie Blackmore's Birthday.

Who, the naive and leaderless might ask, is Ritchie Blackmore?

Randy Eddo liked it when someone asked that question. "Ritchie Blackmore," he said, "is the greatest proponent of pure, heavy rock music alive. He is the man to whom I dedicate my life."

Eddo had found a true hero in Ritchie Blackmore. Blackmore was one of the first English guitarists to begin playing loud hard rock guitar in the late sixties, when Randy was still in the crib. Blackmore went on to form one of the most popular heavy-metal groups of all time, Deep Purple, before finally leaving the band in a fit of rage over the group's commercial successes. He went on to form another, less accessible heavy-metal band, Eddo's favorite, Rainbow.

Eddo had gone to the library and found every old interview with Blackmore he could. He knew every story of every time Blackmore smashed a camera, or threw a steak across a restaurant, or told an interviewer he could "cut any guitarist alive." In making reservations at restaurants, Eddo used the name Blackmore. He had even petitioned Ridgemont High to officially recognize Blackmore's birthday, April fifteenth, if only by playing his music during the two lunch periods.

Randy Eddo's request was denied. So it was that every April fifteenth, Randy stayed home and celebrated Blackmore's birthday *his* way.

At 8:00 on the morning of Blackmore's birthday, Randy Eddo walked through the living room and threw open the imitation oak doors of his family's Magnavox stereo. Then he began playing, one by one, and in chronological order, every record and bootleg record Ritchie Blackmore had ever made or had a hand in.

This year was Randy's second annual observance, and he began as tradition dictated, with the *Screaming Lord Sutch* album. Blackmore, Eddo pointed out, was only sixteen when he performed his first recorded solo on that record.

Eddo's parents had grudgingly decided to go along with the celebration of Ritchie Blackmore's birthday. They simply asked Randy to keep it as low as possible, for the elderly neighbors next door, and take messages if anyone called. Randy himself did no ticket business on this day.

Mr. and Mrs. Eddo would arrive home from work at six in the evening, and Randy would just be getting into the *great* stuff: "Woman from Tokyo" and the *Made in Japan* live album with all those excellent five-minute screams from when Ian Gillan was still in the group.

"Randy!" his mother shouted. "Can't you *go* anywhere?"

"No," said Randy Eddo. "Suffer."

It took about twelve hours total, but on the evening of Ritchie Blackmore's birthday Randy Eddo could always look back on a fulfilling and wonderful experience.

Cadavers

"Shock," lectured Mr. Vargas, "represents your greatest threat to life. Blood collects in the abdominal cavity. A person becomes pale, cold, clammy to touch. Taken to its extreme, death occurs. . . ."

Everyone knew what was coming up in May. Mr. Vargas's biology class had gone through most of the textbook. By process of elimination there wasn't much left on the class schedule. Except . . .

"Now as you know, we'll be taking a field trip to University Hospital before the end of the year. I've set the date for three weeks from today. I want you all here on that day because it is a mandatory attend for this class, and your grade. We'll be able to see every facet of the hospital's life—from birth to death."

The next two-and-a-half weeks were a whirlwind of controversy. Some students were trumpeting the fact that their parents would write a note; others claimed that they would definitely be sick on that day. No way were they going to stick their hands into any cadaver. No way would they even be in the same *room* as a bunch of stiffs. Forget all the scientific details you'd learned all year—doesn't that stuff *rub off?*

But when the day arrived, there was near-total attendance for Mr. Vargas's famed and feared University Hospital field trip. The bus took off after third period. It was an eight-block ride.

The class was met by two representatives of the hospital. The first step of the tour took the students to the floor-one lab, where they were given a complete explanation of all the testing facilities. *When is this going to happen?* The second-floor mental ward was fascinating. They saw the emergency room, an iron lung, a cancer ward . . . *but when was it going to happen?*

"Now," said one of the guides. "I'll leave you with Dr. Albert for your last stop today."

The class was taken to the basement of University Hospital, to the bottom floor, attainable only through a second elevator. The class descended in three shifts.

"What you are about to see," said Dr. Albert, "is the human body in a state of transition. These are the preserved bodies of four deceased individuals—mostly derelicts—who died some two or three days ago. They have willed their bodies to our scientific pursuits, and to University Hospital in particular. So follow me, if you will . . ."

Dr. Albert, along with Mr. Vargas, led the class through the steel doors of the refrigeration room. The bodies were stretched out on metal trays, each covered with a single starched white sheet. Dr. Albert approached one of the cadavers and yanked the sheet down to its waist.

It was the orange crumbling body of an old man. His skin looked as if it might rub off if touched.

"Now, Allen here died of a bad liver a few days ago . . ."

"What can you do with the cadavers?" a student asked.

"We perform operations," said Dr. Albert. "Delicate operations that shouldn't be practiced on a live patient. We study the causes of death . . . it's really not a morbid thing. I believe

Mr. Vargas keeps formaldehyde animals in his room at Ridgemont High . . ."

Vargas nodded and stepped up to Allen.

"Now class," he said, "this is a wonderful opportunity that Dr. Albert provides us with. Let's not cheapen it in any way. This is an opportunity to study and identify actual parts of the human body, which we've been studying from textbooks all year long."

You could tell Vargas was itching to get his hands on those cadavers.

"Now, Steve . . . can you identify the spleen on old Allen here?"

Vargas peeled open Allen's chest cavity. Several girls gasped.

"That blue thing right in there," said Shasta.

"Right!"

"Claudia? Where is the human heart located?"

"I don't see it."

"Right!" Vargas was loving it. "It's covered by lung tissue! But, contrary to where we place our hands during the Pledge of Allegiance, the human heart *is* centrally located and . . ." Vargas pulled out a purplish blue muscle and hefted it in his hand.

"This," he said, "is the human heart."

Steve Shasta immediately turned to three friends. "You each owe me five bucks!"

Linda Barrett ran out of the room, holding her mouth. The rest remained through the entire episode, while Mr. Vargas displayed almost all the human body organs. Afterward, everyone boarded the bus for a quiet and reflective ride home. They returned to school like war heroes.

"What was it like in there?" asked one of the others. Their eyes were full of wonder and fear.

"It was hairy in there," said Shasta on lunch court. "Some of us didn't make it."

The Mist-Blue Newport II

The cars, all washed shiny new, swished slowly past the entrance and into the parking lot. There were Ridgemont students everywhere, all headed for the red carpet leading into the Twentieth Annual Ridgemont High School Senior Prom.

This year the prom was being held at the Sheraton Airport Inn, in the "world famous" Lagoon Room. There was nothing about the location and motif that suggested a lagoon, but the ballroom did have all the essentials of a prom site. There was a splendid view of the city, a bandstand, room for the hors d'oeuvres table, and plenty of space for sitting and dancing. Best of all, the Lagoon Room had cork walls.

It happened to be a Ridgemont tradition to line the walls of the prom site with silver hearts. Each heart bore the names of a prom couple. The idea was to spend your first half hour working your way around the room, squinting at the names and reminiscing with any kids or teachers you met along the way, no matter how well you knew them.

If ever it was a time to drop the hierarchy of the high school lunch court, this was it. The conversations between even the most bitter enemies were the equivalent of verbal yearbook signatures on prom night.

"Oh, Rachel, I know we haven't gotten along much all year. And I stole your boyfriend and badmouthed you all year long, but—I JUST LOVE YOUR DRESS!"

Next, a student was expected to make a pass by the table of Principal Gray and his wife, Nancy. They were seated by the hors d'oeuvres, bright and attentive. Principal Gray looked everyone in the eye as if he knew them. The rumor was that he had studied last year's annual.

"Well hello, *Charles*, how's your science work? Have you

met my wife, Nancy? *Charles* was an excellent basketball player for us . . ."

And a student was expected to toss the bull around a little with the Grays.

"I had a great year, Mr. Gray. I'll always remember the great times and my friends here at RHS."

Most of the faculty chaperones sat together at other tables. On prom night there wasn't a whole lot for them to do. It wasn't like the usual Friday-night dance *orgies*, as they called them. On those nights a chaperone really got to use his flashlight. On one Friday night he might snag thirty groping couples in and under the bleachers.

The senior prom was classier than that. Kids in suits and gowns felt a responsibility to give up the fighting and groping for this night. *This thing cost me forty-nine bucks to rent!*

For most girls the question of what to wear on prom night was a matter that required some thought. To make her own or buy one? And if she bought it, God forbid there was another girl with the same one . . .

For the boys there was only one avenue to travel. A tux. And you got it at Regis. Regis Formalwear carried four basic prom-class tuxedos. The style a kid picked was a statement in itself:

The Black (or Brown) Regency—A standard choice, it was single-breasted and simply cut. Many chose the Regency, and who could say it wasn't a fine conservative suit.

Or Camel Camelot—A brown-and-black velvet affair, as it was called in the Regis brochure, this outfit meant the difference between "arriving and *making an impression.*"

For the more daring, the Yellow Seville—A colorful, Gatsbyesque piece, the Yellow Seville was a "classic vision in soft yellow, with the added comfort of a suppressed waist."

They were impressive offerings for any prom goer. Impressive, but none of the aforementioned tuxes could match the fourth and final Regis selection: There was nothing that matched the Mist-Blue Newport II.

The Mist-Blue Newport II was an awesome tux. It was turquoise, with black lapels like the fins on a '56 Cadillac. They flapped as its wearer walked. The Mist-Blue Newport II cost a little extra, but it was also equipped with a Charleston tailcoat and a ruffled front—the better to go along with the half-size top hat that came with it.

Steve Shasta entered the Ridgemont prom at 8:30 in a Mist-Blue Newport II. He stood briefly in the doorway of the Lagoon Room. Then he turned to his date, Laurie Beckman.

"Come," said Shasta, "let us find our silver heart."

Brad Hamilton arrived a few minutes later with his date, Jody, a junior he'd met two weeks before. Like many prom couples his was a match bred out of necessity. Both shared friends, both wanted to go to the prom, and neither had the right date. They both looked grittily determined to have a good time.

There were many, of course, whose personalities prevented them from attending such an undeniably sosh school event like The Prom. There were still others who had at first dismissed the prom as "useless tradition." Then, faced with an evening home alone, they began madly looking for a date in the last few days. William Desmond, the wrestler-columnist was such a case. He'd been slamming the prom like crazy, then in the last week had asked four girls to go with him. He discovered an odd phenomenon.

"Do you have plans for the prom?" he'd ask.

"Well . . . no."

"*All right!* You're going with me!"

And here was the weird part for Desmond.

"But I can't go with you, William."

"Why?"

"*Because.*"

"Why? I know a couple of people on the prom committee and everything. They'll take care of us. I know the band . . ."

"I can't, William, because *someone* else wants you to ask her."

"Who?"

"I can't tell you who. It wouldn't be right."

"Who!" Desmond would start to get excited. "You've got to tell me!"

"I can't! I promised!" And the girl would scurry off.

Desmond thought about it. It was killing him. He ended

206

up going with no one and spending another evening at the mall. He ran into Jeff Spicoli at Rock City.

"Why aren't you at the prom, Desmond?" asked Spicoli.

"I *hate* the fuckin' prom," said Desmond.

"Why?"

"I'll tell you *why*. Because you have to be a *certain way*. How can I explain it? They want you to be a certain way or they don't accept you in high school. I'd like to get hold of the person who started all this prom and letter jacket and A.S.B. shit and . . ." Desmond crumpled a paper cup sitting on top of Space Invaders. "And KICK HIS ASS."

"You got it," said Spicoli.

Ridgemont High had worked up to its Twentieth Annual Senior Prom with . . . well, a guy like A.S.B. President Kenneth Quan would have to call it *spirit*. There was quite a turnout tonight.

The only trouble was, like Brad and Jody, no one seemed to be having "the time of their lives." Perhaps it came down to the "Hello Richard" thing. When couples began pairing off at the beginning of the year, it seemed that one of the first things said in the heat of passion was, "We'll do this and this and this and then, at the end of the year, we'll go to the *prom* together!"

But during the year they broke up, and when prom time came they reluctantly called each other.

"Hello, Richard. It's *Brenda*."

"I know it's you, Brenda. I recognize your voice. How's it going?"

"Oh, pretty good. I'm getting a little nervous about going to college. I'll be okay. It's just the end-of-the-year blues." Translation: *I didn't get asked to the prom.*

"Yeah. Things are the same with me." *Me neither.*

"Richard, I was driving around the other day, and I heard 'Beast of Burden,' and . . . God, I thought of us! I got a little sad."

"Yeah, me too."

"You know what?"

"What, Brenda?"

"Richard, we should go to the prom together. Wouldn't that surprise a few people!"

And on prom night, just as they were getting through with that expensive steak and lobster dinner, sitting there in tails and gown, all the old irritations would return.

Linda Barrett and Doug Stallworth arrived. It was another obligation, of course. They were fighting when they walked in. Then they had not been able to find their silver heart. By the time they sat down at a table they weren't speaking.

"What took you guys so long?"

"*Men* drivers," said Linda.

They were all sitting at the same table—Linda and Doug, Brad and Jody, Steve and Laurie—all saying nothing. They had come together for the memories. Now they just wished they could get out of there and on to the after-prom parties.

Tina Dellacorte came slithering up to the silent table.

"Hi you *guys!*"

"Tina," said Shasta. "How are you doing?"

"Really *gude*," she said.

"What are you going to do this summer?"

"Stick around!" said Tina. "Go to Mammoth! I don't know!"

"Fantastic."

"Well," said Tina Dellacorte. "S'ya later." She left the table.

"I see her on a desert island," said Shasta. "She's been shipwrecked for two months. The natives have raped her like crazy. A boat comes to pick her up. 'Are you okay?' they say. 'How are you?' And Tina Dellacorte smiles real big and goes, 'REALLY GUDE!' "

Silence at the table. The prom dates looked around restlessly at the other couples.

"Well," said Shasta, "there's always Grad Nite."

Later, in the bathroom, two seniors were discussing Grad Nite in front of the mirror. Grad Nite, it seemed, was the special consolation prize for seniors with post-prom depression. Sponsored by Disneyland for graduating high school students

208

in the western United States, Grad Nite was the one night a year the Magic Kingdom opened its doors only to juniors and seniors. For a $20 entry ticket, you and a date had the run of Disneyland from the usually closed hours of 10 P.M. to 5 A.M. Grad Nite was an experience often spoken about in hushed tones.

"Girls roam in *packs* at Grad Nite," said one senior before the Lagoon Room mirror.

"It's gonna be awesome," said the other girl. "I only came to the prom 'cause everyone makes such a big deal about it."

At midnight, the lead singer of Takoma read aloud the winner of Prom King and Queen voting.

"KENNETH QUAN AND CINDY CARR!"

Gasp. Hands to face again. Cindy Carr, this time in all black, burst into tears and stumbled to the front of the hall in near hysterics. Kenneth Quan accepted back pats from friends and then joined Cindy at the bandstand. A tiara was placed on her head; he was given a crown. Gregg Adams sat resolute at his own table.

"Hey, man," he told his friends, "be *happy* for her."

Takoma played "Three Times a Lady" one more time, followed with a few more Cheap Trick and Van Halen songs, and finished up with "Kashmir" at 12:30.

"Thanks for having us! Good night and drive carefully!"

The Ridgemont couples then spread out in every direction for the second stage of prom night. It was still very early by prom standards. Most of the kids would be roaring all night long, and by 12:50 there was nobody in the Lagoon Room—the site of unimaginable thrills and tears—except for a couple of janitors cleaning up.

The After-Prom

It was an uphill battle all the way, but Evelyn and Frank Hamilton had finally given in on this one. For Brad. The kids wanted to have a prom party at the house, and the Hamiltons agreed to stay in their upstairs bedroom.

Brad had thought ahead to spike the pool with Wisk, and by the time kids started arriving at one o'clock, the whole pool was one big steaming bubble bath. It turned out to be one of the hottest after-prom parties. Everyone was there. Even Lisa was there, with her new boyfriend, David Leach.

There were some—the shy ones—who stayed in the kitchen. *I'm watching the pizza. I don't want to go swimming.* But most went for it on prom night. They stripped out of their carefully chosen gowns and Regis Sevilles and Regencies. Even Shasta took off his exalted Mist-Blue Newport II. Everyone put on bathing suits and dove in.

Graduation time brought in nameless faces from all over. Jerome Barrett, Linda's brain brother, arrived from USC, chain-smoking joints. Then there was Gloria, Linda's best girlfriend from grade school. She'd come in from Chicago for a few days. And there were the usual types whom you only saw at parties.

Mike Damone and Mark Ratner were also at Brad's after-prom party. They hadn't been speaking since last April, but tonight . . . hell.

"Hey, Rat," said Mike. "I'm really sorry about what happened. I know I shouldn't have done that to a buddy. I'm really sorry."

"I understand," said The Rat. "You can't help it. You're just lewd, crude, rude, and obnoxious."

They laughed, shook hands.

Eventually the twenty kids crammed into the Hamilton Jacuzzi. Then Brad, who had finally convinced his date to shed down to her bikini, reached into a bush and withdrew two bottles of rum from Mesa De Oro Liquor.

"ALLRIIIIIIIIIIGHT!"

The first bottle was passed around the Jacuzzi, and before long the glow of teenage drunkenness—however faked or real—came over the cramped little Jacuzzi party.

Damone felt something. Someone had grabbed his dick! He scanned the faces in the Jacuzzi. It wasn't Stacy! Not only wouldn't she do that to Damone, not again, but she was in the kitchen watching the pizza.

Who was it?

"I'm going under," said Damone. He feigned a drowning man. "I'm dying . . . *blub.*"

He slipped underwater, a daring move in the overcrowded Jacuzzi, but he was looking for clues underneath the bubbly water. Who had grabbed his dick? No clues.

He popped back up again. "I'm alive!"

Someone grabbed his dick again.

Later everyone retired to the living room for coffee and making out to a soundless TV. Before long, Brad had passed out by the stairs, rum victim number one.

Damone had gone out by the pool to look at the night sky.

"Hi, Mike."

He turned around. It was Brad's date, Jody. She was still wet, hugging herself to keep from shivering.

"How are you?"

"Pretty good," said Jody. "Brad passed out by the stairs."

"I know."

She stood next to him, breathing softly and saying nothing in the way girls do, Damone knew, when they wanted you to kiss them. It was Jody! It had to be Jody he felt underwater!

He thought. She was great looking. Should he go for it? He sure wanted to.

"I'm going to go inside," said Damone. "And check on the pizza."

Later, the few that were still awake went to nearby Mt. Palmer to watch the sun rise. It never rose on that foggy morning, and nobody seemed to mind.

"You wait till *our* prom," Mike Damone told The Rat. "We'll have an even *better* time."

"Yeah. That was pretty nice of Brad to throw a party. He's probably going to have to clean it up himself."

"When he wakes up."

"Hey," said The Rat. "Let's go to 7-Eleven and get some coffee."

"Great idea," said Damone. "Let's take the Prickmobile."

Damone and The Rat rolled down the hill in Damone's scratch-marked car. It was that magical hour when the mist was still out and the sky was turning deep blue.

Lieutenant Flowers

It was a typical late May morning. The sun was shining. The sound of second-semester typists wafted across the lunch court. Jeff Spicoli was parked out in the Adult School parking lot smoking from his bong. He held a long hit in his mouth, then expelled it slowly, luxuriously, through the window of his blue Malibu.

The billow of smoke caught the eye of Lt. Larry Flowers, who was walking the halls nearby. *Pot.* He decided to investigate this matter, even if it was the Adult School lot. Even if Ridgemont High offered it up pretty much as a free zone. He was going to do something about it.

Lieutenant Flowers saw Spicoli lounging in the driver's seat of his car. He cut straight across the dirt lot.

Someone yelled Spicoli's name. There was something in the tone and urgency that made Jeff instinctively reach down to chuck the bong under his seat. Lieutenant Flowers saw the movement.

"FREEZE!" he shouted.

Flowers advanced rapidly on the car and arrived at the driver's window just as Spicoli had completed the action of flicking the glowing bong well under his seat.

Flowers reacted in a single motion. He pulled his pistol right out of the shoulder holster and jammed it through the crack at the top of the window. With the other hand he grabbed a handful of Spicoli's hair and pulled him up against the window.

"Whatthefuc . . ."

Flowers was cramming cold steel at his head.

"Just get out of the car," said Flowers with a smile. "*Move.*"

Flowers took him to the office and wrote him a referral. When Spicoli told his parents and friends the story, they decided to sue. And sue they did. A quarter-million dollars worth, against Ridgemont and against the Education Center.

Flowers came back from a motorcycle ride one morning two days later and found a gray school board envelope waiting on his doorstep.

"My life was in danger," was the way he explained it to the board's investigators. "That kid could have had a shotgun under that seat. I did what came naturally, what they taught me in Chicago."

"How many students have you seen with a shotgun in your years of education?" they had asked him.

"You only have to see one," said Lt. Flowers.

He was fired by the school board, banished from the California Educational System. He now works a late-shift security job at Knott's Berry Farm.

Aloha, Mr. Hand

It was nearly the end of the line. The school awards were about to be announced, mimeographed caps-and-gowns information had gone out to the seniors, along with Grad Nite tickets. The annuals were almost ready. Jeff Spicoli was counting the hours.

Since Spicoli was a sophomore, an underclassman, there weren't many graduation functions he could attend. Tonight was one of the few, and he wasn't about to miss it. It was the Ditch Day party, the evening blow-out of the June day that underclassmen secretly selected toward the end of the year to ditch en masse. Spicoli hadn't been at school all day, and now he was just about ready to leave the house for the party out in Laguna . He hadn't eaten all day. He wanted the full effect of the special hallucinogenic mushrooms he'd procured just for the poor man's Grad Nite—Ditch Night.

Spicoli had taken just a little bit of one mushroom, just to check the potency. He could feel it coming on now as he sat in his room, surrounded by his harem of naked women and surf posters. It was just a slight buzz, like a few hits off the bong. Spicoli knew they were good mushrooms. But if he didn't leave soon, he might be too high to drive before he reached the party. One had to *craft* his buzz, Spicoli was fond of saying.

Downstairs, the doorbell rang. There was an unusual commotion in the living room.

"Who is it, Mom?"

"You've got company, Jeffrey! He's coming up the stairs right now. I can't stop him!"

There was a brief knock at the door.

"Come in."

The door opened and Jeff Spicoli stood in stoned shock. There before him was The Man.

"Mr. . . . Mr. Hand."

"That's right, Jeff. Mind if I come in? Thank you, Mr. and Mrs. Spicoli," Hand called back down the stairs. He took off his suit jacket and laid it on the chair. "Were you going somewhere tonight, Jeff?"

"Ditch Night! I've gotta go to Ditch Night!"

"I'm afraid we've got some things to discuss, Jeff."

There were some things you just didn't see very often, Spicoli was thinking. You didn't see black surfers, for example. And you didn't see Baja Riders for under twenty dollars a pair. And you SURE didn't see Mr. Fucking Hand sitting in your *room*.

"Did I do something, Mr. Hand?"

Hand opened his briefcase and began taking out lecture notes. He laid them out for himself on Spicoli's desk. "Are you going to be sitting there?"

"I don't know. I guess so."

"Fine. You sit right there on your bed. I'll use the chair here." Mr. Hand stopped to stare down last month's Penthouse Pet. "Tonight is a special night, Jeff. As I explained to your parents just a moment ago, and to you many times since the very beginning of the year, I don't like to spend my time waiting for students in detention. I'd rather be preparing the lesson.

"According to my calculations, Mr. Spicoli, you wasted a total of eight hours of my time this year. And rest assured that is a kind estimate.

"But now, Spicoli, comes a rare moment for me. Now I have the unique pleasure of squaring our accounts. Tonight, you and I are going to talk in great detail about the U.S. Foreign Policy in the 60's . . . now if you can turn to Chapter Forty-Seven of *Land of Truth and Liberty* . . ."

"Would you like an iced tea, Mr. Hand?" Mrs. Spicoli called through the door.

Jeff was still orienting himself to what was happening. Was he too high? Was this real? He was not going to Ditch

215

Night. That was it. He was going to stay in his room tonight with Mr. Hand . . . and talk about Foreign Policy.

"I'd love some iced tea," said Mr. Hand. "Whenever you get the time . . ."

Now Mr. Hand had said they'd be there all night, but at 7:45 he wound up with the Vietnam War and started packing his briefcase.

"Is that it?"

"I think I've made my point with you, Jeff."

"You mean I can go to Ditch Night after all?"

"I don't care what you do with your time, Mr. Spicoli."

Spicoli jumped up and reached to shake Hand's hand.

"Hey, Mr. Hand," said Spicoli. "Can I ask you a question?"

"What's that?"

"Do you have a guy like me every year? A guy to . . . I don't know, make a show of. Teach the other kids lessons and stuff?"

Hand finished packing and looked at the surfer who'd hounded him all year long. "Well," he said, "why don't you come back next year and find out?"

"No way," said Spicoli. "I'm not going to be like those guys who come back and hang around lunch court. When I graduate, I'm *outta* here."

"*If* you graduate."

Spicoli was taken aback. *Not graduating?* No thumbing up the Coast, meeting ladies and moving to Hawaii for the dyno lobster season? More school? "Not graduating?" he said.

Hand broke into the nearest thing approximating a grin, for him. It wasn't much, of course, but it was noticeable to Jeff. His lips crinkled at the ends. That was plenty for Hand.

"Don't worry, Spicoli," said Hand. "You'll probably squeak by."

"All right!"

"Aloha, Spicoli."

"Aloha, Mr. Hand."

Mr. Hand descended the stairway of the Spicoli home, went out the door, and on to his car, which he had parked just around the corner—*always use the element of surprise.* Hand knew one day next year he would look to that green metal door and it would be Spicoli standing there. He'd act like he had a million other things to do, and then he'd probably stay all day. All his boys came back sooner or later.

Hand drove back to his small apartment in Richards Bay to turn on his television and catch the evening's "Five-O" rerun.

A P.R. Problem

Ever since the Lt. Flowers gun incident, Ridgemont High had been all over the front of the local section. Then, if that wasn't bad enough, there had been an accident on the way to a junior varsity baseball game. Two vans, both driven by students, were headed out to the last game of the year when one of the vehicles "just flipped over." None of the students would explain how the accident happened, but three sets of parents were now suing the school.

Mr. Gray, like most principals, took the bad publicity personally. Of course he had an ego. Ridgemont High was *his* school. Egg was dripping from *his* face. Principal William Gray had what was called in his Media Guide a "P.R. problem."

At a time when most other principals were concerned with the details of their own summer vacations, Gray was on the phones. Talking to the board, talking to lawyers, and talking to goddamn parents and reporters. There had even been a picture of him looking haggard in his own school newspaper, the *Reader*, with the caption, "Gray reviews mishaps."

A P.R. problem.

Principal Gray's first move was to take Del Taco, the nearest and most popular fast-food stand for ditchers, by force.

On a lazy afternoon toward the end of school, as students crunched into third-period tacos, the doors were suddenly clamped shut from the outside.

Two county security officers swept in and rounded up twenty-two ditchers. Trouble was, as Gray would soon learn, all but two went to Paul Revere Junior High School.

Even though Gray made a *big deal* about busting the two Ridgemont High ditchers, it was a well-known fact—Principal Gray, as the man himself might say, was P.O.'ed.

The buxom message girl from the front office came swinging into English Literature with a blue slip, a slip that meant you had a personal meeting with the principal at that very moment.

She delivered the slip to the teacher with a flourish.

"Mark Ratner?"

The Rat walked up to the front, got the slip, and headed out the door. Nerves of steel. Now Ratner couldn't imagine what Gray would want with him, what this was all about. He trudged down the hall. Maybe they wanted him to give a speech! Or better yet—of *course*—he was probably going to get the Debate Award. Who else would they give that to? Of course! This was what they did for the award winners. They let Principal Gray slip you the news.

Ratner was ushered into the principal's office.

"Mr. Ratner?"

"Yes, sir. Nice to see you, sir."

"This is the new annual."

"Oh, really?"

"Yes," said Mr. Gray, "it is."

"It looks excellent, sir. That's pretty great. That you get them this early, sir."

Definitely the Debate Award.

"Yes. We do get them early. It's a very nice annual. I like it very much this year."

Ratner nodded his head. Gray sure was acting strange. "Are you sure you wanted to talk to me, sir? I didn't work on the annual staff or anything . . . even though I would have *liked* to. I was pretty busy with Debate."

218

"I don't believe I'm mistaken," Gray said coldly.

Gray then opened the annual on his desk and flipped through it carefully, so as not to break its new binding. Finally he reached a two-page picture and spun it around to face The Rat. The title of the school group shot was What a Way to Go!

"Mr. Ratner, are you aware that you are posed obscenely in this year's *Rapier?*"

The Rat began to get a deep acidic feeling that started in his groin and worked its way up into the very pit of his stomach. He was dizzy.

It was the school group picture, taken last October by Arthur Chubb.

"We have information that this is you, Mr. Ratner."

Circled at the far right corner of the group picture was Ratner, his ass stuck out in the air. They'd printed it all right. No airbrushing for this year's *Rapier!*

The Rat's eyes immediately raced to the opposite side of the shot. There was Damone, smiling serenely in an Arrow sport shirt. His pants were on. His hands were in his pockets.

"It's me." The Rat's teeth started to chatter as he confessed. "It was supposed to be a gag . . ."

An icy stare.

"I was a ham in my time, Mr. Ratner. It's just that *parents* pay for these things and, once in a while, they like to read through their child's annual. And when they see your *butt,* they might be a little *curious.* They might get a little P.O.'ed. And you know what? This phone on my desk *rings.* Quite a bit. And if they were to see this picture in those 1,500 copies sitting in the gymnasium, that phone *would ring.* A lot."

"Are you going to expel me?"

"Well," said Gray. "What I'm going to do is tell you a little secret, Mr. Ratner. A secret between you and me."

"What is that, sir?"

"Those parents aren't going to see your butt this year. Do you know why?"

"Why, sir?"

"Because we have arranged for you to spend this weekend in the school gym. And you will be doing the following. With-

out soiling or breaking the binding on any of these books—
which is to say, VERY CAREFULLY—you will be erasing
your posterior from every one of our new *Rapier*. As you can
see, the bond *is* erasable."

He demonstrated with the tip of a pencil.

"Thank you, Mr. Gray."

"You will supply your own erasers. And, oh yes, Mr.
Ratner. Don't forget to sweep up after yourself. I don't want
eraser shavings all over the floor."

The Rat drifted out of the office. Stunned. A whole weekend of erasing.

"We have information," my ass. The Rat hadn't told anybody *anything*. It could only have come from Damone.

Damone. The Mouth. Mr. All Talk. The Rat walked
straight over to Youth and Law class, where he knew Damone
would be. The Rat walked straight into the room and pulled
Damone out of his seat. Outside the door The Rat began the
first step of the high school prefight ritual. He threw his books
down and beckoned to Damone. Even though Damone was
stockier and in much better shape, Ratner went ahead and
spoke the unretractable words.

"Well, Damone," he said, "COME ON."

"What's going on, Rat? What are you doing? Why do I
want to fight you?"

"Mr. GRAY just called me in to show me the new *Calu-
met*, which features my *ass* hanging out. You fuckin' lied to
me, Damone. You told me to play that joke on Chubb, and
you told me it would be airbrushed. But it wasn't, you *asshole*
. . . SO COME ON."

"I don't want to fight you," said Damone. "No way."

"COME ON." Ratner was as pissed as Damone had ever
seen him. "I've got to spend the weekend erasing all the new
annuals, thanks to you . . ."

"Is *that* all," said Damone. "That'll be a *blast*. We'll do it
this weekend."

Ratner slowly let his hands down. "You'll help?"

"No sweat," said Damone. "It'll be great."

• • •

It was kind of funny, really. A good story for the grand-children, The Rat figured. At the end of the Erasing Ass Weekend, as it would come to be called, Principal Gray had been so proud of the job The Rat and Damone did, that he rewarded them both with the right to go to Grad Nite. Everything, it seemed, was going their way.

The Exer-Gro Plus

The Rat had developed the habit of coming home and checking the mail before anyone else. It was just a little routine he'd gotten into six weeks, to the day, after he'd ordered the Exer-Gro Plus back in March. The Rat knew all the bills by heart, all the junk mail. By now he was sure they'd mailed it to someone else.

On this day toward the end of the year, The Rat walked back to his house after school. He said hello to the kids next door who were always building something in the garage, and casually flipped open the mailbox.

It was a small square package. He knew the instant he saw it what it was. This was it, just in time for Grad Nite, too. The Exer-Gro Plus.

The Rat set down his books, went to the bathroom, did everything he possibly could do to delay the pleasure of opening his package. He wasn't sure what it would be. Perhaps some kind of stretching device, an exercise machine. Whatever, he just hoped it didn't take too long.

Now, to use a penknife or just rip it open? Of course. Rip that thing open. The Rat tore into it, separated the newspaper wrapping that had been used to pack it, and there it sat. The Exer-Gro Plus.

It was a rubber dickhead.

No special formula, no exercise machine, no nothing. Just a rubber dickhead. Phony as hell.

There was a letter with it:

CONGRATULATIONS ON RECEIVING YOUR NEW EXER-GRO PLUS, THE EVER NEWEST IN OUR LINE OF SEXUAL-ENHANCEMENT ITEMS. NOW YOU CAN THRILL AND IMPRESS WOMEN EVERY-WHERE BY WEARING THE EXER-GRO PLUS EVERYWHERE YOU GO, IN ANYTHING YOU DO. LIFELIKE, MADE OF QUALITY NON-TOXIC MATERIALS, THE EXER-GRO PLUS IS GUARANTEED TO LENGTHEN THE DESIRABILITY OF ANY MAN BY AT LEAST THREE INCHES. GOOD LUCK IN YOUR NEW LIFE WITH THE EXER-GRO PLUS.

It was a three-inch-high nine-dollar rubber dickhead. The Rat couldn't believe it. He went back and reread the ad. There was nothing that promised it would be anything else. But it was still a rip-off! And it wasn't like he could write the Action Line about this one. Shit. Besides, it didn't even work. The Rat wore it into Safeway once, and it fell down his pantleg.

Grad Nite

 At the time he should have been leaving the house for Grad Nite, Mike Damone was still shirtless. He was in the bathroom checking himself out in the mirror.

By the time he finally arrived at Ridgemont, the five yellow buses parked along Luna Street were already filled with students.

"Aaaaaaaayyyyyy, Damone!" someone yelled. The Rat. "Glad you could make it. Where's your date?"

"Your mama couldn't make it."

The Rat laughed and continued talking to a girl sitting in the seat next to him.

"You didn't save me a seat!"

"The bus filled up." The Rat shrugged. "There should be a seat somewhere. Ask Mrs. Franks."

Damone straightened his tie, smoothed his three-piece suit, and approached Mrs. Franks, PTA liaison for Grad Nite. She was walking in tight little circles on the sidewalk next to bus 1.

"Mrs. Franks," Damone asked politely. "Where's my seat?"

"There's an extra seat on bus 5," she said briskly. She was lost in thought.

Leslie Franks was once president of the PTA. Her kids had long since grown up and moved (as far away as possible, no doubt), but Mrs. Franks still came back once a year to take the helm at Grad Nite. It was like Jerry Lewis and Muscular Dystrophy, Leslie Franks and Grad Nite. She took it seriously, and something was seriously wrong right now.

"Go try bus 5." She shooed Damone away.

But there was no seat on bus 5. So Mike checked all the other buses. They, too, were filled.

"Mrs. Franks, I hate to bother you again. But I can't find a seat."

"Did you check the other buses, young man?"

"Yes."

"Joseph?" She called out. "Where is Joseph Burke? Please help this boy find a seat! Count students if you have to."

Joseph Burke, ever the subservient A.S.B. advisor when it came to Mrs. Frank's imperious presence on Grad Nite, did so. He counted all the students until they had once again come back to bus 5. Burke counted, and sure enough . . .

"Go ahead," said Burke. "There's an extra seat in there somewhere."

And while The Rat sat in bus 3—The Cool Bus—talking to some girl, Mike was walking down the aisle of bus 5. They looked like ex-convicts on bus 5. He was looking for a seat, anything resembling a seat.

The last available seat on bus 5 was next to a familiar face—Charles Jefferson. He was back for Grad Nite.

"Is this seat taken?"

Jefferson ignored Damone.

"Hey, Charles, is this seat taken?"

After a time, Charles Jefferson looked down at his own muscular legs, which were bowed out to take up the entire spare seat. He moved one of his legs slightly, an indication that Damone could have the corner. He took it.

Meanwhile, Vice-Principal Ray Connors was visiting each bus before it took off. He reached bus 5 and stood in the stairwell.

"Can I have your attention," he said. "Can I have your attention way in the back?" He waited for quiet. "All right, *people*. We're going to be leaving in another minute. I just want to remind you that we are from Ridgemont High School. We've been going to Disneyland for ten years, and the next class would like to go, too. We've never had any real trouble with Ridgemont students . . . and we've always been real proud of that. So let's continue with the program, and we hope you all have a real good time. We'll see you here next week."

And there was thunderous applause, but none of the buses began their journey just yet.

Outside, still pacing the sidewalk, Mrs. Leslie Franks was muttering to herself. The crisis was now obvious—the driver of bus 5 had not arrived.

And then . . . a figure appeared on the horizon.

"Look. Look." Mrs. Franks sighed heavily. "Oh, thank Jesus."

The driver held a sleeping bag across her chest and walked toward the Ridgemont buses. From the distance she looked like a sumo wrestler.

She was a professional bus driver, and her name was Miss Navarro. She greeted Mrs. Franks, PTA liaison to Grad Nite, like this: "Ever year I say no more Grad Nite. And ever yet I end up doin' it again. All I ask is that you don't wake me 'fore five. 'Cause I sleep right there on the aisle. *Alrighty?*" And with that, Miss Navarro instinctively hopped behind the wheel of Big Number Five and gunned her up.

It was just past eight. Time to get this caravan on the road. The five yellow buses lumbered onto the freeway for the two-and-a-half-hour trip down the coast to Anaheim, California, home of Disneyland. It was another Ridgemont ritual, like salmon swimming upstream. Grad Nite. Bad sex, troubled relationships, grades, hassles at work—they all went out the window for Grad Nite. Time out for adolescence!

For twenty bucks, a junior or senior and date had the complete run of Disneyland from 10 P.M. to 5 A.M. All the Magic Kingdom asked in return was that the Grad Nite students follow two simple rules: First, boys were to wear a suit and tie; girls, a formal gown. Ties were to be worn at all times. (They probably figured the last thing any kid in a three-piece suit wanted to do was raise hell and ruin the suit.) Plus, as Disneyland officials stated in the rule sheet that came with a Grad Nite ticket, any display of school colors or clothing would "suggest rivalries . . . and would be entirely unacceptable."

The second rule, for which Disneyland heaped on the special security every Grad Nite, was no alcoholic beverages or drugs.

There were horror stories, told by friends of friends, about that second rule. Rex Huffman's older brother, Mark, who was busted at Grad Nite several years back, had a tale to tell. Mark had smuggled five joints of marijuana into Disneyland in his sock and felt good enough about it to head straight for It's a Small, Small World and light one up.

Halfway through the ride, just as the boat compartment was entering the French sector, an attendant literally swung out of the Disneyland shadows on some kind of security rope and into the compartment. The attendant handcuffed Mark Huffman to the boat and later led him into a Disneyland holding tank for questioning.

And here was the best part—the holding tank, according to Mark, was *beneath* Disneyland. It looked just like the end of "*Get Smart.*"

Once in the holding tank Mark was given the sternest of lectures. What it boiled down to, according to Huffman, was, "You-Can-Fuck-Around-with-Anything-in-This-World-but-You-Can't-Fuck-Around-with-Disneyland." He was kept there until his parents made the three-hour drive from Temple City to take their pothead son away. On Grad Nite, there was nothing more humiliating.

Mike Damone was not about to be that stupid. The Disneyland holding tank was a fate for smalltimers. Damone had studied up; he was playing smart odds. Tonight he would operate like a fine piece of machinery.

It so happened that the Girls' Chorus, which featured the angelic-looking Laurie Beckman as one of its lead vocalists, had sung at the Disneyland Pavilion for Grandparents' Day two afternoons before. Damone had written everything out very carefully—the directions to the perfect hiding spot that Damone's brother, the Toyota salesman, had given him. And Mike had given Laurie the special knapsack containing a fifth of Jack Daniel's whiskey.

She had hidden it under an oath of secrecy, in exchange for Damone's telling her Steve Shasta secrets. (Damone shared the same P.E. class with Shasta.)

Sitting there on bus 5, bouncing up and down with the rumbling bus, Damone knew everything would be fine. Just fine.

"Can I SMOKE?" Charles Jefferson yelled suddenly, with a force unequaled since Malcom X's Lincoln Park speech in '62.

No one answered.

"I *said*, can I *SMOKE?*"

The bus 5 chaperone, someone's mother, stood up and shakily turned to face Charles Jefferson. "Uhhhh . . . I'm afraid smoking is not allowed on the school bus. I'm very sorry."

This suited Charles just fine, and he sat back with rare satisfaction as he knocked out a Kool and had a nice long smoke.

"Hey, *turn* on the radio," someone yelled.

Miss Navarro turned on the radio and found a rock station. She pushed the volume way beyond the point of distortion, to the level where the two small speakers rattled ominously from either side of the bus. Everyone sang along with a vengeance.

At the back of the bus Damone could hear everything that made a 150-foot school bus move down the highway. Every gear shift. Every grind and shudder. The noise lulled Charles Jefferson to sleep, and after a few minutes his leg snapped back open to push Damone even further into the aisle.

After a while Damone made his way to the front of the bus in search of a familiar face. He found a cluster of students gathered around a kid from Bio 3–4.

". . . and so Walt Disney had this friend in Japan," the guy was saying. "This scientist was experimenting with the freezing of cats. He would freeze them, seal the animals in a vacuum-insulated capsule of liquid nitrogen for a few weeks, and then thaw them out. And the cats would be alive!

"So later Walt Disney contracts cancer and knows he's going to die, right? What does he do? He calls up his friend in Japan and says, 'Freeze me!' "

"Total bullshit," said Damone.

Two girls glared at Mike, and that hurt.

"This is all in the medical journals, *Damone*. You're just showing your ignorance."

Damone went back to sit with Charles Jefferson. Lit-up drive-ins and neon restaurants whizzed by. By the end of hour one, most of the male students had dozed off. Somebody's girlfriend had switched the station to The Mellow Sound. The girls were all singing along to a Billy Joel ballad.

Something jarred Charles Jefferson awake.

"TURN THAT SHIT OFF!" he demanded.

Miss Navarro turned the station back to rock.

"The Skating Ramp!"

Heads began to pop up all around. This was an important landmark in the journey to Disneyland. Indeed, there were five times the normal amount of power lines strung along the freeway. All that juice could only be headed for one place.

There, in the distance was the snow-peaked cap of the Matterhorn Mountain and . . .

"The Orange Drive-In!"

The cheering drowned out the rock music. The buses rat-

tled onto a freeway knot that shot vehicles out onto Disneyland Drive. The first glimpse of Disneyland was a truly amazing sight.

Hundreds upon hundreds of yellow buses, all with black
lettering on the side, filled the Disneyland parking lot. The
parking lot was almost bigger than Disneyland itself. There
were buses for miles, for days, all converging into a mass of
yellow.

"DISNEYLAND!"

Bus 5 pulled up to a red parking-lot light alongside a bus
from Las Vegas. The kids all peered at each other. Some pried
their windows open and yelled.

"Meet me at Monsanto, midnight!" Damone blew some
brunette a kiss as the buses pulled away.

The five Ridgemont High buses pulled into their prede-
termined parking spaces. All the students were instructed to
stay put while Mrs. Franks visited each group for another lecture.

"You are to be back here at your bus in your *seat* at 5 A.M.
exactly."

"HOW ARE WE SUPPOSED TO FIND THESE
BUSES AGAIN?"

"You'll find these buses," said Mrs. Franks with weary
resignation, "right here in lanes 121–126. We're not leaving
this spot all night. If you get lost, go to the chaperones' lounge
on Main Street. But try to remember Lanes 121–126. Any
other questions?"

No more questions.

"Okay, please remember the rules, people," said the
Grand Dame of Grad Nite. "And have a great time. We'll see
you tomorrow morning at 5 A.M."

You had to respect a place like Disneyland.

At first not even his business-manager brother would loan
Walt Disney the money to build the park. It was too far-reach-
ing, too self-indulgent, they told him. Too much "the world's
biggest toy for the world's biggest boy." But in the afterglow of
Disney's successful *Snow White*, he went ahead and built it
anyway.

At five-eighths the size, Disneyland is a re-creation of all facets of life on earth—Disney-style. Every continent, every body of water, even the highest and lowest points in the world are all represented just as Walt wanted them.

Employees of the park all attend a special school to learn the Disney policy ("We get tired, never bored"). Even the anxiety of waiting in long lines is eased through the deception of a mazelike series of right-and-left turns that gave a guest (never the word *customer*) a sense of accomplishment. Disneyland today is a study in absolute, almost eerie perfection. Today, many years after Disney's death, the place is still run as if Walt Was Watching.

There was one last lecture, from Vice-Principal Ray Connors, as his students prepared to enter the Magic Kingdom.

"I don't want you getting into any trouble out there tonight. If there's any problem, you tell them to come find me, but I don't anticipate something like that happening. Have a good time, and we'll see you at five. And thanks for leaving your contraband behind."

William Desmond had a pint of tequila stuffed down his pants. Tim Copeland had two grams of cocaine in his wallet. Many others were armed with joints to smoke on the People Mover. Some had fruit injected with vodka.

There were five separate inspection points at which to enter Disneyland on Grad Nite. Three security guards were installed to pat kids down at every station. To the far right of them was the chaperones' entrance. There were no security guards posted there.

William Desmond began to panic. No way he'd get by with a pint stashed down his pants. No human penis was that big. He stood there at the entrance looking for a bathroom. A trash can. Anything. His only hope, he figured, was that his peach-fuzz beard made him appear older, above such shenanigans as booze smuggling. Desmond was right.

A teacher from another school tapped him on the shoulder. "You dropped your chaperone pass."

Desmond turned and saw he was being handed that most golden of Grad Nite items—an all-areas-access chaperone pass. It was fate!

"Thanks a lot," said Desmond. He grabbed the pass in a hurry and breezed through the special chaperone entrance with a mature nod to the agent.

Damone and The Rat passed through the other guard station and into the crush of kids who'd come from all over the western United States in their gowns and three-piece suits.

"It looks like a C&R Clothiers convention," said The Rat.

"Where do you want to go first?"

"Let's get our pictures taken."

"We can't get our pictures taken yet."

Disneyland provided a free old-fashioned sepia portrait taken by a booth photographer on Main Street as a Grad Nite service. "Every jock in the world is waiting in line to get a picture. We'll go later."

"Well," said The Rat. "Where do you want to go?"

"The bathroom. I think my tie's screwed up."

They pushed their way through the hordes of kids and larger-than-life Disneyland figures, toward the first bathroom they could find.

"I can't believe it," said Damone. "Grown up men dressed like Mickey Mouse. What a hell of a way to earn a buck."

In this, the first of 500 Disneyland bathrooms, there were twenty more guys just like The Rat and Damone, shamelessly and meticulously adjusting their hair and ties until just . . . *right*. Some even had hair spray and cologne.

"What's that?" asked Damone.

It was a strange grunting sound, getting closer. A moment later, the bathroom was filled with even more guys. This group did not speak with each other, but instead communicated through fingersnaps and signals. They, too, waited for the mirror, shaping their hair and making furious tongueless sounds.

"Hey *guys*," came the voice of William Desmond. "I got a chaperone pass, you guys!" Desmond entered the bathroom and was showing around the pint he'd smuggled in, and his pass.

The deaf-and-dumb contingent paused in admiration.

230

Then they communicated furiously among themselves again.

Desmond, the wrestler-columnist, ducked into a stall. Rat and Mike looked at each other and tore ass into the ocean of teenagers. They were the picture of sophistication in their three-piece suits. They were ready to experience the gamut of human emotions in the next seven hours. *Grad Nite.*

Inside Disneyland two things were instantly noticeable: Every male in sight wore a gray cardboard gangster hat. It was the only souvenir. Everyone had them. Second item was The Voice.

That mellifluous, folksy Voice. Most people probably thought it was Disney's own voice, that good old Wonderful-World-of-Disney chuckly voice. *Well, 'ol Sparky, you better git, boy!* It was as omnipresent as Mickey Mouse, as familiar as the voice of Time. You couldn't get away from The Voice of Disneyland.

Damone revealed the basic strategy for the evening. Disneyland, he said, was a matter of hitting the most popular attractions first, while everyone else was still wandering around. In the meantime, of course, there was the unspoken quest for girls.

Damone and The Rat chose Pirates of the Caribbean as their first ride. On the way, Damone told The Rat the story of the hidden Jack Daniel's on Tom Sawyer Island. It would be their secret of the night, for use only after they'd found . . . *babes.*

The Rat felt good. He hadn't even seen Stacy tonight. She'd gotten on another bus, and that was more than okay with The Rat. One thing he had to say, when he was through with a girl, he was *through with a girl.* He still hoped he wouldn't run into her, at least not until after he'd found another girl.

The Rat and Damone, armed with the secret of the Jack Daniel's, took a place in line for Pirates of the Caribbean. Directly in front of them in line were Stacy and Linda Barrett.

They turned around. "Oh, hi! Hello, Mike! Hello, Mark!"

"Hi, you guys!" It was all very gracious.

And then the voice from behind. "Hey hey hey. I was looking for you!"

William Desmond had found them again.

"Hi, William."

"What happened to you guys? I finished whizzing, and you guys were gone."

"Nice shirt," said Damone.

"Thanks," said Desmond.

"Was it hard getting the come stains off it?"

William ignored the joke. "Anybody have any *cocaine*?"

"Why don't you shut up, William."

Some other kids joined them in line. They were bright and rosy looking.

"Hi," one of them said. "Where are you from?"

"Ridgemont. It's outside Oceanside."

"Wow. We've heard of you! We're from Notre Dame in Riverside!"

"Isn't that a Catholic school?" asked Damone.

"Yes!"

"Tell me something," said Desmond, addressing one of the girls in the Notre Dame group. "Why did they call the Virgin Mary a virgin if she slept with Joseph?"

The girl cast a vicious look at Desmond. "Because it was the Immaculate Conception."

"Sorry," said Desmond. "It's not easy being the coolest guy in Disneyland."

"Some people get all the luck," said The Rat. "We get Desmond."

"Jesus," said Desmond. "Did you see that girl look at Desmond, Mark?"

"No."

William whipped around. "Where? Who?"

"Just this girl who looked at you."

"Where?"

"Right over there. SEE? Now she turned away 'cause we're looking at her. But William, if I were you, I'd go right over there and stand by the popcorn vendor so she'll walk right past you. I guarantee she'll say something to you."

William Desmond walked casually over to the popcorn vendor.

"Let's get out of here," said Damone, and he and The Rat ran in the opposite direction.

"Where do you want to go? On the bumper cars?"

"The bumper cars are pussy."

They decided on the Haunted House. On the way there, they spotted two girls in the gift shop. Damone wandered in nonchalantly, browsed a moment, then held up a leather fringed jacket to the two girls.

"Is this me?" he asked.

The girls laughed and ran out of the gift shop.

"It's a start," said The Rat. "It's a start."

The Haunted House was a fifteen-minute wait and—as Damone put it—for what? A bunch of kids—or was that sardines—were ushered into a tall-ceilinged room where the doors clanged shut, and, as soon as the room started to shrink and get really scary, here came The Voice again. How could The Voice scare you? You'd been hearing it since you were a baby.

"You're about to experience a disquieting metamorphosis. Is this Haunted Room *actually* shrinking. Or is it just your imagination?" The room filled with exaggerated sounds of horror from jaded teenagers.

"Or consider this dismaying observation. This chamber has no windows! And no doors! And your *challenge* is to find a way OUT."

The Voice let loose with another demented laugh that couldn't scare a child over two. The Rat turned to the attendant. "Who is that guy with The Voice?"

She smiled and shrugged.

The Rat and Mike exited the Haunted House and decided to scout Tom Sawyer Island, home of the hidden Jack Daniel's bottle.

"Let's get the booze," said Damone.

They arrived at the island to find a terrible surprise. Not only was Tom Sawyer Island closed for the evening, it had been partially converted into a stage for a disco dance band.

"FUCK." Damone collapsed on a bench. "I have to think about this."

"Looks like no booze for us tonight."

"Are you crazy? I had to pay for that and everything! Let's go ride the Monorail and figure this out."

The Disneyland Monorail System was built as an ultra-modern transport system in 1965. Meant to "rocket" guests around the perimeter of the Magic Kingdom, it stopped at every quarter of the park and even at Disneyland Hotel across the street.

The Rat and Damone fell into a couple of window seats.

"During our journey," The Voice began, air-transport style, "please see to it that you keep your head and arms inside the cabin at all times. You are riding aboard a Mark III system . . ."

At the next stop two dark-haired girls entered the compartment. One was wearing a red dress, the other a clingy blue gown. They cruised slowly by Damone and The Rat.

The boys offered them nothing less than The Attitude. Supreme indifference.

The girls sat behind them and started talking loudly.

"I couldn't believe our bus, could you? First the clutch went out . . . then the gear shift. We're luuuuuuu-cky to make it here alive."

"At least the radio was good," said the girl in red.

Then they sang a line from a song in unison, probably the last song they'd heard on the bus ride up: "Wa-tching the De-tect-tives. Don' they look *cute?*" Then the girls broke up laughing.

The Voice began again: "Welcome aboard the Disney-land Monorail. America's first daily operating monorail system. We ask only that you keep your head and arms inside the cabin at all times . . ."

The laughing died down, and the two girls realized there was a war of nerves going on. Neither of the couples wanted to let the moment pass, but neither wanted to make the first move.

Finally Red Dress spoke first. "You guys staying for the weekend?"

"Who, us?" asked Damone.

"Yeah."

"No, we're going back tonight."

"Where are you guys from?"

"Ridgemont. How about you?"

They answered in unison. "We're from Flag."

"What's Flag."

"Flagstaff, Arizona!" The boys nodded. "We're gonna be here till Monday 'cause our bus broke down. We're staying at the Wagon Train Motel on the other side of Disneyland."

"Yeah. We're all doubled up, and every third room is a chaperone."

The two girls looked at each other. "Wa-tching the De-tect-ives . . ." Then they broke up again.

The Rat and Mike nodded distractedly. More Attitude for these girls. Why, there was plenty of other things to do than try and get these girls to go back to their motel rooms with them.

The Voice: "We're now in a reentry pattern back into the Magic Kingdom. Destination? Tomorrowland. World of the Future . . ."

"Aren't we supposed to get out here?"

"We'll just tell 'em we got tired and fell asleep on the Monorail." The girl in the blue gown looked at The Rat. "Do you know anyone from Flag?"

"Just you," said The Rat. Damone looked at him approvingly.

They introduced themselves: Becky (blue dress) and Stephanie (red dress).

"Hey, you know what?" said Damone.

"What?"

"We have booze."

"You have *booze*?"

"Yes. I can't even tell you where it's hidden. But why don't we go there?"

"Wow!" said Becky.

"Let's go get the booze," said Stephanie. "And then we'll take it back to our motel!"

The Rat and Joe looked out the window. That would be acceptable.

The fifth of Jack Daniel's was hidden in a small crevice in the southwestern caves on Tom Sawyer Island. The compartment had been made five years earlier by Damone's brother, Art, on vacation no less. It had been a tradition for all of Art's friends to use the hiding place. Now it was Mike's turn.

"You can't go on Tom Sawyer Island tonight," said Becky. "They've got a band out there tonight."

"I have an idea," said Damone. "There is a way."

The only way out to the man-made island at the center of Disneyland was by wooden raft. The raft was ferried back and forth all day by a Disneyland employee in riverboat get-up. And they had chosen *this* Grad Nite to quit running the raft.

But the raft was still there, sitting calmly by the deserted and darkened dock. It was held only by a rope.

Damone gave the instructions. He would untie the rope, and they would float across to the island, lying low on the raft.

"No way," said The Rat. "They'll catch us."

"Come on," said Becky. "Don't be a *wussy*."

"You have that word, too?"

They floated across the moat to the other side, undetected. Once on shore, Damone led them to the back caves, to the site he had meticulously outlined for Laurie Beckman.

Damone reached up, found the compartment, and the knapsack containing a sealed bottle of Jack Daniel's Old No. 7.

They took a few slugs, then quickly returned to the greater Magic Kingdom. Paddling back across the moat, the four hit the dock and scattered in different directions, according to plan. They were to meet at Jungle Cruise.

Damone was just about to round the corner and head out of Frontierland when he felt an arm grab him from behind. Then another arm.

"Come along with us."

He turned to see two Disneyland security officers dressed as old-time coppers. They had already confiscated his Jack Daniel's knapsack.

"Where are you taking me?"

"To the holding office."

The *holding tank!* Shades of Mark Huffman!

236

"I heard about that place," said Damone. "It's underground, isn't it?"

"You're thinking of Disney *World*. That's in Florida. They have an underground security office."

Damone was led to a very-much above-ground office behind Main Street marked JUVENILE SECURITY.

"Hello, young man."

He had been brought before a middle-aged man, kind of like his father. This man spoke in that same folksy tone—but there was no mistaking his authority. This was some kind of behind-the-scenes Disneyland masher. And he was going to try to make Mike *break*. "All we'd like to know is what you were doing out on Tom Sawyer Island tonight. Did you fool around with any equipment out there?"

"No."

"What were doing out there on Tom Sawyer Island?"

"Having some fun."

"You know we don't run Tom Sawyer Island on Grad Nite anymore."

"Didn't know."

The two attendants who'd brought Mike Damone to Juvenile Security remarked that they had confiscated a bottle of whiskey, and that "the boy's breath smelled alcoholic."

"Are you intoxicated at this moment?"

"No, sir. No way."

"May I see some identification, please?"

Damone took out his wallet and showed them his driver's permit.

"Where are your friends, Mike? Are they friends from your high school? Or did you meet them here?"

"I don't know."

"We just want to find your friends and keep them out of trouble, Mike." He was trying another tack. "We know they gooded you into doing what you did out there on Tom Sawyer Island."

Mike said nothing.

"What *did* you do out there on Tom Sawyer Island tonight?"

Mike said nothing.

237

"Mike, I'm going to have to call your parents right now unless you can help us a little."

Mike said nothing.

"All we have to do is check your file. We have all the forms you filled out with the ticket application. We have them all right here."

Mike looked panicked. Inside, he felt relieved. He had listed the request line of a popular AM station in Los Angeles. Just in case. It was always busy.

The juvenile security chief picked up the phone on his desk. "This is Richards. And I'd like to place a *parental* call, W.D. code 1456 to 213-279-1771." He waited a moment. "Could you try it again? Okay."

He replaced the receiver. "It's busy."

"Sorry," said Damone, "my mom talks a lot."

"Mike," said the security chief. "I'm afraid I'm going to have to get in touch with your head chaperone right now . . ." But the words trailed off in the man's mouth. He was looking at Damone, who appeared to be going into some kind of serious spasm. "Are you all right? Are you a diabetic."

Mike didn't respond. He was going into convulsions. He fell off his chair onto the floor and started banging his head against Mr. Richards's desk.

"Quick! Can I get some help in here! This boy is having a seizure! Can I get some help in here?"

But the Disneyland henchmen who brought Damone in had already gone off to nab some other kid, no doubt. So the security chief made the fatal mistake of leaving the room to get some help. He was gone less than thirty seconds, but it was time enough for Damone to pop up and head for the other door, the one he came in through. He disappeared out onto Main Street.

Tired and wasted, Damone wandered into Great Moments with Mr. Lincoln. He couldn't find anyone he knew. He fell into a seat and watched the show. When it ended, he walked back out onto Main Street.

"What time is it?" he asked.

"It's getting near five."

Damone headed for the bus.

"Hey Mike!"

It was The Rat, who was running for him from the Monorail exit.

"Where have you been?" asked The Rat.

"A long story," said Damone. "They got my bottle. Where have *you* been?"

The Rat held up a Wagon Train Motel key, his souvenir.

"Wa-tching the De-tect-tives."

"You're kidding! What happened?"

"I ain't saying!"

"Did you make out?"

"I ain't saying!"

The last thing The Rat and Damone did on their Grad Nite was get an old-fashioned picture taken on Main Street. It was a frozen moment in time. Definitely scrapbook material all the way.

It was The Rat who took the seat next to Charles Jefferson on the way home. He didn't mind. Charles took a long time to notice him, however, pleading for the seat.

"But my teddy bear's sitting there," complained Charles. "Aw . . . go 'head." He, too, was offered a corner, but only after the bus was in motion.

The sun rose while the five buses were still cruising on the freeway, fifty minutes outside Ridgemont. The whole inside of the bus smelled of stale socks. Most of the kids were asleep, though some were still awake and clutching their stuffed animals. Most of the guys were snoring loudly, their gangster hats knocked askew and their mouths pressed against the window.

Back at the Ridgemont parking lot, Damone rolled home and The Rat stood trying to wake up enough to drive his father's car back up the hill.

He saw Stacy Hamilton.

"What happened to you?" she asked.

"Oh," said The Rat, "just had a wild night. Where's Linda?"

"She got a ride. Can I get a ride home with you?"

"Sure," said The Rat.

She crawled in the back of his car, and he drove her

239

home. When they reached Valley View condominiums, he woke her up.

"You'd better let me get out here," said Stacy. "My mother doesn't want anybody to see me in an evening gown being walked home by a guy at seven in the morning."

"I understand."

"Do you?" She rubbed her eyes. "Can I see you over the summer, Mark?"

"If I'm around," said The Rat.

She handed him her Disneyland photo. "Here. So you won't forget what I look like."

The last thing The Rat did before going to sleep was stick the photo in the corner of his mirror.

Have a Bitchin' Summer

The Ridgemont Senior High School annual was made available on Monday of the last week of school. In an effort to keep reasonable order in the few classes still in session, A.S.B. Advisor Joseph Burke announced in the morning bulletin that an Annual Signing Party would be held in the gym during sixth period.

Students came pouring into the gym to find another surprise. Burke had slipped in one more dance sponsored by the administration. The bleachers had been wheeled out, the lights were low, there was even a live band. The T-Birds, featuring one of the Robin Zander lookalikes on lead vocals, were already on stage.

Stacy Hamilton and Linda Barrett walked into the gym slowly, head to head in deep conversation.

"I'm torn," said Linda. "Doug wants to get married. I know I love him. We know each other so well it's the only thing left for us to do."

"Then do it," said Stacy. It was one of the rare times she could give Linda advice. "All your friends would be there. It would be very romantic. You and Doug, finally getting married."

Linda nodded.

Romantic, thought Stacy. *Did I just say that?* At the beginning of the year it seemed that sex was the most fun that she, or any of her girlfriends, knew about. *Did you get him?* Now she was wondering about romance. Well, Stacy figured, some people learn about romance before sex. She just got it the other way around.

"I guess I'd go to junior college," said Linda, "while Doug worked at Barker Brothers. My parents say that I should just be a housewife, but they don't know what they're talking about. They send Jerome—the *smart* one—to college, and tell me to stay home. Doug says the same thing. But maybe I don't *want* to stay at home."

"Linda," said Stacy, "you and Doug were meant for each other. He saved you from a fate worse than death."

"What's that?"

Stacy smiled. "High school boys!"

The two girls walked through the Annual Signing Party, and soon spotted Mike Damone collapsed against the back of the gym. He was letting people approach him. Once the story of the erased bare ass came out, it was Ratner's and Damone's turn at celebritydom. Damone was signing annuals at a furious pace.

"I remember erasing this one," Damone was telling some timid underclassman. "Don't you hate it when people start something in your annual and then cross it out?"

"Yes," said the girl.

"Have a bitchin' summer," said Damone.

He had crossed out "I don't really know you, but . . ." and just left "Take care, Mike Damone."

A friend from Damone's P.E. class slammed down on the hardwood gym floor next to him. He flipped his annual into Damone's lap, nearly cracking him in the nuts.

"Go for it," said the kid.

Damone signed.

"Sheesh," said the kid. "My only fuckin' picture is on fuckin' page 98. I have a partial on 106, but that's bullshit. I look like I weigh about a thousand pounds."

Damone handed the book back. "To the future of America—it's in your hands. Don't splash, Mike Damone."

Mark Ratner showed up and sat down next to Damone. The two held court all Annual Signing Party.

Mr. Vargas passed by, carefully documenting the event with the school's camera equipment.

Linda Barrett was next to come by. She fell down next to Mike in a black low-cut dress. She'd gone home to change. She wrote "I LUST YOU" on the knee of Damone's jeans.

"I'm back with Doug," said Linda. "We're going to get married as soon as I get out of college."

"When is that?"

"In four years, stupid."

"Yeah," said Damone. "Sure. Doug'll be in the old-folks home, and one day you'll come cruising up and say, 'Let's get married.' But he'll be deaf by then so he won't even hear you."

". . . I'll never forget your bod," said Linda. She looked up to see Brad Hamilton standing nearby. "Hi, Bradley!"

"Hi. You see Laurie Beckman and Steve Shasta? Look at that! They're about to go for it right there on the floor."

Several teachers on both sides had already discovered the slow-dancing couple. Plotting their chaperonal strategy, they decided on a double-flashlight attack that pinned two separate beams on the couple. But it did not break Laurie and Steve up. Mr. Burke had to go out there and do it himself.

Jeff Spicoli wandered up, annual in hand. He stopped to look at the band on stage. He stayed there, staring off into space, for several minutes. His hand was frozen in his hair, as if he'd forgotten to let go.

"Hey, Spicoli," said Damone.

Spicoli turned to see The Rat and Damone, Linda Barrett, Brad and Stacy. His head started bobbing. He was on some distant plane, no doubt ripping through the cosmos of his surf-ravaged mind.

"Want us to sign your annual?"

"Ohhhhhhhhhhhh." Spicoli laughed menacingly. "It's so *radical.*" He offered his annual to Damone.

Spicoli's annual was filled with comments like, "Dear Jeff—I'm not real good friends with you, but you will never have any problems in life. There will always be someone to tell you where to get off." Or, "We got high in P.E., didn't we? Fuck class!"

It made Damone feel sorry for the guy. He'd take his annual home to his mom and dad. His dad would ask what he spent the fifteen bucks on, and then he'd flip through the annual by the living-room light.

"Jefffff? Why do all these boys keep thanking you for the drugs?"

Damone signed Spicoli's book. "Good thing you're going to Hawaii," said Damone. " 'Cause you're gonna get kicked out of the house when your parents read your annual."

Spicoli smiled and nodded. "Good luck to all you rats coming back to this crackerjack joint," he said. "I laugh in your face." He had written the same line in any annual he could get his hands on.

Damone and The Rat watched Spicoli drift off to other parts of the Annual Signing Party.

"You just know he's gonna grow up to be a shoe salesman," said The Rat.

The All-Night 7-Eleven Man

Brad could see it. He could hear it in the way people said goodbye and good luck to him. He could read the expression in their eyes. They looked at him and thought, Here's a guy I'll have to visit—*when I come back.*

Everyone was leaving, all his friends. Even the ones who

said they'd never go near college. Well, they were all talking about applications and acceptances these days. Even Linda Barrett, and that had been one of the big surprises for Brad. The way he heard it, Linda had come home from school after the Annual Signing Party when her mother broke the news. She had been dealing with Paula Crawford, Linda's RHS counselor, since last semester. No wonder they'd all talked her into taking the advanced classes.

Linda had been accepted into Students International, the program that allows a select few to study in any college throughout Europe. Linda had thought about it for three seconds, Stacy told Brad, and decided it was exactly what she wanted to do. She started crying right there in her living room.

Doug Stallworth had come over from work at Barker Brothers right in the middle of her crying fit. The Barrett family told Doug the news, expecting him to get all excited for Linda, too. And Doug, unbelievably enough, did get excited. Even though he knew he'd been left behind. They probably would become friends now, Brad thought. Ridgemont guys for life.

"Life," Brad had become fond of saying, "I just don't know . . ."

It was a joke and it wasn't a joke. These were the worst of times for Brad. He had now been reduced to the lowest position in teen life. He was right where, if he recalled correctly, he once said he wouldn't let . . . well, a *dog* work.

He was the all-night man at the Ridgemont 7-Eleven.

It was a slow night and Brad was wide awake. He figured that was the best way to be, especially if you had the kind of job where they showed you where the *shotgun* was. He had too much time to think on this job. That was the problem. But, it was bucks. It was bucks.

Brad had taken to napping in the afternoons after school, and then powering down the coffee once he hit the 7-Eleven. He once said he hated the stuff, would never drink it. Now he couldn't get enough. He reached for the pot without even thinking about it. Drank a cup without even realizing he had.

By 4:15, when Brad got home, he was ready to sleep. When friends asked him how he functioned on three hours' sleep, he told them all the same joke: "I sleep my ass off."

On this particular night he had been leafing through the magazines, listening to the Muzak.

It all happened very quickly. Two men pulled up in a black Camaro. One man in a nylon mask came running into the store and immediately spray-painted the automatic scanning camera above the door. Brad was too stunned to be scared. It had to be a joke.

It was no joke. In another instant, the nylon-masked man stood in front of Brad with a .45—just like in the movie *Dirty Harry*. "Give it to me," he said. "Let's GO."

"They empty and close the big safe at midnight here. I'm just the all-ni . . ."

"BULLSHIT!" the gunman bellowed. "I know this store. I know where the safe is. Why don't you just move over there, real slow, behind the donut case, and GET IT." He waved the gun at the donut case.

It was true, about the hidden safe. Any big bills that came in after midnight—when they closed the big safe in the back—went into the hidden safe. And that was behind a panel at the back of the donut case.

Hamilton walked over to the donut case. He caught a whiff of the fresh coffee he made and felt nauseous.

"I'm instructed to tell you that we are on a video alarm system and there are other hidden cameras in the store . . ."

"JUST CAN IT, OKAY? GIVE ME THE MONEY OR I'LL BLOW YOUR FUCKING BRAINS OUT. DO YOU UNDERSTAND THAT?"

"Okay," said Brad. His legs were now shaking uncontrollably. "I just started here, and they just taught me about this one thing. I don't care if you take their money. Just let me figure this out."

"MOVE!"

Brad opened the phony back of the donut case and fiddled with the strongbox combination. On his finger was the new class ring he'd picked up the other day.

"YOUR TIME IS RUNNING OUT, MR. HIGH SCHOOL . . ."

Brad was just about to get it open, just about there, when the phone rang. The gunman tightened.

"OKAY, ANSWER IT, QUICK!"

Brad looked up at the gunman. He wasn't nervous. He was *pissed*. Pissed at everything. Pissed at life. All he had wanted was a decent senior year. *All he wanted.* All he wanted was to keep his job, his car . . . but that had been too much to ask. He got fired. He got caught beating off. Bad grades. And this guy! This asshole who waved a gun at him and called him Mr. High School.

Tears welled in Brad Hamilton's eyes. "You motherfucker," he said. "Get *off* my CASE!"

And then, just like it was the most natural thing in the world, Brad Hamilton reached for the hot, steaming coffee he had just made and poured it onto the gunman's hand.

"AAAAAAAAAAARRRRRRRRRRRRR!"

The .45 rattled to the floor. The gunman was still looking in horror at his red, swelling hand when Brad snapped up the gun.

The gunman's accomplice, poised behind the wheel of the black Camaro, spotted the foul-up and screeched out of the parking lot.

"There goes your ride *home*, mister," said Brad, gun trained on the 7-Eleven robber. "Look at the big man now! Look at Mr. I-Know-Where-the-Strongbox-Is!"

The gunman managed, in all his pain, to heave a carton of Butterfingers at Brad as he howled around the front of the store. But Brad was on a roll, now.

"Why don't you just show me where the police alarm is now . . . come on, *guy.*"

And that was the story of how Brad Hamilton got his old spot back on lunch court. There wasn't that much time left to enjoy it, but it felt good nonetheless.

Even better was how the local reporters started hanging around, and Janine Wilson from local news, and all the stories started coming out. Even Mr. Hand told him he'd done The

American Thing—when your back is against the wall, all you can do is fight. Brad won. And damn if that phone didn't ring at the Hamiltons' late one night.

"Hello?"

"Hello, Brad!"

"Yes? Who's calling?"

"Bradley, this is Dennis Taylor down at the Ridgemont Drive Carl's. Listen, I hope I'm not bothering you right now."

"I'm pretty busy," said Brad.

"Brad, listen, I'm going district here in a couple weeks, and I was wondering if you wanted to come back down here and work with us again. You can have your old fryer back. We'd love to have you here. Everyone wants you back, buddy!"

The nerve. The ultimate nerve of the guy.

"Last time I talked to you," said Brad, "you wanted me to take a lie-detector test. Now it's 'Am I disturbing you?'"

"I know what's eating you, Brad. That incident with the money. Well, that money turned up in the dumpster after you left. I am sorry. I should have called."

"Yeah, you should have." Brad paused. "And I probably would have taken your lousy job back if I hadn't taken a district supervisor job myself—with 7-Eleven."

The Last Bell

On the last day of school, Mike Damone stood at his locker and cleaned out the last mimeographed sheet crammed into the back corner.

"If this paper could talk," he said.

Standing next to him was The Rat. "Well, Damone. In the end, it looks like it comes down to just you and me."

"Looks like it."

Damone clanged the locker door shut. "A very touching

moment," he said, "I feel like I just ripped my heart out. A whole year I spent in that little box. It's like a brother to me."

"You could get the same locker next year."

"I considered it. It's a pretty good location. I'll have to see where my classes are. This is a good sosh area, though. You get a good crowd that comes by."

The school was all tank tops and t-shirts, red faces and Frisbee discs. You knew it was almost over when people actually saved the last issue of the *Reader*. For once it wasn't blowing all over campus.

"Stacy wants you, you know," said Damone. "You should go for it."

"No way, man," said The Rat. "I can't wait to get my car and head for Flagstaff."

"She should come to you," said Damone.

"Says who?"

"Says The Attitude."

"The Attitude," said The Rat, "is only good until you meet the right girl."

"Whatever you say, Rat."

Students were still signing their annuals, hanging lazily out the windows, and talking with friends. Mr. Bates was playing his ukulele in social studies class. On this day, school was a countdown.

There were many rumors of an elaborate end-of-the-year stunt for the last day. But the fact was, given the chance of staying and pranking or getting out ... Ridgemont students *went*.

Across the commons, Damone saw Steve Shasta striding down the hallway in all his glory. Shasta had been selected for a Yale scholarship, their first for soccer. They had pulled him out of class to tell him, and his mom was sitting there in the office and everything. Teachers were giving him investment advice. They had given him the treatment in the local press, too.

Now, Damone wasn't in the habit of asking a lot of people to sign his annual, but it *was* Shasta. You couldn't help but yell something at the guy.

"Hey, Shasta! You hear about the big party on Marine Street?"

Shasta caught a look at who was calling his name. "Yep," he said.

Mike Damone trotted up with The Rat following behind. "Sign my annual, Shasta."

"Yeah," said Shasta, bored.

"Bet you're happy."

"Yep."

Shasta opened Damone's annual to a soccer shot and signed, right under his picture: "Best wishes, Steve Shasta."

Damone laughed as if it were a joke. Okay, he felt like saying, now sign it for real. But that was it. Shasta was already a big soccer star. No time for personal messages that might be worth something someday.

"Thanks," said Damone.

The Rat had to go to class, so Damone sat out on lunch court for a time. Brad Hamilton was sitting out there too, finishing an assignment for Mrs. George's Project English class. It was the ten-year letter she asked all her seniors to write. The letter was meant for yourself, and Mrs. George was going to mail it back to you (at your parents' address) in ten years. "Be relaxed," she'd said. "Be natural. Say exactly what's on your mind today. This is one paper that will not be corrected for grammar."

Damone decided to take a walk by the 200 Building, where Mrs. G. taught class. What he found was no real surprise at the end of any semester. It was a full speech class. They were all there on the last day, the last-chance students appearing to get their grades. Damone took a seat by the open door.

The final on this last day was a five-minute career speech, to have been prepared on 3×5 cards. The speech was meant to hit on all the points listed on the board in Mrs. George's neat script.

1. What is my career?
2. Do I like my career?

3. What are its financial rewards?
4. What kind of schooling does it require?
5. Did I enjoy this class?

Damone watched as Jeff Spicoli, the last of the Ridge-mont surfers, stood at the front of the class reading from a three-page manuscript. It was a speech about the sixties, which was the wrong topic, and it had probably seen more than one teacher this year, but Spicoli read it with passion. He read it, in fact, like it was the first time he'd had a chance to look at it.

"Everything was going great in the sixties," Spicoli said. "Diseases were being cured. We were winning the space program." He looked up, for eye contact. "Then everything went off balance. A president was assassinated. The divorce rate approached one marriage in two. A president was caught in an attempt to lie and cover up with more lies. A nation was shocked and dismayed." He looked up again and appeared to ad-lib. "It was awesome.

"What has happened to the generation or two earlier that was dedicated to answering all the unanswered questions? For the latter part of the seventies it appeared America gave up asking."

Some clapped, but the speech was not over. Spicoli had just lost his place in the manuscript.

"With the care-free life of the fifties and the problems of the sixties and all the even larger problems of the seventies and eighties, who knows what will happen in the future? With nu-clear power and gas shortages and many other problems, I doubt that it can get much worse. Hopefully the past has taught us we should not give up before finding the solutions."

Spicoli mumbled a last line, but it was drowned in applause. The clock was inching closer to the 2:00 mark that meant The End of School.

"And I really like this class, Mrs. George."

"Thank you, Jeff," said Mrs. George. "But you didn't say anything about your career."

"Well, I'm glad you asked me about that," said Spicoli. "It just so happens that I was going to go to Mexico this summer. I had it all planned and everything. But the time came around, and I looked at the bottom line, and you know what? I just didn't have the bucks. It was a total drag. So I had to go find a place to work. And I just want to warn you that you may see me this summer . . ." He gulped, threw his hair out of his eyes. "Working at Alpha Beta." He paused. "And it's only for six weeks, so don't hassle me."

Mrs. George smiled. "Is that the truth, Jeff?"

"Any amount of money," said Spicoli, holding out his hand.

"Okay, well thank you for your speech. Have a nice summer, Jeff." Spicoli took his seat, bowing to applause. "Now where's Valerie?"

"Oh," said a girlfriend of Valerie's. "She went to Mission Viejo's prom last night. She knew she wouldn't be here today."

"Well. Her grade goes down from an A— to a B+."

"I don't think she cares," said her girlfriend.

It was at that moment that Brad Hamilton walked into the classroom to deliver to Mrs. G. his ten-year letter. The speech class stopped in silent respect. A buzz passed through the class. *That's the guy! That's the guy who poured coffee on the armed robber!!*

"Sorry I'm late with this, Mrs. G.," said Brad. "I wanted to do some extra thinking about this letter."

Brad Hamilton placed his letter on Mrs. G.'s desk. Here was the lunch-court king of last September, toppled from grace in October, back on top in June. He made it look easy. Looking back, he had been struggling all year long just to make his car payments, cover his schoolwork, and just stay even. He had been busting his *ass*, he figured, when his parents, at the same age, were probably busy just being seventeen.

College could wait another year, Brad had decided. He was going to put in a full summer at the 7-Eleven, keeping those little guys out of the store and pulling in the coin. Who knew where it would take him, but he was ready for the ride.

All Brad knew right now was that sometime ten years from now he would be visiting his parents, and they would say, "Oh Brad, something came for you in the mail." And Brad would open a decade-old letter, this record of his tumultuous senior year:

Dear Brad:

This graduation business sure sneaks up on you. Every year I get my annual back, and it's filled with "Have a nice summer." Now it's "Have a nice life." That's going to take some getting used to. If I could go back and do this year over, there are a few things I wouldn't have done. I wouldn't have bought a gas guzzler, and I wouldn't have worked at Carl's. I would have taken another class with Mr. Hand. I would have taken Dina Phillips to Hawaii for three weeks, and I then would have married Linda Barrett. As for my friends, I wouldn't change one of them, for they are the best group of friends a guy could have.

Sincerely,
Brad Hamilton

He walked out of speech class and over to the parking lot, to The Cruising Vessel. Stacy was waiting for him by the car.

"Let me guess," said Brad. "You want a ride home."

"Mind reader," said Stacy.

Brad opened her car door first, a grand gesture for him, and then walked around to his side. He got inside The Vessel and gunned the engine.

"All in all," he said, "an excellent year."

"I know it was," said Stacy. "Just wish me luck. I have *two more years* here."

They headed down Ridgemont Drive, past fast-food row. As he drove, Brad spotted a couple of unkempt underclassmen loitering on the street corner. He stuck his head completely out of the window to shout at them.

"HEY," he yelled, "WHY DON'T YOU GET A JOB!!!"

Back at Ridgemont High, a motorcycle ripped along Luna Street. There were war cries coming from the parking lot.

The third bell had rung.

Grateful Acknowledgments

David Obst, Irving Azoff, Art Linson, Neal Preston, Bob Bookman, Joel Bernstein, Fred Hills, Danny Bramson, Ron Bernstein, Kathy DeRouville, Erica Spellman, Jackie Snyder, Cindy Crowe, Alan Hergott, David Rensin, Virginia Johnstone, Tom Pollock, Bill Maguire, Leslie Ellen, Louise Goffin, Judy Boasberg, George Cossolias, Judd Klinger, Susan Blond, The Thugs, Debbie Gold, Richard C. Woods, Karla Bonoff, Harold Schmidt, Daniel Kortchmar, Shaun Daniel, Thom Mount, Susan Bolotin, Abigale Haness, John Dodds, Kevin McCormick, Lori Zech, David Bernstein, Barry Steinman, Jann S. Wenner, Riley Kathryn Ellis, Martha Cochrane, and Wendy Sherman.